# NONCOGNITIVIS

C000000452

'*Noncognitivism in Ethics* is the best introduction to noncognitivism and to the complex philosophical issues it generates that I have seen. It is written with teaching in mind. While the discussion is advanced enough to maintain the interest of even a professional reader, it presupposes very little. Schroeder always takes care to explain the point of any philosophical technique that might otherwise put off newcomers.'

Mark van Roojen, *University of Nebraska*, USA

'*Noncognitivism in Ethics* combines sparkling clear presentation and balanced critical assessment with extremely thoughtful and well-crafted sets of exercises that accompany each chapter. This is an ideal book for undergraduates beginning serious study of metaethics, while the more advanced exercises and masterful overview of the challenges confronting noncognitivist views also make this a perfect text for graduate seminars.'

Mark Timmons, *University of Arizona*, USA

According to noncognitivists, when we say that stealing is wrong, what we are doing is more like venting our feelings about stealing or encouraging one another not to steal, than like stating facts about morality. These ideas challenge the core not only of much thinking about morality and metaethics, but also of much philosophical thought about language and meaning.

*Noncognitivism in Ethics* is an outstanding introduction to these theories, ranging from their early history through the latest contemporary developments. Beginning with a general introduction to metaethics, Mark Schroeder introduces and assesses three principal kinds of noncognitivist theory: the speech-act theories of Ayer, Stevenson, and Hare, the expressivist theories of Blackburn and Gibbard, and hybrid theories. He pays particular attention both to the philosophical problems about what moral facts could be about or how they could matter which noncognitivism seeks to solve, and to the deep problems that it faces, including the task of explaining both the nature of moral thought and the complexity of moral attitudes, and the 'Frege–Geach' problem.

Shroeder makes even the most difficult material accessible by offering crucial background along the way. Also included are exercises at the end of each chapter, chapter summaries, and a glossary of technical terms - making *Noncognitivism in Ethics* essential reading for all students of ethics and metaethics.

**Mark Schroeder** is Associate Professor of Philosophy at the University of Southern California. He is the author of *Slaves of the Passions* (2007) and *Being For: Evaluating the Semantic Program of Expressivism* (2008).

# New Problems of Philosophy
**Series Editor:** *José Luis Bermúdez*

The New Problems of Philosophy series provides accessible and engaging surveys of the most important problems in contemporary philosophy. Each book examines either a topic or theme that has emerged on the philosophical landscape in recent years, or a longstanding problem refreshed in light of recent work in philosophy and related disciplines. Clearly explaining the nature of the problem at hand and assessing attempts to answer it, books in the series are excellent starting points for undergraduate and graduate students wishing to study a single topic in depth. They will also be essential reading for professional philosophers. Additional features include chapter summaries, further reading, and a glossary of technical terms.

Also available:

Forthcoming:

# NONCOGNITIVISM IN ETHICS

*Mark Schroeder*

Routledge
Taylor & Francis Group

LONDON AND NEW YORK

This edition published 2010 by Routledge
2 Park Square, Milton Park, Abingdon, Oxon OX14 4RN
Simultaneously published in the USA and Canada
by Routledge
711 Third Ave, New York, NY 10017

Routledge is an imprint of the Taylor & Francis Group, an informa business

© 2010 Mark Schroeder

Typeset in Joanna and Scala Sans by
Bookcraft Ltd, Stroud, Gloucestershire

British Library Cataloguing in Publication Data
A catalogue record for this book is available from the British Library

Library of Congress Cataloging in Publication Data
Library of Congress Cataloging-in-Publication Data
Schroeder, Mark Andrew, 1977-
Noncognitivism in ethics / by Mark Schroeder.
p. cm. -- (New problems of philosophy) Includes
bibliographical references and index.
1. Ethics. 2. Cognitive science. 3. Emotivism. I. Title.
BJ45.5.S37 2010
170'.42--dc22
2009036228


ISBN 13: 978-0-415-77343-0 (hbk)
ISBN 13: 978-0-415-77344-7 (pbk)
ISBN 13: 978-0-203-85629-1 (ebk)

# CONTENTS

# ACKNOWLEDGEMENTS

This book has benefited from over eight years of thinking seriously about noncognitivism, and much of it therefore depends on my earlier work. This is particularly the case for Chapters 6 and 7, which rely heavily in places on 'What is the Frege–Geach Problem?'; Chapter 8, which benefited from being composed alongside 'The Moral Truth'; Chapter 9, which is derived from 'How Not to Avoid Wishful Thinking'; and Chapter 10, which relies on the arguments in 'Hybrid Expressivism: Virtues and Vices'. Portions of other chapters also benefit from 'Expression for Expressivists', 'How Expressivists Can and Should Solve Their Problem with Negation', 'Expressivist Truth', *Being For*, and 'Reflection, Disagreement, and Invariance', co-authored with Jake Ross.

Work on this project was made possible by the time I spent in the Moral Psychology and Moral Realism working group at the Institute for Advanced Studies at the Hebrew University in Jerusalem, organized by David Enoch and generously further supported by the College of Arts and Sciences at the University of Southern California, as well as by a further semester of support through USC's program for Assistant Professors' Paid Leave, which USC was kind enough to allow me to defer until after tenure. Early drafts of some of the material benefited from exposure to my graduate seminar on expressivism at USC in the fall of 2006, and its earliest ideas were tested in my graduate seminar on expressivism at the University of Maryland College Park in the spring of 2006.

In addition I am especially indebted to Andrew Alwood, Be Birchall, Daniel Boisvert, Mark Budolfson, David Copp, Jamie Dreier, Billy Dunaway, David Enoch, John Eriksson, Stephen Finlay, Ryan Hay, Jeff King, Matt King, Barry Lam, Mike McGlone, Tristram McPherson, Indrek Reiland, Michael Ridge, Jake Ross, Johannes Schmitt, Scott Soames, David Sobel, Jussi Suikkanen, Mark van Roojen, two blind referees for the publisher, and others I am sure that I have missed, for motivation, important ideas, and/or in some cases quite extensive feedback. In particular, Andrew Alwood, Daniel Boisvert, Mark Budolfson, John Eriksson, Matt King, and Tristram McPherson all provided very useful feedback on up to two-thirds of the manuscript, and Justin Snedegar compiled the index. Where I haven't benefited sufficiently from their input, the fault lies with me. I may not have taken on this project at all if not for the encouragement of Jamie Dreier, and I am particularly grateful to Tony Bruce of Routledge for his forbearance, and for his willingness to entertain and support my experiment with the exercises. Finally, my deepest debts are to my wife, Maria Nelson, for time, support, understanding, encouragement, and, above all, willingness to put up with a little bit of philosophy.

# PREFACE

In 1968 J.O. Urmson published *The Emotive Theory of Ethics*, writing as 'an admirer, but not an adherent'. After more or less forty years of the noncognitivist tradition in English-speaking philosophy, it was, then as now, the only critical but sympathetic book-length discussion of the range of issues, as Urmson then saw it, facing emotivist views, the earliest wave of noncognitivist theorizing. Urmson's book, however, is very much a product of its time and place. Some of its most important lessons – about the differences among emotivist views, about the general kinds of motivation for noncognitivist views, and about what is ultimately the basic problem facing the earliest sorts of emotivism – still stand. But other parts of its discussion now seem less relevant, and he has very little or nothing to say about the main issues that have occupied attention over the last forty years, including the development of expressivism as we now understand it, the issues surrounding deflationism about truth, and various developments in our appreciation of the Frege–Geach problem.

But despite the centrality of noncognitivism to the last eighty years of philosophical thinking about morality, nothing has since come to take Urmson's place. The only existing discussions which bring together a wide range of the issues and problems raised by noncognitivist theories are written by proponents of particular such theories. This has two unfortunate consequences. The first consequence is that these discussions tend to focus on the particular *version* of noncognitivism propounded by their respective authors. And the second consequence is that the problems facing noncognitivism can sometimes tend to be framed in ways such that these authors have something to say about them, and which are consequently less than fully perspicuous with respect to appreciating the full range of these problems.

Each of these consequences is, I think, in its own way a considerable drawback when it comes to using these discussions for pedagogical purposes. Moreover, I think the same drawbacks for pedagogy are also drawbacks when it comes to helping us collectively, as the practitioners of metaethics, to come to and consolidate a shared understanding of where we are and what investigation to date has accomplished: an appreciation, at the least, of the relative costs and advantages of different sorts of view, and ideally, a clearer sense of what work remains.

I write this book with the surely over-ambitious hope that it can serve these dual purposes: of pedagogy and of consolidation. It is an opinionated and critical but broadly sympathetic guide to the terrain, which I hope will be of use to everyone from the uninitiated to the professional researcher. If it does not consolidate the terrain in quite such a way that everyone can agree on, it at least aspires to present a clear and consistent picture of what such a consolidation might look like, and which might serve as a backdrop for competing – perhaps better – ways of mapping out the terrain. And it is designed to get the reader fully engaged in the project of trying to see what it would take to get noncognitivism to work.

The book does not by any means cover every important issue related to noncognitivism – I could not do so and still respect my goal of broad accessibility. Among the notable topics which do not receive detailed discussion in the main text are the problem of 'creeping minimalism', the 'moral attitudes problem', and various parts of the literature on the relationship between noncognitivism and mind-dependence. But the book is self-contained, and in each case I think that the issues I do not discuss would be much better served by being informed by a better understanding of the issues that I do discuss. My goal has therefore not been to achieve complete coverage, but rather to equip the reader with the tools to think about the resources available to noncognitivist theorizing. I've done my best to organize the issues that I think are most important in order to understand both noncognitivism's prospects, and what must be done in order to make good on them. I've also presented some issues in ways that are in some cases oversimplified; I hope that this makes for fewer distractions for novice readers, and that experienced readers will recognize many of these instances and make appropriate allowances.

The Routledge New Problems of Philosophy series has a broadly 'interdisciplinary' focus, paying special attention in particular to new work on how philosophy connects with other disciplines. In this book I do note periodically how the issues about noncognitivism connect up with various issues related to linguistics, but in the apt terminology of David Enoch and Ralph Wedgwood, my main focus in the book is aggressively inter-*sub*-disciplinary, in the sense of crossing the sometimes artificial subdisciplinary boundaries that we erect around the areas of the philosophy of language, philosophy of mind, metaphysics, epistemology, logic, and normative ethics. In fact, the chapters are actually mostly arranged around the issues which arise for noncognitivism in each of these areas of philosophy. Like the division among the subdisciplines themselves, this is sometimes somewhat artificial, but my hope is that it calls attention to the inter-sub-disciplinary nature of the subject. In my own mind, this is both what makes the subject exciting, and what lends me optimism that there are many places to look in order to make progress.

As I write, it has been another forty years since Urmson. I write with the hope that this book, too, will before long be perceived as a product of its time and its place. If so, then that will be because as a field we will have made some kind of clear progress at least in coming to a better understanding of the issues at stake. I write in the hope that a clearer sense of where we are now – even a somewhat controversial one – will help us to get there sooner.

## Note for instructors

Noncognitivism and the problems which face it are intrinsically difficult and theory-laden issues. A full appreciation of the Frege–Geach problem, for example, requires a fair bit of antecedent understanding of philosophical logic and mainstream semantic theorizing. All of this makes it difficult to present these issues to undergraduates, and anyone teaching the material from articles must do a lot of spadework simply in order to provide the necessary background. It's been one of my primary aims in developing this book to try to make this material accessible to undergraduates by explaining what students need to know about the background ideas from logic and semantics, and to try to explain and introduce new and unfamiliar terminology and notation along the way. There still end up being a lot of new concepts and notation which appear in this book, particularly for students who haven't first taken a logic course, for example. And the material is still challenging. But my hope is that what is needed in order to understand it is at least all present, and I hope that my explanations along the way will resonate familiarly but not be redundant for students who have taken an introductory logic course.

Chapter 1 is a general introduction from scratch to the questions of meta-ethics and to the issue of noncognitivism that may be safely skipped by anyone familiar with the issues in metaethics, or by any teacher using this text in a course in which such issues are covered separately, but is included to make the book self-contained. A two-week unit on noncognitivism in an upper-division undergraduate course might read Chapter 2 and Stevenson (1937) in the first week, and Chapters 3 and 4 in the second week, or alternatively might skip the earlier noncognitivist views directly for expressivism, and read Chapters 4 and 6, together with a couple of supplementary readings. A longer undergraduate unit might make it further into the book without supplementary readings, or might proceed at a slower pace, with more supplementary readings. Many more flexible choices about what to cover also make good sense given the text; for example, in many cases, for students with less philosophical background it may make sense to skip the introduction of Hare's views in sections 5–6 of Chapter 2, so as not to over-load students with too many different options at once. And some instructors may find the material on the Frege–Geach problem in Chapters 3, 6, and 7, can be woven into a course in which they use other materials in order to introduce expressivism. It should be noted that Chapter 7 is the most challenging in the book, and may not be appropriate for many undergraduates, and that Chapter 8 builds in some ways on Chapter 7. Chapters 9 through 11 can be covered even if Chapters 7 and 8 are skipped.

When I teach this material to graduate students, I proceed at a rate of approximately one chapter per week, supplemented with a full load of primary text materials roughly along the lines of what I suggest in the 'further reading' section at the end of each chapter, with further reading optional. A graduate course covering noncognitivism as just one topic in metaethics might cover chapters a little bit faster with a little bit less required primary reading, for example doing Chapters 2–7 in three weeks, with Chapters 2 and 3 together with Ayer and Stevenson the first week, Chapters 4 and 5 together with a little bit of Gibbard (1990) and Horgan and Timmons (2006) the second week, and Chapters 6 and 7 together with chapter 6 of Blackburn (1984) and chapter 4 of Gibbard (2003) in the third week. A four-week unit might split the third week and add Hale (1993) or van Roojen (1996) to Blackburn (1984) in week three and add Unwin (2001) and Dreier (2006) to Gibbard (2003) and Chapter 7 in week four. Any such course would cover the most central topics.

Each chapter is supplemented not only by a list of suggested further (and ideally contemporaneous) reading for more advanced study, but by a series of pedagogical exercises, classified both according to difficulty and according to purpose. Some of these exercises extend the discussion in the main text in natural ways – for example by asking the reader to apply a lesson to one noncognitivist theory which in the text was discussed in connection with another. But others serve largely to introduce new and more sophisticated complications that are left out of the main text, to avoid hiccups for readers with less philosophical background. And still others pose new problems or objections to specific noncognitivist theories, or set up potentially prom-ising paths of inquiry.

In order that readers may easily ascertain which exercises may be of interest, they are rated on a scale from Easy (marked 'E') through Medium ('M') and Difficult ('D'), to Advanced ('A'). Exercises rated 'D' and 'A' in many cases presuppose background philosophical knowledge not covered in this book. As a general rule, exercises rated 'E' and 'M' are appropriate for most undergraduates, and those rated 'M' through 'A' are appropriate for graduate students. Each exercise is also characterized as testing Comprehension, providing Qualifications of the text, offering Extensions of the text, Branching out from the text, or posing a New problem, though in some cases more than one of these labels would have been appropriate. For selective exercises I provide sample partial answers or hints, and where necessary I try to say explic-itly what moral I think can be drawn. I'm sure the exercises are far from perfect, but my hope is that they are at least a good initial stepping-stone from 'finding out' (what other philosophers have had to say about these issues) to 'doing' (the philosophy oneself), and you will have skipped a lot of content if you skip them entirely.

For Maria

# 1

# THE PROBLEMS OF METAETHICS

## 1.1 What is metaethics?

Each year, as many as 300,000 girls undergo a procedure known as 'infibulation'; the World Health Organization calls it 'type III' genital cutting.[1] Extensive tissue is removed from their genitalia and the labia are stitched together so that after the procedure, nothing remains except a small opening for urine and menstrual blood. In many cases, infibulation is performed by a village midwife, with no anesthesia. There are no known health benefits of this procedure, but it can lead to bacterial infection, open sores, recurrent bladder and urinary tract infections, and increased risk of transmission of HIV. It also substantially raises the risks involved in childbirth: a 2006 study by the WHO found that infibulation raises the risk of the death of a child in pregnancy by 55 percent, raises the risk of cesarean section by 31 percent, and is associated with a 69 percent increase in the risk of postpartum hemorrhage, compared to women who have not undergone any genital cutting procedure.[2] Infants also need to be resuscitated in childbirth 66 percent more often, and their birth weight is on average 9 percent lower.[3]

Many people – you may be one of them – believe that it would be wrong to take one's pre-adolescent daughter to have this procedure performed, for no medical reason. Of those who think so, many believe that it is wrong to allow others to have this procedure performed on their children, and as a result of views like these, the WHO has long sought to discourage procedures like this one. But some people disagree. They believe not only that it is wrong to prevent people from having procedures like this one performed on their daughters, but that it is permissible, or even a duty, to have this procedure performed on one's own daughter. Hundreds of thousands of parents choose to have the procedure performed on their own daughters every year, and millions more choose to have less drastic genital cutting procedures performed on their daughters.

What people disagree about, in this case, are *moral* questions: whether it is wrong or not to take one's daughter for infibulation, and whether it is wrong or not to *allow* people to take their daughters for infibulation. We are all familiar with moral questions, and we all have views about at least some of them. Sometimes the answers to moral questions seem easy or obvious – for example, most people find it obvious that killing an innocent person in cold blood in order to steal their DVD collection is wrong. You are not likely to find someone to disagree with you about this moral question, unless she is simply being disingenuous. But other times, even when the answer to a moral question seems obvious, you discover that other people disagree with you. For example, you discover that up to 300,000 girls each year are willingly subjected by their well-meaning parents to infibulation – parents who do not believe that what they are doing is wrong. Though you may find it obvious, they apparently do not. (Perhaps you are among those who do not find it obvious that infibulation is wrong – in that case, you disagree with the many people who do!)

Moments like this one tend to provoke a kind of existential paralysis known in philosophical circles as 'interest in metaethics', for reasons I'll explain in a moment. A first thought that you might have is: maybe taking one's daughter for infibulation is wrong *for us*, but all right *for them*. If you haven't had this thought, you are bound to have encountered someone who has. This is the idea that wrongness is *relative* – that actions are not simply right or wrong *simpliciter* – that is, all by themselves – but relative to a person, or relative to a cultural group, or relative to a time and place. Maybe, this idea claims, infibulation is wrong relative to our time and place, but all right, relative to the time and place of northern Sudan, where it is estimated that over 90 percent of women have undergone some variety of genital cutting procedure or other, and infibulation is very common.[4] The idea that wrongness is relative is a thesis about the *metaphysics* of morality. It is a thesis about what we are talking, thinking, or disagreeing *about*, when we talk, think, or disagree about a moral question – that it is something relative, rather than absolute.

If you do not conclude that wrongness is relative, then next you are likely to wonder why you are so certain that infibulation is wrong, when other people are so equally certain that it is not wrong, and even that it is a duty. What makes you so sure, after all, other than that it seems obvious to you? But the opposite answer seems obvious to people with the opposing view. So what makes you think that what is obvious to you is a better guide to the truth than what seems obvious to them? If you are particularly reflective, you may add to these considerations the observations that given your upbringing and social circumstances, you were practically determined to find it obvious that infibulation is wrong, and that you would likely have found the reverse obvious, had you grown up in northern Sudan. These observations are bound to increase your puzzlement about how you really know that it is wrong, if your thinking that it is wrong is just a product of your upbringing and social circumstances. If you have ever wondered about any of these things, then you have been thinking about the *epistemology* of morality – the question of whether and how we do or can know the answers to moral questions.

Philosophers classify these questions about the metaphysics and epistemology of morality as belonging to the area of 'metaethics', so called because many people believe that the questions of metaethics are not questions *within* ethics – that is, they are not themselves moral questions – but are rather questions *about* moral questions – so they are 'meta' questions. Not everyone agrees with this characterization of what metaethics is about, but we have the name, nevertheless. Along with questions about the metaphysics and epistemology of morality, metaethics is concerned with questions about moral thought and questions about moral language. Since metaphysics, epistemology, the philosophy of mind (that is, of thought), and the philosophy of language are sometimes called the 'core areas' of philosophy, metaethics can therefore be characterized as what happens when we ask questions from the 'core areas' of philosophy about the subject matter of morality.

This book falls under the heading of 'metaethics' because it is primarily a book about moral *language*. But to appreciate the reasons why philosophers have been attracted to some of the theories about moral language that we will encounter in later chapters, it is important to see these questions about moral language as situated among related questions about moral reality (moral metaphysics), moral knowledge (moral epistemology), and moral thought (the philosophy of mind). And in fact, the questions about moral reality and moral knowledge are easier to understand.

## 1.2  The core questions (i): metaphysics and epistemology

We have already encountered one question about moral metaphysics, when you first entered your state of existential paralysis: it was our question as to whether wrongness is relative or absolute. But there are other, and more central, questions about moral metaphysics. <u>The biggest is: what are moral questions about?</u> The answer, of course, is that they are about morality – about what is right or wrong. But what kind of thing is that? Compare: if the question that we are interested in is whether sugar is soluble in water, there is more that we can say about what this is. For sugar to be soluble in water, after all, is for it to have the property that, very roughly, if you put some of it in water, then, other things being equal, it will dissolve. Now, that is not a very exciting answer to what questions about solubility are *about*, but it is an answer nonetheless. Metaethicists – people who spend their time thinking about metaethics – disagree a great deal over whether any answer at all can be given to the question, 'what are moral questions about?' other than the trivial one, 'they are about what is right or wrong', and if so, what kind of answer can be given.

*what is morality?*

One major concern that many people have had about the answer to this question is that they have noticed that morality is not a very scientific topic. Physicists and psychologists and biologists and chemists do not have very much to tell us about what is right and wrong – at least, not in virtue of the experiments or theories specific to their disciplines. Moreover, it is hard to see what sorts of experiments *would* be able to tell us the answers to our most important moral questions. People who believe that science is our best guide to what is true about the world therefore worry that we have a choice: either moral questions are really, ultimately about something that science can help to shed light on, or they are at best only about something spooky or unscientific.

The problem, however, is that it is hard to see how moral questions could possibly be about something that science can help to shed light on. Scientific investigation might reveal that babies do not, after all, die if they touch the clitoris during childbirth, as is reportedly believed by some in Burkina Faso.[5] Consequently, scientific investigation might *help us to settle* the question of whether it is wrong to not surgically remove a woman's clitoris before she is ready to give birth. But this kind of scientific investigation helps only if we know in advance that if a child will die if it touches the clitoris and if there is a high risk, if a woman with an intact clitoris gives birth, that the infant touches it, then it must be wrong to not surgically remove a woman's clitoris before she gives birth. Since that is moral knowledge that we have to have *before* we do the scientific investigation, similar reasoning shows that not all moral knowledge can come from science — some of it has to come from somewhere else. And that, in turn, makes it seem to many people that moral questions can't really be about something that science can ultimately shed light on, and hence that if they are about anything at all, it is something spooky. Many metaethicists disagree with this conclusion, of course, but many also worry about it, to at least some degree or another.

We have also already encountered one of the main questions from moral epistemology: how do we know what we know about morality? It is important not to confuse this question, 'how do I know?' with the question, '*do* I know?' Just as you can see that when you press the button on a drinking fountain water comes out the spout, and be fully confident that it works while still wondering *how* it works, you can see that you know some things about what is right and wrong while still wondering *how* you know those things. The question of *how* we know what is right and wrong is the central question in moral epistemology.

Still, even though the questions, 'how do I know?' and '*do* I know?' are different questions, and we can ask the former while being confident that the answer to the latter is a robust 'yes', many philosophers have believed that the question of how we know what is right and wrong is particularly *hard*. And some people who are particularly impressed with how difficult this question is to answer have found themselves wondering '*do* I know?' after all.

To see why this question can seem to be particularly difficult, compare it to the question of how you know that there is a book in front of you. The sciences of optics, anatomy, neuroscience, and cognitive psychology have all contributed to helping us to understand how you could know such a thing. First, some light bounces off of the book and into your eyes. Then, it bounces off of your retina, where it encounters the photoreceptors that we know as rods and cones. From there, a signal passes through your optic nerve which corresponds to the pattern of stimulation of your rods and cones by different wavelengths and intensities of light, which is resolved by your visual cortex into a book-like shape. This is just part of the story, and a very sketchy part at that, but these and related sciences help to fill it in, so it turns out that scientists in fact know quite a lot about how you know that there is a book in front of you.

The problem is that there does not seem to be any similar such story that we can tell about how you know that it is wrong to take one's eight-year-old daughter for infibulation. Unlike the book-like shape of the book in front of you, and the book-like pattern of inked text on its pages, the wrongness of taking one's eight-year-old daughter for infibulation is not, at least on the face of it, something that we can see. For that matter, it does not seem to be something that we can hear, or something that we can taste, touch, or smell, either. So how, exactly, do we find out about it? Recent research in anthropology, evolutionary biology, primatology, social psychology, brain imaging studies, and other fields adds to this worry, by telling us what *does* lead us, in general, to have the moral views that we do. Much of this research lends itself to the conclusion that we are evolutionarily destined to have certain views, that the reasons for which we think we hold them are really simply post hoc rationalizations, and that our moral thoughts are driven by our emotions, much more than by any kind of reasoning or reflective thought.[6]

When science gives us this kind of picture of where our moral views come from, it appears, at least initially, to contrast sharply with what science tells us about where your belief that there is a book in front of you comes from. And this is what makes it look hard to understand how, by processes like these, we ever manage to find out about anything – let alone about what is right or wrong. And that, in turn, leads some people who start with the question of *how* we know, to end up with the question of whether we know, after all.

## 1.3  The core questions (ii): mind and language

So far we have encountered one major question from moral metaphysics, and one major question from moral epistemology. We also need to introduce an important question from each of the philosophy of mind and the philosophy of language. These problems are somewhat more theory-laden than the problems we've just discussed from moral metaphysics and moral epistemology, so you may not have encountered them before. But they are questions that philosophers have become deeply puzzled about, and so it is important to at least see what they are. Fortunately, they are closely related to one another.

To see what these questions are, first notice that we have been talking about moral reality as something that moral questions are *about*. When you disagree with a man from northern Sudan about whether it is wrong to take one's daughter for infibulation, you are disagreeing *about* something. You are *talking* about this thing if you decide to go to Sudan to discuss it with him, and you are thinking about this thing, when you ponder it at night. But just as we can wonder how you manage to find out about this thing – that is, how you know what is right or wrong – we can also wonder how you manage to talk and think about it. The question of how you manage to talk about it is a question from the philosophy of language, and the question of how you manage to think about it is a question in the philosophy of mind. These questions sound very similar, and in fact they are closely related.

To see how to become puzzled about these two questions, notice that many, many of the things that we manage to talk and think about are things with which we have become *acquainted* in some way – either directly or indirectly. For example, you have thoughts about the book in front of you (for example, you either think that it is pedantic, or that it is arcane, depending on your relative background in philosophy), and you are acquainted with it directly, by seeing it in front of you. You also have the ability to talk and have thoughts about Julius Caesar, one of which I have just gotten you to exercise. This is not because you are acquainted with him directly, but rather because you have heard about him from people who have heard about him from people ... and so on, down to people who were directly acquainted with him. Hence, you are *indirectly* acquainted with Julius Caesar.

Acquaintance, either direct or indirect, or at least something like it, seems to play an important role in your ability to have thoughts about something. I can show this by giving you the ability to think about something that you have never before been able to think about. Unless you fall in a very small class of readers, you have never before had the ability to think or talk about my childhood dog, Chocolate Chip. But now you have the ability to both think and talk about Chocolate Chip; I have just given it to you, by giving you a name that I and my family used to refer to Chocolate Chip, while we were acquainted with him and his antics. So the ability to think or talk about someone or something doesn't come for free; it comes only under certain conditions, and the idea of direct and indirect acquaintance is one way of trying to spell out what those conditions involve, which gets the right results in the cases of this book, of Julius Caesar, and of Chocolate Chip.

But it is hard to see how rightness and wrongness are things that we can be acquainted with, either directly or indirectly in ways like these. If you can't see them, hear them, taste them, touch them, or smell them, then how does anyone become acquainted with them in the right sort of way? Thinking along these lines has made some philosophers who started with the question, 'how does it happen that we manage to think and talk about what is right or wrong?' to become worried about the further question, 'do we manage to think or talk about what is right or wrong, *after all?*'. Certainly not all philosophers are worried about this question, but reflection on the difficulty of answering the 'how?' question has definitely made some people worry.

We've now encountered one major question from each of moral metaphysics, moral epistemology, the philosophy of moral language, and the philosophy of moral thought – each of the 'core areas' of philosophy as they apply to the subject matter of ethics. These questions were: what are moral questions *about?*; how do we *find out* about that?; how do we manage to *talk* about it?; and how do we manage to *think* about it? Similar questions from the 'core areas' of philosophy come up when philosophers think about many other topics, outside of ethics – for example, when philosophers think about mathematics, or causation, or material objects. So I will call them the *core questions*.

To understand one of the important reasons why at least some philosophers have been attracted to the kinds of theories about moral language that we will encounter in this book, it suffices to notice that <u>each of the core questions contains a *presupposition*</u> – an idea that it assumes to be true, such that it wouldn't make sense if that idea were not true. In all four cases, each question is based on the presupposition that moral questions are *about* something. If moral questions are not, really, *about* anything, then there is no real question to be answered as to *what* they are about. Likewise, if moral questions are not really about anything, then there is no real question to be answered as to how we find out about it. And similarly, there would be no real questions as to how we manage to talk about it or think about it. Hence, some philosophers who have thought that the core questions are difficult to answer in a satisfactory way have become attracted to the idea that the presupposition of these questions is in fact false – because moral questions aren't really *about* anything at all. If moral questions aren't really about anything, then we don't have to answer the difficult core questions – we can simply avoid them. And that is one of the main ideas whose consequences we are going to investigate in this book.

Because similar questions to our core questions come up when philosophers think about many different topics, there is an analogous move that is sometimes made in those other areas of philosophy. Just as some metaethicists conclude that moral questions are not really *about* anything, in order to avoid the presupposition of the core questions of metaethics, some philosophers of mathematics conclude that mathematical questions are not really *about* anything – or at least, not really about numbers – in order to avoid the presupposition of the core questions of mathematics. And similarly, for other topics. Since this pattern happens in so many different places, in different areas of philosophy, it is useful to give it a name, and it is commonly called nondescriptivism, a usage I'll follow here. Hence, a nondescriptivist view about some subject matter holds that questions in that subject matter are not really *about* anything – at least in whatever sense is presupposed by the core questions. That is, they don't 'describe' anything – hence the name.

## 1.4  The motivation problem

There are many kinds of nondescriptivist theories in philosophy, about many different subject matters. And though the core questions constitute a *general* or *domain-neutral* motivation for nondescriptivism – which applies in many different areas of philosophy – some topics lend themselves to *special* or *domain-specific* motivations for nondescriptivism. For example, one of the most important problems in metaethics is called the motivation problem, and I'll explain what it is in just a moment. The motivation problem has led many philosophers to think that nondescriptivism about moral questions must be true. But the motivation problem doesn't arise in the philosophy of mathematics or in the philosophy of causation. So the reason it provides to believe in nondescriptivism is *special* or *topical*, in the sense that it trades on specific features of moral questions – things that seem to be true about moral questions but not about mathematical questions. That is what I will mean when I say that it is *domain-specific*, as opposed to the *domain-neutral* reasons for accepting nondescriptivism provided by the idea of avoiding the core questions by denying their presupposition.

The motivation problem starts with the following observation. Suppose that you and your friend have been discussing whether she ought to donate money to CARE, a highly rated international poverty-fighting organization.[7] She thinks not. Maybe she thinks that her money works more effectively to fight poverty if given to Oxfam,[8] or maybe she thinks that it is more important to donate to the political campaigns of the party she believes will make a larger difference than she can with her donation. Or maybe she simply thinks that it is her right to spend her money as she pleases, and prefers to spend it on soy lattes and sugar-free biscotti.

Whichever of these is the case, part of the point of engaging in this discussion with her is probably that you expect it to make a difference, if you convince her. Suppose, for example, you really do convince her that you are right, and that she ought to donate money to CARE. If the next thing that happens is that a representative of CARE comes knocking on the door soliciting donations, you will expect that she will not be indifferent. Having decided that donating is what she ought to do, you will expect her to at least feel some motivation to donate. Before you convinced her, maybe she, felt indifferent, but after you convince her, you expect her to feel indifferent no longer. If your friend really feels no such motivation, you are likely to wonder whether she was really just being insincere in agreeing with you, perhaps just hoping that you would get off her back.

So far, so obvious; all we've noted so far is that we typically expect people to feel at least some motivation to do what they think they ought to do. But I haven't gotten to the problem, yet. The problem is that this appears to make moral beliefs very different from other sorts of beliefs. If you are discussing with your friend whether the Alcove serves onion rings the size of dough-nuts, for example, you might expect your friend to be motivated to eat lunch at the Alcove, but that depends on whether she has a hankering for outsized onion rings. If she goes in for such things, then she will be motivated to have lunch at the Alcove, if you suggest it, but if the thought of such onion rings disgusts her, then she will be motivated to go somewhere else. So in general, when you convince your friend of some ordinary, non-moral matter, there is nothing in particular that you expect that to motivate her to do (besides, of course, to admit that you are right about it) – what she will be motivated to do depends on what she wants or likes, what disgusts her or for what she hankers. But moral questions are different. If you convince your friend that she ought to donate to CARE, then there is something in particular that you expect this to motivate her to do, even if she has no special desire to do what she ought. You expect her to have some motivation to donate money to CARE.

The fact that moral beliefs seem, at least, to be different from non-moral beliefs in this way – that is, in terms of their motivational properties – is one that has struck philosophers as important for approximately as long as we have written records of anyone thinking about philosophy at all. The idea that moral beliefs *do* have a special connection to motivation that non-moral beliefs do not is called <u>motivational internalism</u>. Not everyone thinks that motivational internalism is true; a number of philosophers believe that there is something hasty and uncareful about the reasoning that I went through in the last two paragraphs in order to try to give you the idea of motivational internalism. They believe that if you think more carefully about how moral beliefs moti-vate, you will see that they are not, in fact, all that different from non-moral beliefs. These philosophers accept what is known as *motivational externalism*.

Still, even though there is much disagreement about the truth of motivational internalism – that is, about whether moral beliefs have a special
connection to motivation that non-moral beliefs do not – people who do
think that it is true are led next to wonder why it is true. So even if you, like
the motivational externalists, doubt that there is any very deep difference
underlying the two examples that I just gave, suppose for just a moment
that you really were convinced that there is such a deep difference between
moral beliefs and non-moral beliefs. So what we want to know is: why?

The most influential answer to this question has been that moral beliefs
have a special connection to motivation that non-moral beliefs do not because
moral beliefs are a different kind of mental state from non-moral beliefs. Proponents
of this answer often pair it with a picture of how these two kinds of mental
states differ. According to the picture, non-moral beliefs are about something.
They are like maps, which tell us the lay of the land, where 'the land' is a
metaphor for what they are about. Whereas moral beliefs, according to this
picture, are not maps to anything. They are more like goals we have, about
which destination on the map we want to reach. According to this picture,
ordinary, non-moral beliefs do not correspond to any particular thing that
they motivate someone to do, because even once we know where we are
on the map, what we do next depends on what destination we are trying to
reach. Whereas according to the picture, moral beliefs do correspond to a
particular thing that they motivate someone to do, because having a moral
belief is a matter of having some particular destination as your goal.

The picture that I have just sketched, according to which some mental
states are like maps of the world, and other mental states are like goals
about which destination we are headed for, is sometimes called the Humean
Theory of Motivation. It is called that because, in the eighteenth century, David
Hume drew this picture in a very compelling way.[9] A different metaphor
sometimes used to describe what is essentially the same picture, is that of
direction of fit.[10] According to this metaphor, some mental states 'try' to match
to the world, and are unsuccessful if they do not change in order to match
the world. Whereas other mental states 'try' to get the world to match themselves, and are unsuccessful if they do not get the world to change in order
to match them. The difference between these two sorts of mental states is
therefore like the difference between the notepad of a detective who follows
a grocery shopper, trying to keep track of what goes into her cart, and the
shopping list of that shopper. Both lists try to match what is in the cart, but
the detective tries to do it by changing his list, and the shopper tries to do
it by changing what is in the cart.

So put in terms of the Humean Theory of Motivation, the most influential answer to the question of *why* moral beliefs have a special tie to motivation that non-moral beliefs do not, is that non-moral beliefs are like the detective's list, and have what is called 'mind-to-world' direction of fit, because they try to match – to *map out* – how the world is. Whereas moral beliefs have a special tie to motivation, because they are like the shopper's list, and have what is called 'world-to-mind' direction of fit, because they try to get the world to match themselves. These are just metaphors, but they are helpful metaphors, because they give us a picture that different theories fill out in different, more concrete ways.

## 1.5 Noncognitivism in ethics

We now know enough to be able to say what the motivation problem has to do with nondescriptivism, the view that we encountered in the last section. If moral beliefs contrast with non-moral beliefs in not being maps to anything – in there being nothing about the world that they try to match – then in a natural sense they are not about anything. After all, intuitively the thing that a belief is about, is the very thing that it tries to match, and is unsuccessful if it does not match. So the influential answer to the question of why motivational internalism is true turns out to be the same as the strategy for avoiding the core questions, by denying their presupposition. Both involve the idea that, in at least some sense, moral beliefs are not really *about* anything.

This means that the strategy for avoiding the core questions and the influential answer to why motivational internalism is true lead to the same place. They both lead to *nondescriptivism*. Because of its connection to the motivational problem, nondescriptivism about morality often goes by another name. It is called noncognitivism. If 'cognitive' means 'having to do with belief', the idea is that moral thoughts are not of the same kind as ordinary beliefs – at least, ordinary *non*-moral beliefs. So they are in that sense 'noncognitive', and hence the name for the view.

Philosophers have offered many different definitions for the term 'noncognitivism' over the last seven decades or more. Some have defined it as the view that moral sentences cannot be true or false. Some have defined it as the view that there is no such thing as a moral belief. Some have defined it as a special version of *expressivism*, a particular theory that we will encounter in Chapter 4. So when you read other books and articles about this topic, you will see that the word is used differently by different people. But one thing that people generally agree on, is who counts as a noncognitivist. It is agreed by most philosophers that the theories of A.J. Ayer, Charles Stevenson, R.M. Hare, Simon Blackburn, and Allan Gibbard all count as part of the 'noncognitivist tradition'. Since we don't have a better name for this tradition, that is how I will use the word 'noncognitivism' in this book.

We will begin to encounter the views of these theorists in Chapter 2, where we will see that as a matter of fact, there is not very much that they can all agree on. But they do agree on this much: that we don't need to worry about the core questions, because they have a false presupposition, and that as a result, we can explain why moral thought and language are more intimately connected to motivation than non-moral thought and language. So I will understand noncognitivism in ethics to be a family of nondescriptivist theories about morality which try to explain a special connection between moral thought and motivation.

And so I can now (at last!) say what this book is about: it is about the problems and prospects facing noncognitivist theories. So far, we've seen in this chapter that noncognitivist theories can be perceived to have certain advantages in the core areas of philosophy, and that they can apparently provide a neat explanation of motivational internalism, which is at least very plausible as an observation about moral thought. These are the main attractions of noncognitivism – the reasons why a variety of philosophers are tempted to think that it is true. Now, you may not find these particular features attractive. For example, you may think that there are satisfactory answers to what moral questions are about, and as to how we find out about and manage to talk and think about what they are about.. And you may think that there was something misleading about my examples in which you convince your friend that she ought to donate, as compared to the case in which you convince her that there are doughnut-sized onion rings at the Alcove, and hence you might think that motivational internalism is a big exaggeration. If you think those things, then noncognitivism will not be attractive to you. But many people have become convinced that the core questions are particularly difficult in the case of morality, and that motivational internalism is true. So noncognitivism is attractive to them. (And you may, in fact, be one of them.)

So how, then, do we figure out who is right? If we disagree about how difficult the core questions are to answer satisfactorily, and about whether motivational internalism is true, then how do we decide whether noncognitivism is true? Well, there are essentially two ways that we can go. On the first strategy, we spend our efforts trying to figure out what the right answers are to the core questions, assuming that noncognitivism is false. If we *can* answer these questions in a satisfactory way (even if they are quite difficult), then we learn something: we learn that at the very least, these questions are not *too* hard to answer. And that removes one kind of reason – the reason based on the strategy for avoiding the core questions – to think that noncognitivism is true. Similarly, as part of this strategy we can spend our efforts trying to determine whether motivational internalism is true – that is, just what the nature of the connection is between moral belief and motivation, and whether we can explain it by any less drastic measures than those proposed by the noncognitivist. If we can, then again, that removes one of the reasons to think that noncognitivism is true.

So the first strategy is *indirect*. It says: find out the answers to everything else in metaethics, and if we can reach satisfactory answers, then there may be no reason to think that noncognitivism is true. But the second strategy for trying to figure out whether noncognitivism is true is more direct. Setting aside whether it is well motivated, on the second strategy we spend our efforts trying to figure out what things would be like if noncognitivism were true, and checking to see whether things could really be that way. In order to explore this strategy, we need to know more of what noncognitivist theories are like. We need to begin to develop the details of these theories, and to see whether they have testable predictions.

Nearly any other book about metaethics will tell you some of the things that you need to know in order to work on the first strategy. In this book, we will take the second strategy. Having explained some of the reasons why people are tempted to think that noncognitivism is true, I am now going to set those reasons aside for the remainder of the book, except when we are trying to figure out whether a given noncognitivist theory really achieves the main purported advantages of noncognitivism, after all. Instead of trying to figure out whether noncognitivism is a *tempting* view, we will spend our time trying to figure out whether it *could* be true.

In particular, as we'll see in Chapter 2 when we learn more about what individual noncognitivist theories look like, it will turn out that just as noncognitivism is thought to *solve* various problems from the core areas of philosophy, noncognitivist theories also *face* important problems in each of the core areas of philosophy. The general reason why noncognitivism faces these problems is simple: if moral questions are not *about* anything, and we are not talking about anything when we discuss them – any special subject matter of morality – then what *are* we doing?

We do, after all, have moral thoughts. You and I both think, for example, that it is wrong to kill an innocent person in order to steal their DVD collection. So if this thought is not *about* anything in particular – the wrongness of this action – then what exactly *is* involved in having this thought? Similarly, we do use moral language – we say to each other sentences like, 'Infibulation is wrong' or 'It's not wrong to take one's daughter for infibulation'. So if these sentences are not *about* anything in particular – the wrongness or lack of it attaching to a certain surgical procedure – then what do they *mean*, and what use are they? Noncognitivist theories in ethics face a special burden to answer these questions – to tell us what kind of thoughts moral thoughts are, and what kind of *meaning* moral sentences have, if they aren't about anything in particular. It is in answering these questions that noncognitivist theories run into their problems.

So in later chapters, we will look at problems faced by noncognitivist theories in the philosophy of mind (Chapter 5), in the philosophy of language (Chapters 3, 6, and 7), in metaphysics (Chapter 8), and in epistemology (Chapter 9). Along the way, we'll gradually learn about what different kinds of noncognitivist theory are like (Chapters 2, 4, and 10). Unless noncognitivists can solve these problems that face their theories, noncognitivism *can't* be true, even if it could help us to solve many philosophical problems if it *were* true.

## Chapter summary

In this chapter we introduced the *domain-neutral* core questions of metaphysics, epistemology, the philosophy of language, and the philosophy of mind, as well as the *domain-specific* motivation problem from metaethics. We introduced noncognitivism as a kind of *nondescriptivist* theory about what kind of meaning moral words have, if they are not about anything. And we previewed what to expect in the remainder of the book.

## Further reading

An alternative take on the central problems of metaethics can be found in Darwall, Gibbard, and Railton (1997); Miller (2003) provides a fairly typical introduction to the field and its various topics. Both are written at a somewhat more advanced level than this chapter. Urmson (1968, chapter 2) is also recommended. I follow Urmson in distinguishing between domain-neutral motivations from the core areas, and the domain-specific problem about motivation.

## Exercises

1    E *Comprehension*: In section 2 we distinguished between the question of *whether* we have moral knowledge and the question of *how* we get that knowledge, and in section 3 we distinguished between the question of whether we manage to talk and think about moral questions and how we manage to do so. Provide examples of two other topics about which you might wonder both whether something is true, and how it is true. Choose one example about which you wonder how something is true, without that making you doubt that it is true. Choose another example, for which wondering how something could be true makes you wonder whether it really is true.

2    E *Qualifications*: In the main text, I characterized noncognitivist views as holding that moral sentences are not really about *anything*. This characterization was somewhat sloppy. Consider the following four sentences:

1    Infibulation is wrong.
2    Infibulation is common.
3    Infibulation is both common and wrong.
4    Aww, infibulation!?

For each sentence, list the things that sentence is intuitively about. Can you list the same number of things for each sentence, or do you get different numbers for different sentences? How do these numbers compare?

3    E *Branching out*: The Open Question argument. Rank the following four questions from most to least interesting or 'live' feeling (ties are allowed):

5    I know it's wrong, but is it wrong?
6    I know it's wrong, but is it harmful?
7    I know it's harmful, but is it wrong?
8    I know it's harmful, but is it harmful?

Do your rankings change if you substitute 'against God's will' for 'harmful'? If you substitute 'untraditional' for 'harmful'? Can you think of anything that you could substitute for 'harmful' that would make your rankings change?

4    E *Extensions*: Rank the following four questions, as you did in the previous exercise:

9  I know it's a triangle, but is it a triangle?

10  I know it's a triangle, but is it a shape with three straight sides?

11  I know it's a shape with three straight sides, but is it a triangle?

12  I know it's a shape with three straight sides, but is it a shape with three straight sides?

Do these questions seem the same or different? 'Shape with three straight sides' seems like a pretty good definition of 'triangle'. Could there be a definition for 'wrong'?

5    M *Extensions*: We noted in the main text that the motivation problem is *domain-specific*, meaning that it does not come up in every area of philosophy. In order to test whether this is true, try to construct an example like the one that we used to introduce motivational internalism for each of two other subject matters: mathematics and beauty. Try to construct a case of a mathematical question – for example, from arithmetic, algebra, or calculus – such that there is something that you expect your friend to be motivated to do, if you convince her of the answer to that question, and not just because of what she wants or likes. And try to construct a similar example for a question about what is beautiful. Is one of these harder to do than the other? How do they compare to the moral case?

6    M *Branching out*: It is natural to wonder whether there are domain-specific problems that motivate nondescriptivism about other topics. For a good example, see Gibbard (1981), who offers a simple argument for nondescriptivism about *conditionals* ('if ... then' sentences) that doesn't apply to other topics. Another good example is the case of truth. Why might the following sentence make someone puzzled about how there could be anything we are saying about the world when we say that a sentence is true?

Liar: The sentence named 'Liar' on page 17 of *Noncognitivism in Ethics* is not true.

## Morals

2    In addition to being about wrongness, sentence 1 is about infibulation with excision. Noncognitivist views don't deny that sentence 1 is about infibulation with excision; just that it is about something else – wrongness. So

it is sloppy to say that according to noncognitivist views, moral sentences are not about anything. What is important about noncognitivist views, is that a sentence is not about *more* things, in virtue of having a moral word like 'wrong' in it, because 'wrong' does not *contribute* to what the sentence is about.

3    One reason some philosophers have been skeptical that there is any answer to the question of what it is to be wrong is because of an argument advanced by G.E. Moore known as the *Open Question argument*. Moore believed that no matter what is substituted for 'harmful', question 7 feels 'open' in a way that questions 5 and 8 do not. This led Moore to believe that they are different questions, and since they are different questions, to believe that whatever is substituted for 'wrong' can't be the answer to what it is to be wrong. Some philosophers believe that even if these sentences all ask the same question, the use of different words to ask it can make 6 and 7 feel 'open', even though 5 and 8 do not. This view predicts that 6 and 7 should feel *equally* 'open'. Did you say that they are equally live questions? Does it matter what we substitute for 'harmful'?

4    One good way to test Moore's Open Question argument to see whether it is a good argument is to check and see whether true definitions feel 'open'. Another good kind of definition to test is the fact that water is $H_2O$. Do the questions in exercise 3 feel 'open' in a way that the analogous questions with 'water' substituted for 'wrong' and '$H_2O$' substituted for 'harmful' do not? Or do they feel the same? Some philosophers believe that it is just the same, and some believe that there is something special and different going on in the moral case, which makes it harder to say what 'wrong' is about than what 'triangle' or 'water' are about.

## References

Anscombe, Elizabeth (1957). *Intention*. Oxford: Basil Blackwell.

Darwall, Stephen, Allan Gibbard, and Peter Railton, eds. (1997). *Moral Discourse and Practice: Some Philosophical Approaches*. Oxford: Oxford University Press.

de Waal, Frans (1996). *Good Natured: The Origins of Right and Wrong in Primates and Other Animals*. Cambridge, MA: Harvard University Press.

Greene, J.D., and J. Haidt (2002). 'How (and Where) Does Moral Judgment Work?' *Trends in Cognitive Sciences* 6: 517–23.

Greene, J.D., R.B. Sommerville, L.E. Nystrom, J.M. Darley, and J.D. Cohen (2001). 'An fMRI Investigation of Emotional Engagement in Moral Judgment.' *Science* 293: 2105–8.

Haidt, Jonathan (2001). 'The Emotional Dog and Its Rational Tail: A Social Intuitionist Approach to Moral Judgment.' *Psychological Review* 108: 814–34.

Joyce, Richard (2006). *The Evolution of Morality*. Cambridge, MA: MIT Press.

Miller, Alexander (2003). *An Introduction to Contemporary Metaethics*. Cambridge: Polity.

Nichols, Shaun (2004). *Sentimental Rules*. Oxford: Oxford University Press.

Smith, Michael (1994a). *The Moral Problem*. Oxford: Basil Blackwell.

Urmson, J.O. (1968). *The Emotive Theory of Ethics*. New York: Oxford University Press.

# 2

# THE NONCOGNITIVIST TURN

## 2.1 Where we are

In Chapter 1 we encountered the basic ideas that motivate noncognitivist metaethical theories – that is, the ideas which make philosophers wonder whether noncognitivism might be true. As we saw, the main idea of such theories is *negative* – we characterized noncognitivism as the idea that moral thought and language are not *about* anything in particular. And that left us with one big question: if moral thought and language are not *about* anything, then what are they for? To this question, different noncognitivists have given different answers. The best way to start to get a sense for what these answers are like is to start to look at some of them. Since noncognitivist theories have gotten progressively more subtle and complicated over the years, it's best to start with some of the earliest noncognitivist theories.

In this chapter we'll first encounter the emotivist theories of A.J. Ayer and Charles Stevenson, and begin to develop a picture of how their theories of the meaning of moral words contrast with the dominant paradigm in theorizing about linguistic meaning, by learning a little bit about what motivates that paradigm and how it works. Then in the later part of the chapter, we'll contrast Ayer's and Stevenson's emotivist views with the prescriptivism of R.M. Hare, and begin to compare some of their relative merits. The main goals of the chapter are to acquaint the reader with what noncognitivist theories actually look like, and to emphasize how different they can be from one another.

## 2.2  What the heck was emotivism?

The earliest noncognitivist theories were called emotivist. We now associate this name with the idea that moral language had centrally to do with the emotions, but this idea was not shared by all views which at the time were called 'emotivist'. A better etymology might relate the name to the verb, 'to emote'.[1] The most colorful statement ever given of an emotivist theory (or any noncognitivist theory, for that matter), and also one of the most illuminating, is that of A.J. Ayer:

> The presence of an ethical symbol in a proposition adds nothing to its factual content. Thus if I say to someone, 'You acted wrongly in stealing that money,' I am not stating anything more than if I had simply said, 'You stole that money.' In adding that this action is wrong I am not making any further statement about it. I am simply evincing my moral disapproval of it. It is as if I had said, 'You stole that money,' in a peculiar tone of horror, or written it with the addition of some special exclamation marks. The tone, or the exclamation marks, adds nothing to the literal meaning of the sentence. It merely serves to show that the expression of it is attended by certain feelings in the speaker.
>
> If now I generalise my previous statement and say, 'Stealing money is wrong,' I produce a sentence which has no factual meaning – that is, expresses no proposition which can be true or false. It is as if I had written 'Stealing money!!' – where the shape and thickness of the exclamation marks show, by a suitable convention, that a special sort of moral disapproval is the feeling which is being expressed. It is clear that there is nothing said here which can be true or false. (1936, 107)

Ayer is clearly claiming, in this passage, that a moral word like 'wrongly' contrasts with non-moral words, in how it contributes to the 'factual meaning' of a sentence, or to what kind of 'statement' one makes with a sentence. What he is saying, then, contrasts with what we might expect him to say about 'quickly':

> Thus if I say to someone, 'You acted quickly in stealing that money,' I am stating something more than if I had simply said, 'You stole that money.' In

adding that this action was quick I am making a further statement about it. I am saying that it had the feature of having been done quickly, in contrast to having been done slowly. 'Quickly' *does* add something to the literal meaning of the sentence. It serves to describe what something was like, independently of the speaker. It serves to say that it happened at a relatively fast speed.

When he says that the word 'wrongly' is sort of like a special kind of exclamation mark, or a 'peculiar tone of horror', Ayer means to be contrasting it with words like 'quickly'. He means to be saying that it has a different kind of meaning, and hence affects the meanings of sentences which involve it in a different way.

It is very important that Ayer doesn't simply mean that 'wrongly' and 'quickly' have different meanings, which is obviously true. 'Quickly' and 'slowly' have different meanings, but share the same kind of meaning. He means to contrast 'wrongly' with both of these other words – to be saying that we use 'wrongly' to do a different sort of thing from what we use 'quickly' or 'slowly' to do. It has a different kind of meaning. Ayer's analogies to special exclamation marks and the 'peculiar tone of horror' is supposed to help to give us a picture of what kind it has, instead, and how these two kinds are different. The analogies suggest that Ayer thinks that 'wrongly' contributes to the meaning of 'you acted wrongly in stealing that money' in the same sort of way that 'the heck' contributes to the meaning of 'what the heck was emotivism?'.

So Ayer's negative view is very clear. It is very clear that Ayer thinks that moral words are not *about* something. When we add a moral word to a sentence, we don't change what that sentence is about. Hence, whatever kind of meaning moral words have, it can't be a matter of what they are about. It is less clear exactly what Ayer's positive view is about the kind of meaning that moral words do have. What he gives us is an analogy. The analogy is illuminating, because it helps us to see what it might be for moral words to not be about something. They might be for the same purpose as a horrified tone of voice, or might be like 'the heck' in 'what the heck was emotivism?'. Even if we don't have a theory about the meaning of 'the heck', we can all appreciate that it is a useful thing to be able to say, and also that it has *some* kind of meaning. After all, 'what the heck was emotivism?' means something different from 'what kiz hooziwud was emotivism?'. So 'the heck' is meaningful in a way that 'kiz hooziwud' is not. 'Wrongly', according to Ayer, has a meaning like that.[2]

## 2.3 Stevenson

On Ayer's theory, as we've seen, moral words are not about anything, which is why their meaning can't consist in what they are about. According to his contemporary and fellow emotivist Charles Stevenson, in contrast, moral words may be about something, but knowing what they are about does not *suffice* to understand their meaning. Rather than their meaning consisting in something *other* than what they are about, Stevenson held that moral words' meaning consists in something *more* than what they are about. Stevenson first introduced his theory by contrasting it with what he called 'traditional interest theories':

> Traditional interest theories hold that ethical statements are *descriptive* of
> the existing states and interests – that they simply *give information* about
> · interests. ... Doubtless there is always *some* element of description in ethical
> judgments, but this is by no means all. Their major use is not to indicate
> facts but to *create an influence*. Instead of merely describing people's inter-
> ests they *change* or *intensify* them. They *recommend* an interest in an object,
> rather than state that the interest already exists. ... The difference between
> the traditional interest theories and my view is like the difference between
> describing a desert and irrigating it. (1937, 16)

We'll learn more about what some of the 'traditional interest theories' that Stevenson mentions were like in Chapter 4. But we can already see from this passage that unlike Ayer, Stevenson is willing to grant that 'ethical judgments' – that is, moral sentences – may in fact be about something. That is what he means by saying that '[d]oubtless there is always *some* element of description in ethical judgments'. Yet clearly the main point of the passage is also to say that this is not *all* there is to the meaning of moral sentences, because it leaves out '[t]heir major use'.

Whereas Ayer's view amounts to the claim that knowing what a word is about is not *necessary* in order to understand its meaning (because some words, like 'the heck', are meaningful without being about anything), Stevenson is advocating the view that knowing what a word is about is not *sufficient* to understand its meaning (because some words, though they are about something, are not *merely* about it, but have an additional 'major use'). So they depart in each of two different ways from the idea that knowing what a word is about is both necessary and sufficient in order to understand its meaning. We'll have occasion in section 4 to look in more detail at this idea which both Ayer and Stevenson are committed to rejecting. But first, let's look in a little more detail at the other features of Stevenson's view.

Because Stevenson does not really deny that moral words are about something, you might suspect that he was more concerned about the *domain-specific* motivations for noncognitivism that we encountered in Chapter 1, rather than with the *domain-neutral* motivations, which turned specifically on denying the presupposition that moral words are about something. And that's mostly correct. Whereas Ayer thought mostly about the core questions, and saw moral language as just one among many topics to which to apply a set of very general ideas, Stevenson was specifically interested in meta-ethics. And whereas Ayer seems not to have thought about the motivational problem – at least, not carefully – for Stevenson the motivational problem is one of the main reasons why he is attracted to his brand of emotivism. So Ayer and Stevenson really illustrate how theorists with very different background ideas and philosophical motives have come to converge on very closely related sets of ideas.

But it is not exactly true to say that Stevenson was not motivated by the core questions. The ability of his view to help with the core questions is one of the things that he does emphasize in his original (1937) paper, under the heading of trying to make sense of why scientific methods do not seem to help us to answer moral questions. And that, of course, sounds like a familiar worry from Chapter 1. So the question for us to ask is: how could Stevenson avoid having to explain why scientific methods don't help us to answer moral questions, if he still granted that they are about something – something that we would need to find out about, in order to answer them?

To see the answer to this puzzle, we must look in more detail at Stevenson's positive characterization of his theory. Once we get beyond the metaphor of irrigating the desert, Stevenson offers two different 'patterns of analysis' of moral language. It is important to understand that Stevenson did not think that it is possible to state definitions which tell us what 'good' means, by giving paraphrases which have essentially the same meaning, in the way that a dictionary might tell us that 'bachelor' means 'unmarried man'. He thought this both because he simply did not think that there *are* any other words with exactly the same meaning,[3] and because he believed that it is *vague* exactly what ordinary natural-language words like 'good' mean.[4] So what Stevenson offered instead was two different 'patterns', neither of which was exactly right, but each of which illustrated an important dimension or aspect of the meaning of moral words. Each 'pattern' allowed that moral words are about something – indeed, Stevenson thought, about two things. And each pattern insisted that there is more to the meaning of moral words than what they are about. The two patterns differed over which thing that moral words are about was taken to be primary and which derivative.

According to Stevenson's first pattern of analysis, the sentence, 'This is  good' means something roughly like, 'I approve of this – do so as well'. From his very earliest work onward, Stevenson emphasized that this was overly simplistic as a literal account of what 'this is good' really means. But he used it in order to *illustrate* two important things which he held to be true. The first was that on some uses of 'this is good', it *is* about something – it is about what the speaker approves of. In this, Stevenson agreed with the 'traditional interest theories' that we will encounter in Chapter 4. But the second thing that Stevenson wanted to emphasize was that 'this is good' is not merely a report of what the speaker approves of; it is also an endorsement of so approving, or used to *encourage* or *invoke* the listener to approve. Stevenson goes back and forth between different characterizations like these, but the important thing for him is that a moral sentence like this one does not merely describe, but is also used to 'create an influence'.

Stevenson (1944) describes the 'second pattern of analysis' as follows:

> 'This is good' has the meaning of 'This has qualities or relations X, Y, Z ...,' except that 'good' has as well a laudatory emotive meaning which permits it to express the speaker's approval, and tends to evoke the approval of the hearer. (1944, 207)

It is clear from the context that Stevenson has a very specific idea of what we should expect X, Y, or Z to be in a given situation, even though he doesn't really say so. For example, earlier he writes:

> A clergyman tells us 'what a very good girl' Mary is, and we feel confident, on his testimony, that Mary is chaste, kind, and pious. (1944, 85)

His thought appears to be this: sometimes we use the word 'good' to say that we approve of something and to endorse approving of that thing. In such cases, listeners who know which sorts of things we approve of can also learn more about what that thing is like. If, for example, a clergyman so uses the word 'good' to describe a girl, and we happen to know that clergymen generally tend to approve of girls only if they are chaste, kind, and pious, then we can work out that she must be chaste, kind, and pious. That's on

the first pattern of analysis. On the second pattern of analysis, we understand 'good' to be primarily associated with the information that Mary is
chaste, kind, and pious, and then we work out for ourselves that the speaker
approves of her. So things are the other way around. Stevenson seems to
think that moral words are sometimes used more in the former way, and
sometimes more in the latter way, and that we need to reflect on both, in
order fully to appreciate their meaning.

To return to our puzzle, on neither of these patterns of analysis does it
turn out that what moral words are about is something that we can't find
out through ordinary methods. Ordinary empirical methods are perfectly
appropriate for figuring out what people approve of, as well as for ascer-
taining whether Mary is chaste, kind, and pious. So even though Stevenson
thinks that moral words are about something, he doesn't think that this
is anything which leads to special puzzles about what that thing is, about
how we find out about it, or about how we manage to talk or think about
it. What makes it *seem* like the thing that moral words are about is something that ordinary methods don't suffice to find out about, is that ordinary
methods don't suffice to *answer moral questions*. And the reason why they don't
is that there is more to answering moral questions than finding out about
what the moral words are *about*. To answer a moral question, you have to also
decide what *attitude* to have.

## 2.4 Truth-conditional semantics

To appreciate the significance of these ideas of Ayer and Stevenson, and
to understand some of the most important challenges that noncognitivist
views face, it is important to contrast their ideas with a Very Big Idea that
they are committed to rejecting.[5] This Very Big Idea is that it is necessary and
sufficient to understand the meaning of a word to know what that word
is about. I use capital letters because though I'm simplifying somewhat,
something very much like this Very Big Idea is at the heart of the dominant
paradigm for theorizing about meaning, lies at the heart of the development of modern logic at the turn of the last century, and is central to most
of the insights into linguistic meaning in natural languages like English over
the last forty to fifty years.

In order to illustrate the appeal of the Very Big Idea, I'm going to do two
things. First, I'm going to explain two things that we ought to hope for
from any adequate theory about what words mean. And then I'm going to
show how easy it is to accomplish these two things in the case of ordinary

non-moral words like 'red', 'rectangular', and 'aluminum', which Ayer and Stevenson would both agree are uncontroversially about something. The way that this is done is one of the basic insights of an approach to theorizing about meaning called truth-conditional semantics, and although most versions of truth-conditional semantics are much more sophisticated and technically complex than the simple sketch that I will use as an illustration, and though many theorists who fall into the 'truth-conditional' family would insist on qualifications to or more careful formulations of these ideas, all of the more sophisticated developments are built on ideas pretty much like the ones I will state here.

So what might we hope for from a theory about what words mean (usually called a semantic theory)? The first thing that we should hope for is that whatever the theory tells us about what sentences mean, it had better be useful when it comes to explaining how speakers manage to use those sentences in order to accomplish their communicative purposes. After all, we use sentences in communicating with one another, and we use sentences that mean different things to communicate different things. In general, sentences with different meanings are useful for communicating different things, so an adequate theory of meaning had better help us to explain how the meaning of a given sentence makes it suited for the actual communicative or other conversational purposes to which we put it. I'm going to call this first thing that we should hope for from a theory of meaning, the communicative constraint.

The second thing that we ought to hope for from a theory of meaning is that whatever the meanings of sentences are, they had better follow from the meanings of their parts and how those parts are arranged. This is because there are infinitely many sentences in any natural language, and if you understand the meanings of just a few words, we can construct arbitrarily many new sentences that you have never seen before – but which you will immediately understand. For example, the majority of sentences which appear in this book are ones that you have never seen before. (That is why it is worth your time to read the book, after all.) But that is no obstacle to your understanding them, because you can figure out their meaning on the basis of their parts and how those parts are put together. This is usually called the compositional constraint.

To see why truth-conditional semantics has been such a fruitful research program for understanding meanings, all we need to do is to see how easy it is to satisfy both of these constraints for the case of words that we can understand as being about something, in at least a certain limited sense.

Ordinary non-moral words like 'red', 'rectangular', and 'aluminum' are about something, at least in the sense that they serve to demarcate differences and similarities in how things are. For example, 'red' picks out a similarity that is shared by fire trucks and cinnamon sticks and British post-boxes but not by igloos or iguanas. 'Rectangular' picks out a similarity shared by football fields, the façade of the Lincoln Memorial, and Wyoming, but not by footballs or Massachusetts. And 'aluminum' picks out a similarity shared by Boeing aircraft and Coke cans, but not by alligators or by the Declaration of Independence.

The words 'red', 'rectangular', and 'aluminum' are predicates – in particular, they are adjectives. But ordinary names are also about things – the things they name or refer to. For example, 'Colorado' is about a mountainous western state, and 'Air Force One' is about the plane in which the president of the United States travels. Given that we know which similarity is demarcated by 'rectangular' and which thing 'Colorado' refers to, it is easy to figure out what it would take for the sentence 'Colorado is rectangular' to be true. For it to be true, the thing 'Colorado' refers to needs to share the similarity that is demarcated by 'rectangular'. Similarly, to figure out what it would take for the sentence 'Air Force One is aluminum' to be true, all that we need is to know what thing 'Air Force One' refers to, and which similarity 'aluminum' demarcates. For the sentence to be true, that thing needs to share in that similarity.

These observations can sound banal if you haven't encountered them before. But they are important, because they constitute a pattern. If I give you a new name, 'Max', and a new predicate, 'kibochuk', you have a recipe for figuring out what it would take for 'Max is kibochuk' to be true. For that sentence to be true, it would have to be the case of whoever 'Max' refers to, that he shares the similarity demarcated by 'kibochuk' – whatever that is. This recipe means that if the meaning of a name is what it is about – its referent – and if the meaning of a predicate is what it is about – the similarity that it serves to demarcate – and the meaning of a sentence is what it takes for that sentence to be true – its truth conditions – then we can satisfy the compositional constraint for simple name–predicate sentences like 'Colorado is rectangular' and 'Max is kibochuk'. That is because if that is what the meanings of names, predicates, and sentences are, then our recipe is a recipe for finding out the meaning of a sentence from the meanings of its parts, and how they are put together.

Moreover, the very same idea lets us satisfy the compositional constraint for larger and more complicated sentences. For example, if we know what it would take for 'Colorado is rectangular' to be true, and we know what it would take for 'Max is kibochuk' to be true, then it is not hard to figure out what it would take for 'Colorado is not rectangular' to be true, or for 'Colorado is rectangular and Max is kibochuk' to be true. The former is true whenever 'Colorado is rectangular' is not true, and the latter is true whenever 'Colorado is rectangular' and 'Max is kibochuk' are both true. It turns out that these generalizations apply, no matter which sentences we are talking about. They provide a recipe to get from the truth conditions of simpler sentences to the truth conditions of more complex sentences. So if $S+S+S=C$ truth conditions are meanings, then this turns out to be a recipe to get from the meanings of the parts to the meaning of the whole, which is what the compositional constraint requires.

Now, all of this would not be very interesting, if the hypothesis that the meaning of a sentence consists in what it would take for it to be true did not also satisfy the communicative constraint by helping us to make sense of how a sentence's meaning allows us to use it to communicate what we do. But it is easy to see how this hypothesis satisfies the communicative constraint. This is because in normal cases what we communicate in uttering a sentence is precisely that the world is the way that it would have to be in order for that sentence to be true! For example, someone who says 'Colorado is rectangular' uses that sentence to communicate that the world is the way that it would have to be in order for 'Colorado is rectangular' to be true. So if that just is the meaning of the sentence, then the step from linguistic meanings to our communicative purposes is straightforward. We use a sentence to communicate that its truth conditions are satisfied.

So the ideas that the meaning of a sentence consists in what would make it true and that the meaning of a word consists in what that word is about are powerful and productive ideas. As a hypothesis about meanings, they have led to an enormously productive and successful research program in both linguistics and philosophy, which has shed great light on the meanings of a great variety of kinds of linguistic expressions. Different approaches differ very widely in how they implement these ideas, but they are at the heart of the standard, very productive paradigm for understanding linguistic meaning.

In contrast, both Ayer and Stevenson reject both of these ideas. Ayer denies that it is necessary, to know what a word means, to know what it is about, and Stevenson denies that it is sufficient. Ayer believes that 'you acted wrongly in stealing that money' is different in meaning from 'you stole that money', but not by making a different statement, or being true under different conditions. Stevenson thinks that 'I approve of that' and 'that is good' may be true under the same circumstances, but insists that they still mean something different. It is part of their views that a complete theory of meaning must do more, and must do it differently, than merely assigning truth conditions to sentences. It is part of their view, moreover, that the extra things that it must do will particularly come in handy when it comes to accounting for the meaning of moral words like 'good' and 'wrong'.

This is why noncognitivism is such a significant view in the philosophy of language. It is a major departure from the Very Big Idea of truth-conditional theories of meaning. The difference between the idea that meaning can and should be explained by what words are about and what makes sentences true, on the one hand, and the noncognitivist idea that meaning cannot be so explained and must instead be explained directly by how we use words, is a very important difference to understand. If you are still hazy on this difference, you should read this section again, and be prepared to return to it while you are reading later chapters.

## 2.5 Hare's prescriptivism

Before the 1930s, noncognitivism was not a particularly familiar idea, at least among most English-speaking philosophers, and so Ayer, Stevenson, and their early emotivist contemporaries needed to use colorful examples and analogies in order to get people to understand the basic idea. This led them, in most cases, to exaggerate the similarities between moral language and their illustrative examples, such as Ayer's 'peculiar tone of horror' and Stevenson's metaphor of 'irrigating a desert'. These were colorful analogies, and they help to give us the idea of how a word could be meaningful, independently of or in addition to what it is about.

But if taken too seriously, these analogies start to seem very problematic. Ayer, for example, *seems* to suggest that we could do just as well by going around shouting, 'stealing money!!' at each other and raising our eyebrows in a funny sort of way, as by having our MBA students take classes in business ethics or discussing the moral issues associated with the inheritance tax. It's not clear that Ayer really believes this, but the tools that he uses in order to make clear to his readers what the distinction is between his view and the views that he rejects strongly serve to create this impression. Similarly, Stevenson's first-pattern paraphrase, 'I approve of this – do so as well!', is helpful in getting us to see the basic idea of how there could be more to the meaning of 'good' than what it is about, but if taken too seriously it makes puzzling what is going on when people with the same moral views talk to one another, or when we say things like, 'he's a good thief'. It makes sense why Ayer and Stevenson used these colorful analogies, even if they did not themselves believe that they were fully analogous. After all, they were trying to make space for a new kind of theory – to get people to see what it could be like. But they are still misleading analogies, in some ways, if taken too seriously.

By the time the 1950s rolled around, noncognitivist views had become quite familiar, and so when R.M. Hare wrote *The Language of Morals*, he didn't any longer see the need to make space for noncognitivist theories. Rather than needing to use colorful examples in order to illustrate what his view was like, Hare took it as more or less settled that some kind of noncognitivist theory was correct. He saw his task as to explain how that could be so, and to get people to stop taking Ayer's and Stevenson's analogies and colorful descriptions of their views too seriously. Thus, after intensely criticizing Ayer and Stevenson, among others, for a few pages in his first chapter, he writes:

> I wish to emphasize that I am not seeking to refute any of these theories. They have all of them the characteristic that, if put in everyday terms, they say nothing exceptionable so far as their main assertions go. (Hare 1952, 11–12)

Hare's more cautious view takes as its model a different feature of language from either Ayer or Stevenson. His main idea is that the distinction between moods is one whose semantic significance truth-conditional theories of meaning are not very well cut out to explain. On a traditional classification, the moods of English include indicative, imperative, interrogative, and they differ in the following way:

indicative:   You will bring me my slippers.
imperative:   Bring me my slippers.
interrogative:   Will you bring me my slippers?

Now Hare understood that someone can use any of these sentences in order to suggest or order someone to bring him his slippers. But Hare also noted that the imperative mood is specially suited for issuing suggestions or orders, in a way that the indicative and interrogative moods are not.

*ToM is linked to specially-suited moods*

Hare held that an adequate theory of meaning for English needs to recognize that sentences in the imperative mood are specially suited for issuing suggestions or commands in this way, just as interrogative sentences are specially suited for asking questions – even though not all interrogative sentences are used to ask questions. Now, there is an initial puzzle about how a truth-conditional semantics – that is, a theory of meaning according to which the meaning of a sentence consists, roughly, in what it would take for it to be true – can explain this. After all, on the face of it, it doesn't seem like 'Bring me my slippers' is the kind of sentence that *can be* true or false. At least, we ordinarily don't describe imperative sentences that way. Moreover, even if it *could* be true or false, it's hard to see how what would make it true or false would be different from what would make the corresponding indicative or interrogative sentence true or false. And hence it is hard to see how what would make it true or false could explain the fact that it is suited by its meaning to be used to issue orders or suggestions.

Hare doesn't care so much whether or how a truth-conditional theory, or any other theory of meaning for that matter, can explain the way in which the imperative sentence's meaning differs from that of the indicative sentence. What he cares about is the idea that whatever theory of meaning allows us to explain this, he wants to use that very same kind of theory in order to explain how moral sentences like the following differ from their corresponding non-moral sentences:

    moral:   You behave well.
    non-moral:   You behave.

Adding 'well' to 'You behave', according to Hare's idea, is like adding the imperative mood. The imperative mood and moral words like 'good' and 'well' belong, according to Hare, to the same family.

The idea is not that adding 'well' makes this an imperative sentence – it clearly is not. Nor is the idea that 'You behave well' has the same meaning as the one-word imperative sentence, 'Behave'. Rather, the idea is that the ways in which the contributions that 'well' and the imperative mood make to the meaning of a sentence are very *similar in kind*. Both suit sentences for issuing prescriptions. Prescriptions come in many kinds, Hare thought. Some are commands, and imperative sentences are specially suited for those. Some are polite suggestions, and imperatives are also suited for those. Others, however, are neither commands nor suggestions. For example, the one-sentence slogan for Hare's view was that the word 'good' is used to commend.

Commendation is different both from commanding and from suggesting. Like commanding and suggesting, you can accomplish it with different kinds of sentence, but there is a certain kind of sentence that is *suited by its meaning* to be used for commendation, and that is the kind which contains the word 'good' (and its correlates, like 'well').

Hare thought that the word 'good' is always suited for commendation. For example 'that is a good chronometer' is suited for commending the chronometer. So Hare thought that the account of 'good' applies to 'good' everywhere that it appears with its ordinary meaning, even when its meaning doesn't have anything to do with morality, strictly construed. It turns out that Hare did believe that some uses of the word 'good' – *moral* uses, such as in 'St. Francis was a good man' – are special, because we use them to commend not only St. Francis, but anyone else who might be relevantly like him. This part of his view was called *universalized* prescriptivism, but I won't have anything more to say about it, here.

## 2.6 Noncognitivism recharacterized

Earlier we saw that Ayer held that instead of being used to make what he called a 'statement' about matters of fact, moral words are used to express the emotions, feelings, or attitudes of the *speaker*. We also saw that Stevenson held that to understand the meanings of moral words, we need to understand the effect that they have on the *audience*. This difference – between *speaker*-oriented purposes for which we use moral sentences and *audience*-oriented purposes – is striking and important. And it is more striking that Hare thinks that moral language serves *neither* of the roles that we saw in Ayer and Stevenson – it does not *express* the speaker's attitudes, and its meaning does not consist in its *creating an influence* with the listener, as with Stevenson.

On the first point, he specifically claims that any talk we have about the right kind of emotions or attitudes could only be parasitic on our understanding of prescriptive sentences. For example, he specifically says that 'unless we understand "Shut the door" we are unlikely to understand "I want you to shut the door"' (1952, 6), modeling this on the idea that 'I believe that you are going to shut the door' is not a report of one's own mental state, but a sort of qualified version of 'You are going to shut the door.' He holds a similar view about the relationship between 'I want you to shut the door' and 'Shut the door', so he doesn't think that in any of these cases the attitude could be used in order to explicate the meaning of the non-attitude sentence.[6]

Hare is particularly harsh on the idea that a sentence's 'expressing' an attitude or being imperative-like is any kind of *causal* relation, as if 'we have welling up inside us a kind of longing, to which, when the pressure gets too great for us to bear, we give vent by saying an imperative sentence' (1952, 10). Hare's humorous counterexample to this is the following imperative sentence, which is the kind of thing to come from an instruction manual: 'Supply and fit to door mortise dead latch and plastic knob furniture' (1952, 10). It is possible that for the truly passionate this sentence may be preceded by an upwelling of longing for the door to be so fitted, but certainly not necessary that it be used in that way, and likely that it never has been.

But second, Hare does not think, as Stevenson does, that the role of moral sentences is to effect a change in listeners. He specifically rejects the view, which he attributes to Ayer and Carnap as well as Stevenson, that it is part of the meaning of ethical terms that their role is to have a certain effect. He emphasizes that '[t]he process of *telling* someone to do something, and *getting* him to do it, are quite distinct, logically, from each other' (1952, 13). Hare believes that Stevenson collapses this distinction, because it is part of Stevenson's view that the meaning of a moral word consists in its ability to *cause* listeners to have certain attitudes. Some of the exercises ask you to look in more detail at whether Stevenson really has a problem here.

The important moral for us is that the functions of giving voice to the speaker's attitudes or emotions, of trying to create an effect in the listener, and of serving as a prescription of a certain kind, are all *different* positive stories about what moral language is for. Each leads to its own positive theory about the kind of meaning that moral words like 'good' and 'wrong' have, but each of these theories is substantially different from the others. That is why I call noncognitivism a *family* of theories about moral language, rather than saying that it is itself a theory. What the theories in this family have in common is the idea that to understand the meaning of moral words like 'wrong' and 'good' we need to understand that they have an importantly different kind of meaning from ordinary non-moral words, including words like 'quick', 'rectangular', and 'aluminum', and their prospects to help us avoid some of the traditional core questions of metaethics and to solve the motivation problem.

It is important to recognize that there are many different ways of carving up the territory of metaethics. Even the word 'noncognitivism' is not uncontested and is sometimes defined by philosophers in such a way that Stevenson's or Hare's views don't even count. I've chosen to carve up the territory in such a way as to include all three of Ayer, Stevenson, and Hare, as well as more recent theorists like Simon Blackburn and Allan Gibbard whom we will encounter in Chapter 4. I've done this first of all because despite the differences between their views, these theorists belong to a shared historical tradition which in the English-speaking world began with Ogden and Richards (1923), proceeded through Ayer and Stevenson to Hare, from Hare to Blackburn, and from Stevenson and Blackburn to Gibbard. It is worth understanding this shared tradition and why it has developed in the way that it has, so that is one good reason to consider these views together.

But another good reason to consider them together is that even the very minimal idea that moral words need to have a different kind of meaning from ordinary non-moral words is enough to lead to a shared set of challenges – challenges that are shared by all noncognitivist theories. We'll encounter the first and most important of these challenges in Chapter 3.

## Chapter summary

In this chapter we introduced the emotivist theories of Ayer and Stevenson, and saw that both depart from truth-conditional theories of meaning. We saw that a theory of meaning needs to be able to satisfy the compositional and communicative constraints, and observed how truth-conditional theories of meaning accomplish that. In order to get a sense for how different noncognitivist theories are from one another we also introduced Hare's prescriptivist theory.

## Further reading

It is suggested that this chapter be read along with chapter 6 of Ayer (1936) and chapter 1 of Hare (1952). Stevenson (1937) is also appropriate – and somewhat more challenging, but I recommend waiting for Chapter 4 to look at Stevenson. Another excellent resource is chapter 3 of Urmson (1968), and Urmson's chapters 4–6 contain discussion of Stevenson that should be clear with this chapter as background. I've drawn much of my discussion of Stevenson from his (1944), which is a must-read for those with a serious interest in noncognitivism, but not important for those taking a first look at the territory. Satris (1987) contains a historical overview which traces the roots of noncognitivism in non-English-speaking philosophy in the late nineteenth and early twentieth centuries.

# Exercises

1    E *Comprehension*: For each of the following sentences, say what statement Ayer would say that it is used to make:

    **1**    It was good of you to come.
    **2**    You dance well.
    **3**    Murder is wrong.
    **4**    You did it while I wasn't looking.
    **5**    He came when he ought to.

2    E *Comprehension*: Suppose that Al is a NASCAR fan and subscribes to *Hot Rod* magazine. You've never seen Maggie's car before, but Al tells you, 'Maggie drives a good car.' What, according to Stevenson's 'first pattern' of analysis, have you just found out about the car that Maggie drives? What, according to Stevenson's 'second pattern' of analysis, have you just found out about it?

3    E *Extensions*: In section 4 we saw a recipe for how to find out, on the basis of knowing what it takes for 'Colorado is rectangular' to be true, what it takes for 'Colorado is not rectangular' to be true. Suppose that you know what it would take for 'Colorado is rectangular' to be true and what it would take for 'Colorado is kibochuk' to be true. State a recipe that lets us use this information in order to find out what it would take for 'Colorado is not both rectangular and kibochuk' to be true. State another recipe to find out what it would take for 'Colorado is either rectangular or kibochuk' to be true.

4    E *Extensions*: In the main text, we noted that Hare accused Stevenson of confusing *telling* someone to do something with *getting* him to do it. Shortly after Hare wrote, J.L. Austin introduced an important distinction which helps us to understand this difference. Austin (1962) called the act of *telling* someone to do something an *illocutionary act*. Illocutionary acts are things that we do *in* saying something. In contrast, *perlocutionary* acts are things which we achieve *by* saying something, but depend on the results of what we say. Hence, a given illocutionary act of telling someone to do something may or may not succeed in being a perlocutionary act of getting her to do it. Classify each of the following in terms of whether it is an illocutionary act or a perlocutionary act, and justify your answer:

    **1**    Promising to meet someone for lunch.
    **2**    Inciting a riot.

3   Asking a question.
4   Reminding someone of something.
5   Asserting that you know something.
6   Issuing a command.

5   M *Extensions* (continuing from exercise 4): Austin also distinguished between illocutionary and *locutionary* acts, which turns out to be useful for understanding Hare as well. A locutionary act is an act of uttering a sentence with a given meaning. In the main text we saw that utterances of three different kinds of sentences – an indicative sentence, an imperative sentence, and an interrogative sentence – could all be used to issue the same command. That is, the same *illocutionary* act can be done with any of three different *locutionary* acts. It is also true that the same locutionary act can be used to perform different *illocutionary* acts. Explain how the same sentence, 'I'm out of milk', can be used to perform at least four different kinds of illocutionary act. For concreteness, make one an assertion, one an offer, one a request, and one a question.

6   M *New problem*: Some philosophers have believed that just as the imperative mood makes sentences suited by their meaning for issuing commands, and just as the interrogative mood makes sentences suited by their meaning for asking questions, the indicative mood makes sentences suited by their meaning for making assertions about matters of fact. Explain why this is a potential problem for Hare.

7   M *Extensions*: For each of the following sentences, try to say what statement Ayer would say that it is used to make. If you have trouble, try to explain what you think makes it so hard in each case:

1   It is wrong to act wrongly.
2   It is never right to do the wrong thing.
3   Everything he does is wrong.
4   The good thing is that he came when he ought to.
5   Either murder is wrong, or I've been lied to.

8   M *Qualifications*: In the main text, I characterized Ayer as holding that 'you acted wrongly in stealing that' has a different *meaning* from 'you stole that', even though they are used to make the same *statement*. In doing so, I went somewhat beyond the text. Ayer doesn't actually use the word 'meaning', and the most closely related word that he does use is 'significant'. Ayer

makes it quite clear that the sentence 'stealing is wrong' is *not* significant at all, and that 'you acted wrongly in stealing that' does *not* differ in significance from 'you stole that'. The reason that Ayer thinks this is that he accepts what is called the *verifiability criterion* on significance. The verifiability criterion says that no sentence is significant unless 'it is possible for experience to render it probable' (Ayer 1936, 37), and it was the most important idea of *logical positivism*, a philosophical movement of the 1920s and 1930s of which Ayer's book was basically a popularization. It follows from the verifiability criterion that if there is in principle no way to empirically check and see if something is true, it cannot be a 'significant' claim. Come up with four examples of claims for which you cannot see how there could be any way of empirically checking to see whether or not they are true.

9   D  *Qualifications* (continuing from exercise 8): If Ayer meant 'meaningful' by 'significant', then he would be committed to holding that 'what the heck was emotivism?' is no more meaningful than 'what kiz hooziwud was emotivism?', which uses nonsense words. Some logical positivists, including Moritz Schlick, embraced this result and called many things 'nonsense', and Ayer sometimes uses that word, too (1936, 34). So Ayer faces a problem. He wants to criticize philosophers who are interested in abstruse metaphysical questions, such as those about the nature of experience-transcendent reality, on the grounds that the sentences that they are using are not significant. But he does not want to *criticize* moral language for not being significant; on the contrary he seems to think that it is useful for something different, which does not require its being significant. How could the accusation that metaphysicians' language is not significant be a criticism of them, even though the thesis that moral sentences are not significant does not amount to a criticism of people who use moral language? Once you have an answer, try to use it in order to explain why Ayer can still have his criticism of metaphysicians, even if he allows that their sentences are meaningful.

10   D  *Extensions* (continuing from exercise 5): Stevenson did not make any of these distinctions, between locutionary and illocutionary, or between illocutionary and perlocutionary acts. He had a *causal* theory of meaning, according to which the meaning of a sentence is a matter of whatever utterances of that sentence are disposed to *cause*. Now, there are a number of problems with causal theories of meaning like Stevenson's. One is

that it is hard to see how it could satisfy the compositional constraint (see section 4, above). But Hare (1952) and Urmson (1968) complain specifically that Stevenson's view leaves too much to chance, because it builds everything associated with *perlocutionary acts*, which are only contingently successful, into the meaning of words. Stevenson (1944), however, already anticipated this objection. In response, he emphasized that the meaning of a word is not what it *does* cause, but what it is *disposed* to cause. Try to reconstruct Stevenson's response to the objection from Hare and Urmson, by appealing to this distinction, and evaluate whether it is successful.

11    D *Extensions* (continuing from exercise 10): Philosophers and linguists usually distinguish between *semantics* and *pragmatics*. Roughly, the distinction is between what goes specifically into the *meaning* of words and sentences and what speakers and listeners are able to *interpret* from words and sentences, given what else they know. Explain why Stevenson's causal theory of meaning appears to collapse this distinction, and evaluate whether he can still maintain it. We noted in the main text that Stevenson thinks that the meaning of 'good' is vague. What he appears to mean, however, is not that 'good' has a definite meaning, which is vague, but rather that it is vague *what* the meaning of 'good' is. Decide whether the causal theory of meaning helps to make sense of how this could be, by making vague the boundary between semantics and pragmatics. Do these seem like tolerable conclusions? If not, why not?

## Partial answers

3    Hint: There are four possible cases, depending on which of 'Colorado is rectangular' and 'Colorado is kibochuk' is true. Your recipe for the truth conditions of each sentence should say whether it is true or false in each of these four cases.

5    'I'm out of milk' could be used to make an offer, if someone first asks, 'does anyone else who's out of milk want to pick some up for me while they're at the store?' In that circumstance, you might offer to pick up milk for her by saying, 'I'm out of milk'. Provide similar answers for the others.

## Morals

7    Moral words do not always simply comment on non-moral words, in such a way that we can split off the part of the sentence that is non-moral to look and see what statement it makes. In some sentences, moral words and non-moral words *interact* in complex ways. This is a problem we'll discover more about in later chapters.

## References

Austin, J.L. (1962). *How to Do Things with Words*. Oxford: Oxford University Press.

Ayer, A.J. (1936). *Language, Truth, and Logic*. New York: Dover.

Hare, R.M. (1952). *The Language of Morals*. Oxford: Oxford University Press.

Ogden, C.K., and I.A. Richards (1923). *The Meaning of Meaning*. New York: Harcourt Brace.

Satris, Stephen (1987). *Ethical Emotivism*. Dordrecht: Martinus Nijhoff Publishers.

Stevenson, C.L. (1937). 'The Emotive Meaning of Ethical Terms.' Reprinted in Stevenson (1963), *Facts and Values*. Westport, CT: Greenwood Press.

—— (1944). *Ethics and Language*. Oxford: Oxford University Press.

Urmson, J.O. (1968). *The Emotive Theory of Ethics*. New York: Oxford University Press.

# 3

# THE FREGE–GEACH
# PROBLEM, 1939–70

## 3.1 The basic problem

In Chapter 2, we encountered the earlier generations of noncognitivist theories – both the emotivist theories of Ayer and Stevenson and Hare's prescriptivism. We also saw a little bit of how truth-conditional semantic theories work, and why they are able to satisfy the compositional and communicative constraints – and hence why they do some of the most important things that we should hope that a theory of linguistic meaning would be able to do. We also saw that the views of Ayer, Stevenson, and Hare all conflict with the basic ideas of truth-conditional semantics in important ways, and I suggested that this is the most important shared characteristic of their otherwise quite different views.

We now know enough about noncognitivist theories to be ready to understand the biggest and most famous problem they face. At bottom, this problem confronts all noncognitivist theories, and it confronts them precisely because they reject truth-conditional theories of meaning. One of the main attractions of truth-conditional theories of meaning, we saw, was that they made it easy to satisfy the compositional constraint. It was easy to construct recipes which told us, once we knew the meanings of the parts of a sentence, how to put those together in order to figure out the meaning of the whole sentence. And this was important, because as speakers of the language, we must at least implicitly understand such recipes because we are able to understand new and unfamiliar sentences. We can understand them even though we have never encountered them before, by putting together the meanings of their parts, which we do understand.

Now, if noncognitivist theories are going to be successful accounts of the meaning of moral words, they need to be able to do the same sorts of things that truth-conditional theories can do. In particular, they must be able to explain what complex sentences mean, and how those meanings follow from the meanings of their parts and how they are put together. But by far the best-known problem facing noncognitivist theories is that it is not at all clear what the meaning of most complex sentences containing moral words could be, and hence it is not at all clear how those meanings could follow from the meanings of their parts.

Take, for example, Ayer's theory. Just to see the force of the problem, let's take him seriously when he says that 'stealing money is wrong' has the same sort of meaning as 'stealing money!!', with a special 'shape and thickness of the exclamation marks'. So far, so good – on the face of it, that makes for a nice theory of the meaning of 'stealing money is wrong', because it seems to tell us how that sentence is suited, by its meaning, to our communicative purposes. We can use it, just as we would use 'stealing money!!', to express a 'special sort of moral disapproval'. But how does this help us understand what 'stealing is not wrong' means? And how does it help us understand what 'stealing is wrong or my parents lied to me' means?

Let's take the latter example to illustrate. One might suppose that Ayer's view leads to one of the following paraphrases:

1    Stealing money!! or my parents lied to me.
2    Stealing money or my parents lied to me!!

Unfortunately, because it is far from clear what either of these two sentences means, neither is a very useful analogy for shedding light on the meaning of 'stealing money is wrong or my parents lied to me'. For example, do these sentences express a 'special sort of moral disapproval' of stealing money? That's odd, because someone who does not think that stealing money is wrong might say, 'stealing money is wrong or my parents lied to me'. She might say this, because she isn't sure which is true – that stealing money is wrong, or that her parents lied to her. If she *did* think that stealing money was wrong, she might disapprove of it, but since she isn't sure, she might also be unsure whether to disapprove of it.

Moreover, this problem does not go away even if we interpret Ayer more cautiously and treat his remark about exclamation marks as a sort of hyperbole. Even on a cautious interpretation, Ayer thinks that it is not sufficient to know the meaning of 'you acted wrongly in stealing that money' to know what would make it true. The statement that one makes in uttering this sentence, according to Ayer, is true just in case the person one is addressing stole the money which is referred to by 'that money'. But that is not all the sentence means; in addition, to understand the sentence, we need to understand that it is used to express a certain emotion on the speaker's part toward stealing that money. But then what is the meaning of the sentence, 'either you acted wrongly in stealing that money, or my parents lied to me'? It does not simply mean the same thing as 'either you stole that money, or my parents lied to me'. Nor does its meaning consist in this plus something else.

In short, it is far from clear how to generalize Ayer's story about the meaning of 'stealing money is wrong' to a story about the meaning of bigger, more complex, sentences of which it is a part. But that means that he hasn't really told us what it means. An *adequate* account of the meaning of a word must satisfy the compositional constraint, by telling us how, given the meaning of that word and the meanings of other words, to determine the meanings of complex sentences of which they are parts.[1] It is not hard to see that we can raise similar problems for Stevenson and Hare. The problem arises because what was *attractive* about truth-conditional semantics was that it straightforwardly satisfied the compositional constraint. Since noncognitivist theories depart from truth-conditional semantics, they need to come up with a *different* way of satisfying the compositional constraint. And their accounts of the meanings of simple sentences don't lead to any obvious way of doing that.

This problem is usually called the *Frege–Geach problem*, because it is usually attributed to Peter Geach, who in turn credits it to a point made by the German philosopher Gottlob Frege at the end of the nineteenth century. And in fact, we'll see that Geach gave one of the most influential and general statements of the problem. But in one form or another philosophers have been aware of this problem and related issues since the very beginning of noncognitivist theorizing. For example, Ross (1939) gave it a very clear formulation two decades before Geach. I've begun by trying to introduce the problem in its most general form; in the remainder of this chapter we're going to look at some of the history of how people have thought about this problem up through 1970, and at some of the evidence about how hard or easy a problem it is. Then later, in Chapters 6 and 7, we'll trace what has happened in thinking about the Frege–Geach problem in the years since 1970.

## 3.2 Geach

At around the same time as the early noncognitivists were developing their views about moral language, a number of philosophers – sometimes the same ones, and sometimes different ones – were developing similar ideas about other kinds of language. For example, some suggested the idea that talk about what is true or false is not *about* anything – truth or falsity – but is instead used to 'affirm' or 'deny' the thing said to be true or false.[2] And some suggested that mathematical talk about numbers is not about anything – the numbers – but is rather a way of making prescriptions to each other about what conventions to follow in counting things.[3]

These views were akin to noncognitivism in more than one way. First, they shared with noncognitivism the idea that truth-conditional approaches to understanding meaning are inadequate, because to understand the meanings of certain sorts of words, we need to understand how those words are to be *used*. And second, they shared many of noncognitivism's domain-neutral motivations. It was puzzling what numbers are and how we find out about them, for example, as well as puzzling why we would need to find out about them in order to do what we use number-talk *for*. These other views even had some of their own domain-*specific* motivations. For example, the 'liar' paradox makes it seem puzzling what sort of similarity among things 'true' could be picking out:

Liar:  'Liar is not true.'

Liar is a sentence which says of itself that it is not true. And it presents us with an ancient puzzle. If we assume that Liar is true, then what it says must be true. But what it says is that it is not true, and that can be true only if it is not true. So if we start by assuming that it is true, we get a contradiction. But if we suppose that it is *not* true, that is, after all, what it says. So what it says is true. But that means that it is true after all. It therefore seems that no matter which way we classify Liar, we are forced to classify it the other way. So on which side of the similarity demarcated by 'true' does Liar lie? On the 'true' side? Or not? Neither answer is satisfactory. This is a domain-specific motivation – a motivation that applied in the case of 'true' and not, for example, in the case of morality or mathematics – to suspect that there is not, after all, any genuine similarity that is demarcated by 'true'.

In the late 1950s and early 1960s, Peter Geach offered a very general argument against all of these related theories – these theories about truth, mathematics, and other things, as well as noncognitivist theories in ethics. Each of these theories has the form of telling us the meaning of some word by telling us what it is used to do. For example, Ayer told us that 'wrong' is used to express disapproval, Stevenson told us that 'good' is used to elicit approval, and Hare told us that 'good' is used to commend. So Geach understood these theories as committed to the following claim:

> Geachian performativism:   what makes a *particular instance* of 'stealing money is wrong' mean that stealing money is wrong, is that it is used to perform Φ.

Geachian performativism is a *schematic view*, which means that it isn't really a view, until you plug in something else for 'Φ'. But Geach understood Ayer, Stevenson, and Hare to be espousing *instances* of Geachian performativism, in the sense that Ayer accepted it with 'the act of expressing disapproval' plugged in for 'Φ', and Stevenson accepted it with 'the act of eliciting disapproval' plugged in for 'Φ', and so on. So Geach's argument was designed to be an argument that no instance of Geachian performativism could be correct.

The argument goes like this. The first step is to notice that 'stealing money is wrong' can appear in many different sorts of sentences. Here are some examples:

3    Stealing money is wrong.
4    Is it the case that stealing money is wrong?
5    If stealing money is wrong, then killing is definitely wrong.
6    I wonder whether stealing money is wrong.
7    It is not the case that stealing money is wrong.

In each of sentences 4–7, 'stealing money is wrong' appears as part of a *bigger, more complex* sentence. So much for the first step. The second step of Geach's argument is to notice that someone who says any of sentences 4–7 does *not* perform whichever action Ayer, Stevenson, or Hare thinks that 'stealing is wrong' is used to perform. For example, someone who says sentence 4 is not expressing disapproval of stealing money, nor is she trying to elicit disapproval of stealing money in her audience. Someone who sincerely asserts sentence 7 is certainly not doing so. And the third step of Geach's argument is to observe that 'stealing money is wrong' *means the same thing* in each of these sentences, as it does when it is uttered all by itself. Together, these three observations make an argument against Geachian performativism:

**P1**    In sentences 4–7, 'stealing money is wrong' has the same meaning as it does in sentence 3.

**P2**    Whatever action is performed by someone who utters sentence 3 is not performed by someone who utters sentences 4–6.

**C**    Therefore, what makes 'stealing money is wrong' mean that stealing money is wrong is *not* what action it is used to perform.

This is an excellent argument, if we accept its premises. Geach thought that premise P2 was obvious, but in case you were in doubt about premise P1, he offered further arguments. We know that 'stealing money is wrong' *has* to mean the same thing in each of these sentences, Geach held, because each of these sentences has a *semantic property* – that is, a feature of its meaning – which makes sense only because 'stealing money is wrong' means the same thing in both places. For example, sentence 3 is an *answer* to the question posed by sentence 4. That is not a coincidence; if your friend asks you, 'is the bank next to Main Street?', meaning *financial institution* by 'bank', you haven't really answered her question if you say, 'the bank is next to Main Street', meaning *edge of a river* by 'bank' – even if you mislead her into thinking that you have. The reason you haven't really answered her question is that your words meant something different than hers did. So since sentence 3 really *is* an answer to the question posed by sentence 4, 'stealing money is wrong' must mean the same thing in both sentences. Geach gave similar arguments for the other sentences, and his argument in the case of sentence 5 became particularly famous. We'll have occasion to look in more detail at the examples of each of sentences 5, 6, and 7 later in this chapter and in later chapters.

Geach's argument is clearly a very compelling argument that no version of Geachian performativism can be true. So to evaluate whether it is a successful argument against noncognitivism in *general*, what we need to know is whether noncognitivists are *in general* committed to accepting Geachian performativism. It is clear that the early emotivists did not clearly distinguish their views from Geachian performativism. And we'll see in the exercises that Geachian performativism doesn't come from nowhere; there is in fact at least *some* philosophical pressure for many kinds of noncognitivist views to accept it, because it would solve a certain sort of problem that they face. But it is also clear that some of the more sophisticated later noncognitivists, including Hare, were explicitly careful to avoid endorsing Geachian performativism.

Urmson (1968) explains this very nicely. Not only are sentences 4–7 used to perform different speech acts than sentence 3 is usually used to perform, Urmson points out that even sentence 3 is not always used to perform this speech act. For example, someone who utters sentence 3 sarcastically is not expressing disapproval of stealing money, nor attempting to elicit such disapproval in others. In this way, sentence 3 is no different from our example of an imperative sentence from Chapter 2: 'bring me my slippers'. This sentence, since it is in the imperative mood, is *suited* by its meaning to issue a command or suggestion, but it, too, might be uttered ironically or in jest, or used not to issue an order, but to say that it is time for bed. Hare was well aware that imperative sentences are not always used to issue commands, and similarly he was well aware that 'good' sentences are not always used to commend. His view was not that what makes a particular instance of 'good' mean what it does is that it is used *on that occasion* to commend, but rather that the meaning of 'good' is, at least in part, that it is *suited* for use in commendation, in the sort of way that the imperative mood is suited for issuing commands, even though imperative sentences are not always used to issue commands.

## 3.3 Hare and compositional semantics

So Geach's argument, as it was originally formulated, does not successfully target all noncognitivist theories. It may have successfully refuted some *actual* noncognitivist theories, but as it stands, it did not refute all *possible* theories, and among those theories, it did not refute Hare's actual theory, even though it was among Geach's main targets. Still, Geach's argument points the way to the very general problem that we've already seen.

To see how, notice that we have already seen a much more direct argument that 'stealing money is wrong' must mean the same thing when it appears as part of a more complex sentence, as it does when it appears all by itself. This is the argument from *compositionality*. It is our ability to understand the meaning of 'stealing money is wrong', along with our ability to understand the meanings of the other words in those sentences, that allows us to understand the meanings of sentences 4–7. But in order for us to do that, of course, we have to know what 'stealing money is wrong' does mean – even in those sentences. It is our grasp of this single meaning of 'stealing money is wrong' that we employ in determining the meanings of sentences 4–7. So though *one part* of the problem is to ensure that 'stealing money is wrong' has the same meaning when it appears as part of more complex sentences as when it appears by itself, there is more to the problem than this. The remainder of the problem is to show how to say *what* the meaning of complex sentences is, in terms of the meanings of their parts. Geach was not unaware of this further, more general problem about compositionality. In fact, this further, more general problem is precisely why he credits the point that he is making to Frege. Frege made a distinction between the *force* and *content* of a sentence precisely in order to satisfy the compositional constraint, and it was that distinction to which Geach was referring when he credited Frege with making his point. So even though he formulated his argument in a narrower way, we should really understand Geach as being concerned with the more general problem.

In an important paper in 1970 that was a response to Geach and to John Searle, who had offered an argument very similar to Geach's at approximately the same time, Hare explained in the most general way how noncognitivists can do this. Truth-conditional theories of meaning, Hare pointed out, allow us to determine the meanings of complex sentences on the basis of the meanings of their simpler parts, because they offer us *recipes* to construct, given the truth conditions of an arbitrary sentence, 'P', the truth conditions of more complex sentences involving 'P', such as 'it is not the case that P'. In Chapter 2 we saw what this recipe is: it is that 'it is not the case that P' is true whenever 'P' *isn't*. What Hare pointed out was that noncognitivist theories can do this, too – they can provide recipes which tell us how to determine the meaning of a complex sentence on the basis of the meanings of its parts. The only difference between the noncognitivists' recipes and the truth-conditional theorists' recipes will be that for truth-conditional theorists the meanings of sentences are truth conditions, and so these recipes will tell us how to get from the truth conditions of the simpler sentences to the truth conditions of the more complex sentence. Whereas since on Hare's view the meaning of a sentence consists in what speech act it is suited to perform, Hare's recipes will have to tell us how to get from the speech acts that the simpler sentences are suited to perform to the speech acts that the more complex sentences are suited to perform.

Hare's move tells us exactly what we should expect from a noncognitivist theory of meaning that satisfies the compositional constraint. For each way of taking some simpler sentences and making a more complex sentence out of them, the noncognitivist theory of meaning needs to give us a recipe that tells us how to get from the meanings of the simpler sentences to the meaning of the more complex sentence. If we can do that, then we satisfy the compositional constraint. In fact, there is no other way to satisfy the compositional constraint. Hare's answer to Geach and Searle is really just a redescription of what it takes to satisfy the compositional constraint. But it is important to see that Hare is right – there is no in principle bar to noncognitivists giving us such recipes, just because they do not accept truth-conditional semantics. They will just have to provide us with different recipes than are provided by truth-conditional semantics.

One might hope that the next thing that Hare would have done would be to tell us what some of these recipes are. After all, clearly not just any old recipes will do. For example, consider the following two descriptively named recipes:

> crummy recipe 1 for 'not':   For any sentence 'P' that is suited to perform speech act Φ, 'it is not the case that P' is suited to perform speech act Φ.

> crummy recipe 2 for 'not':   For any sentence 'P' that is suited to perform speech act Φ, 'it is not the case that P' is suited to perform the speech act of endorsing genocide.

Both of these recipes tell us how to get from the speech act that a simpler sentence is suited to perform to the speech act that the more complex sentence is suited to perform. But they are both clearly crummy recipes, and not just because I called them that. 'It is not the case that P' is not, in general, used to perform the same speech act as 'P', nor is it in general suited to endorsing genocide (except in the special case where 'P' is 'genocide is not good').

These are obvious points. But the point is that it is not enough for the noncognitivist to tell us just any old recipes for getting to the meanings of complex sentences from the meanings of simpler ones. They must give us recipes which get the right results. So it turns out that this is where the action is. The problem facing noncognitivist views is to give us recipes for the meanings of complex sentences which 'get the right results'. In section 4 we'll look in more detail at what it means to 'get the right results', and at why this looks harder for noncognitivism than for ordinary truth-conditional theories of meaning. Then in section 5 we'll look at why some noncognitivists remain optimistic, and at how far that optimism should extend.

## 3.4 The contrast with truth functions

In order to see at least part of what it would mean to 'get the right results' from a set of recipes which tell us the meanings of complex sentences on the basis of the meanings of their parts, it will help to look in just a little bit more detail at how truth-conditional theories work. Again, just as in Chapter 2, the details of different truth-conditional approaches vary widely, and the simple ideas presented here are not meant to be understood as shared in specifics by every truth-conditional theory. But they are representative of the *very basic* ideas behind the truth-conditional approach, of which more sophisticated theories provide variations, qualifications, or developments.

The simplest truth-conditional recipe that we've encountered so far is that for sentences containing the words 'not' or 'it is not the case that'. The recipe tells us that no matter what sentence we use to replace 'P', the sentence 'it is not the case that P' is true whenever 'P' is not true – so that whatever would make 'P' true would make 'it is not the case that P' not true, and whatever would make 'it is not the case that P' true would make 'P' not true. Logicians and truth-conditional semanticists long ago introduced a simple tool in order to make it easier to say how to follow this recipe. It is the following picture:

| 'P' | 'It is not the case that P' |
| --- | --- |
| true | not true |
| not true | true |

This picture is called a *truth table*, because it is a table that lets us 'look up' whether 'it is not the case that P' is true, on the basis of our knowledge of whether 'P' is true. It constitutes a *picture* of the recipe for determining what it takes for 'it is not the case that P' to be true, on the basis of what it takes for 'P' to be true, because it tells us how the truth of the former varies with the truth of the latter. In order to figure out what it takes for 'it is not the case that P' to be true, you look up whether 'P' is true on the left-hand side of the table, and then you look across to see whether that makes 'it is not the case that P' true or not, on the right-hand side of the table. This is a *general* recipe, because it works for *any* sentence 'P' – so long as we already know what it takes for 'P' to be true.

Sometimes philosophers make this table look even simpler by writing '~P' as a less cumbersome abbreviation for 'it is not the case that P', writing 'T' as an abbreviation for 'true', and writing 'F' as an abbreviation for 'not true' (think 'F' for 'False') as follows:[4]

| 'P' | '~P' |
|---|---|
| T | F |
| F | T |

These abbreviations make for a tidier-looking picture, but these two tables say exactly the same thing. One is simply tidier looking than the other. The abbreviations that it uses are a kind of specialized notation, so it can seem unfamiliar at first. But the payoff of writing things in this way is that because it is tidier, it makes it easier to see the structure of the table, rather than being distracted by the words.

The table tells us the truth-conditional recipe for 'not'. This recipe is called a truth function, because the inputs it takes are truth values ('true' or 'not true'), and what it spits out is a truth value ('true' or 'not true'). To apply the recipe, we stick in a truth value for the smaller part of the sentence, 'P', that we already understand, and use the table to look up the truth value for the sentence 'it is not the case that P'. If you haven't encountered truth tables before, they may seem like much ado about nothing. But the very same concept allows us to provide simple statements of the recipes for the truth conditions of much more complicated sentences, like the following:

| 'P' | 'Q' | 'R' | 'Either Q and R, or P and ~Q, but not both' |
|---|---|---|---|
| T | T | T | T |
| T | T | F | F |
| T | F | T | T |
| T | F | F | T |
| F | T | T | T |
| F | T | F | F |
| F | F | T | F |
| F | F | F | F |

In this case, it is easy to see that it is easier to follow the recipe as shown by the table, than to try to say in ordinary English just what this recipe amounts to. You look up the truth values of the parts, 'P', 'Q', and 'R', on the left-hand side of the table, and then look across to see whether that makes the complex sentence true or not. This example is an illustration not only of why truth tables are a useful piece of notation, but of how flexible and powerful the truth-conditional approach to meaning really is. The truth-conditional approach has no more trouble assigning truth conditions to complicated sentences like that on the right-hand side of the last table, than it does to sentences that merely add the word 'not'. Both kinds of recipes can be spelled out using truth tables.

But truth tables don't only make the recipes to determine the meanings of complex sentences on the basis of the meanings of their parts easy to describe. They also allow us to *predict* certain important features of the meanings of complex sentences, on the basis of how they are put together. For example, one pretty obvious feature of the meaning of the word 'not' is that for any sentence, 'P', 'it is not the case that P' and 'P' are *inconsistent*. That is, it can't be that both are true at the same time and in the same place. We can call this a *semantic property* of sentences containing 'not'; it is, in fact, the semantic property of sentence 7, above, that Geach appealed to in his argument that 'stealing money is wrong' means the same thing when by itself as in 'it is not the case that stealing money is wrong'. The inconsistency of these sentences, Geach argued, has to do with the fact that 'stealing money is wrong' means the same thing in both places.

The truth-conditional recipe for constructing the meaning of sentences containing 'not' from the meanings of its parts makes it very *easy* to see why sentences containing 'not' have this property. In fact, we can read it off directly from the table. The reason why 'P' and 'it is not the case that P' cannot both be true, no matter what sentence 'P' really is, is that the truth table guarantees that whenever 'P' is true, 'it is not the case that P' is not true (which we can see from the first row of the table), and also guarantees that whenever 'it is not the case that P' is true, 'P' is not true (which we can see from the second row of the table).

This is a nice prediction! It means that the truth-conditional account of the meanings of sentences containing 'not' tells us something informative and correct about those sentences' semantic properties. And that is good. The *reason* why 'it is not the case that P' and 'P' are inconsistent has something to do with the relationship between their meanings, after all. So an adequate account of their meanings should allow us to predict and explain this. The truth-conditional approach does so, and does so in a very straightforward way.

Let's do one more example. The most famous example from Geach was his example of sentences like sentence 5 – sentences which contain an 'if ... then' construction. Such sentences are usually called *conditional sentences*, because they say that something is true provided that a certain condition obtains. Geach argued that 'stealing money is wrong' needs to mean the same thing in 'if stealing money is wrong, then killing is wrong' as it does when all by itself, because the following argument is *valid*:

**P1**    Stealing money is wrong.
**P2**    If stealing money is wrong, then killing is wrong.
**C**    Killing is wrong.

To say that an argument is valid is to say that its conclusion *follows from* its premises, in the sense that if they are true, then it has to be true, too. Geach pointed out that this argument is valid *because* 'Stealing money is wrong' means the same thing in both premises. If it meant something different in one place than in the other, then the argument wouldn't be valid. So, he concluded, it must mean the same thing in both places.

Just as Geach used the validity of this argument in order to argue that 'stealing money is wrong' means the same thing in both places, however, we can use it in order to isolate an important *semantic property* of conditional sentences. That property is that for any sentences 'P' and 'Q', the sentence 'if P, then Q' is, together with the sentence 'P', a valid argument for the conclusion, 'Q'. That is, conditional sentences *always* make arguments that have the same structure, or form, as this one valid. This particular form of argument has a very long and distinguished history, and so it has a very old Latin name. It is usually called *modus ponens*. *Modus ponens* is just a name for any argument that has the structure, 'P', 'if P, then Q'; therefore 'Q'.

Since all such arguments are valid, we might hope that our account of the meaning of the conditional sentence in terms of the meanings of its parts could help to explain why. And again, this is a great success story for truth-conditional semantics. The following is a truth table for 'if P, then Q' which allows us to explain this:

| 'P' | 'Q' | 'if P, then Q' |
|:---:|:---:|:---:|
| T | T | T |
| T | F | F |
| F | T | T |
| F | F | T |

This truth table both tells us how to determine the meaning of 'if P, then Q' on the basis of the meanings of its parts, if we accept a truth-conditional theory of meaning, *and* allows us to explain why *modus ponens* arguments are always valid. To see how, notice that the only row of the table on which 'P' and 'if P, then Q' are both true is the first row. And notice that on that row of the table, 'Q' is also true. What that tells us, is that the only circumstances under which 'P' and 'if P, then Q' are both true, are circumstances under which 'Q' is also true. So if the premises of the argument, 'P', 'if P, then Q'; therefore 'Q', are both true, that guarantees that the conclusion has to be true, as well. Moreover, it guarantees this, no matter which sentences we substitute for 'P' and 'Q' – simply on the basis of our recipe for determining the meaning of 'if P, then Q' from the meanings of its parts.

Its explanations of the inconsistency of 'P' and 'it is not the case that P' and of the fact that *modus ponens* arguments are always valid are some of the great success stories of truth-conditional semantics. Moreover, the success doesn't stop here; truth-conditional semantics allows us to tell similar stories about the semantic properties of many other, often much more complicated ways of constructing sentences, as well. So when we observe that not just any recipe for a noncognitivist account of the meaning of complex sentences will 'get the right results', these are some of the things that we mean. A recipe for constructing the meaning of 'it is not the case that murder is wrong' on the basis of the meaning of 'murder is wrong' needs to lead to an explanation of why those two sentences have to be inconsistent. Similarly, a recipe for constructing the meaning of 'if stealing money is wrong, then killing is wrong' needs to lead to an explanation of why our *modus ponens* argument is valid.

Philosophers writing about the Frege–Geach problem often suggest that it is a problem specifically about explaining the validity of arguments like the one we've just been looking at. As we've seen, however, this is a very narrow way of understanding the problem. The problem is that noncognitivists must provide us with *recipes* for how to construct the meanings of *any* kind of complex sentence from the meanings of their parts, and that these recipes must 'get things right', in the sense that they must allow for an explanation of the features that the resulting complex sentences have, in virtue of their meaning. These are what we have been calling 'semantic properties'. For the special case of conditional sentences, these properties have to do with validity, but for other kinds of complex sentences, the relevant semantic properties needn't have to do with validity at all – for example, the fact that sentence 3 answers the question asked by sentence 4 is an important semantic property of sentence 4, but doesn't have anything to do with validity.

## 3.5 The Hare–Smart argument from license for optimism

So far, we've seen that nothing *prevents* noncognitivist theories from offering recipes which tell us how to determine the meanings of complex sentences from the meanings of their parts. But we've also seen that as of 1970, when

Hare replied to Geach and Searle, no noncognitivists had seriously tried to offer any such recipes, and by looking at the case of Ayer, we saw that it is hard to see exactly what such a recipe would look like. Moreover, we've seen that by failing to actually offer these kinds of recipes, noncognitivist theories contrast sharply with truth-conditional theories of meaning, whose recipes for determining the meanings of complex sentences easily yield fruitful and correct predictions about the semantic properties of those complex sentences – for example, by correctly predicting which other sentences they are inconsistent with, and in which kinds of valid arguments they figure. So that leaves us with an important question: how optimistic should we be that noncognitivists will be able to come up with recipes that can do all of the same sorts of things as the recipes of the truth-conditional theories of meaning?

Even though Hare did not himself do any serious work toward providing these kinds of recipes (other than to tell us that providing them is all that a noncognitivist needs to do in order to solve the Frege–Geach problem), he did make one of the clearest cases for why we should be *optimistic* that this can be done. In fact, Hare had done so in 1952, long before Geach or Searle ever posed their versions of the Frege–Geach problem. (J.J.C. Smart [1984] offered a very similar argument, which is why I call it the 'Hare–Smart' argument.) Like other features of his view, his argument for *license for optimism* was based on comparison with the case of imperative sentences. Hare's central observation was that just as there are both simple and complex indicative sentences, there are also both simple and complex imperative sentences, and moreover such imperative sentences bear logical relationships to one another in very similar ways to how the corresponding indicative sentences do. To use his favorite example, the command, 'shut the door' is contradicted by the command, 'don't shut the door'. So just as adding 'not' to an indicative sentence leads to a sentence that is inconsistent with the one you started with, adding 'not' to an imperative sentence seems to lead to an imperative that is inconsistent with the one that you started with.

Moreover, 'not' is not the only word that we can use to construct complex imperatives; for example, 'shut the door and open the window' is also a complex imperative. Just as 'Max shut the door and Leila opened the window' is inconsistent with both 'Max didn't shut the door' and with 'Leila didn't open the window', the imperative, 'shut the door and open the window' is inconsistent with both the imperative, 'don't shut the door' and with the imperative, 'don't open the window'. Considerations like these led Hare to believe that since imperatives obviously *do* work in these ways and have such logical relationships with one another, there has to be *some* theory of meaning or other which can explain why – and that one will do, he held, for moral sentences. Just as it gives us a recipe for determining the meanings of complex imperative sentences from the meanings of their parts, it would give us a recipe for determining the meanings of complex moral sentences from the meanings of their parts. And just as it would predict and explain the logical relationships among imperative sentences, so it would explain the similar logical relationships among moral sentences.

Hare's argument for license for optimism should lead us to expect that there will be *some* kind of recipes that noncognitivists can offer that will explain *many* of the things that are true of the meanings of complex moral sentences – even if we don't, yet, know exactly how to say just what those recipes are. But it is not clear exactly how far this license for optimism should extend. The first reason why this is not clear is that it does not seem that indicative and imperative sentences can be combined in all of the same ways that moral and non-moral sentences can be combined. Try, for example, the following sentences (sentence 11 combines two imperative sentences, rather than one imperative and one indicative):

8    Shut the door and I'm running late.
9    Shut the door or I opened it yesterday.
10   Shut the door and I'll give you a dollar.
11   If shut the door, then open the window.
12   If shut the door, then I'm running late.

Of these five 'mixed-mood' sentences, only sentence 10 makes any sense. But even sentence 10 doesn't license very much optimism about how imperative and indicative sentences can combine together, because in sentence 10 'and' doesn't seem to mean what it usually does. It appears to really mean, 'if … then', as in 'if you shut the door, then I'll give you a dollar'. But it is easy to construct mixed moral/non-moral sentences just like these:

13   Stealing money is wrong and my parents told me so.
14   Stealing money is wrong or my parents lied to me.
15   Stealing money is wrong and I'll give you a dollar.
16   If stealing money is wrong, then don't steal.
17   If stealing money is wrong, then I'm confused.

We'll see in the exercises that there are other mixed-mood sentences which make more sense than sentences 8–12. But the comparison between sentences 8–12 and sentences 13–17 does not license very much optimism that whatever recipes suffice to account for the meanings of complex sentences involving imperatives will also suffice to account for the meanings of complex sentences involving moral words in some of their parts.

So Hare's grounds for optimism about the prospects for noncognitivist theories to successfully satisfy the compositional constraint extend only so far. That is why since 1970, philosophers interested in defending noncognitivist theories have invested much more effort in trying to spell out the kinds of recipes for the meanings of complex sentences that Hare promised, but did not provide. It turns out, however, that nearly all of the theorizing about the Frege–Geach problem since 1970 has been done by philosophers who were thinking about a new kind of noncognitivist theory called *expressivism*, which we haven't yet encountered.

So rather than moving directly to see what kinds of recipes people have tried to spell out, in order to solve the Frege–Geach problem, we're going to first take a break and see what expressivism is, where it comes from, and why it has been widely thought to be more promising than the earlier sorts of noncognitivist theories that we have been discussing so far. So that's what we'll do in Chapter 4. Then, since expressivism is a view not only about moral language but about moral thought, we'll take a further detour in Chapter 5 to explore some of the biggest challenges facing noncognitivist theories in the philosophy of mind. Once we know what expressivism is, and have seen how some of these issues work in expressivists' account of moral thought, we'll have the necessary background to return in Chapters 6 and 7 to see what has happened in terms of progress on the Frege–Geach problem since Hare wrote in 1970.

## Chapter summary

In this chapter we introduced the *Frege–Geach problem* – the problem of how noncognitivists are to account for the meanings of complex sentences, in accordance with the *compositional constraint* from Chapter 2. We illustrated the general problem with Ayer's account, looked at the original way that Geach framed the problem, and saw the outline of Hare's response. We also learned more about how easily truth-conditional theories of meaning can explain the very same things which Geach's argument challenges noncognitivist theories to explain. Finally, we closed by looking at the Hare–Smart argument for *license for optimism*, and trying to evaluate how much optimism it should give us.

## Further reading

It is suggested that this chapter be read along with Geach (1965) and chapter 2 of Hare (1952). Searle (1962) and Hare (1970) are an essential next step for anyone who wants to pursue these issues further, and one of the exercises requires looking at Searle (1962). For Urmson's contemporary take on the problem, see chapter 11 of Urmson (1968).

## Exercises

1    E *Comprehension*: For each of sentences 4–7 from section 2, explain why someone who uses that sentence would not ordinarily be performing the same speech act as someone who uses sentence 3.

2    E *Extensions*: Using Ayer's notation of specially shaped and thick exclamation marks, try to give an account of the meaning of 'stealing money is not wrong'. If you think your results are satisfactory, explain why. If you think they are unsatisfactory, explain why not.

3    E *Comprehension*: Construct a truth table for 'and'. Philosophers sometimes write 'P&Q' as an abbreviation for 'P and Q'.

4    E *Extensions*: Construct a truth table for 'P or Q or both'. Then construct a truth table for 'P or Q but not both'. The former is what is called the *inclusive 'or'*, because it includes the possibility of both being true, and the latter is what is called the *exclusive 'or'*, because it excludes the possibility of both being true. Logicians usually use the inclusive sense of 'or'.

5    E *Extensions*: Construct a truth table for 'Q or ~P', understanding 'or' in its inclusive sense (see exercise 4). Then construct a truth table for '~(P and ~Q)'. (Treat the parentheses as you would in arithmetic, where '6 + (3 × 2)' is different from '(6 + 3) × 2'.) Compare each truth table to the truth table for 'if P, then Q', from section 4.

6    M *Extensions*: In the main text, we characterized important semantic properties for each of sentences 4, 5, and 7. Geach used those semantic properties in order to argue that 'stealing money is wrong' means the same thing as it appears in those sentences as it does in sentence 3. Come up with an example of a semantic property of sentence 6 that can

play a similar role. Your strategy should be to first think about what makes you confident that 'stealing money is wrong' does mean the same thing in sentences 3 and 6. Then try to make that into a description of an important feature of sentence 6. Finally, appeal to that feature of sentence 6 in an argument that 'stealing money is wrong' means the same thing in 6 as it does in 3.

7    M *Extensions*: For this exercise, imagine that we can paraphrase imperative sentences as explicit performative sentences, so that 'shut the door' paraphrases as 'I hereby command you to shut the door' and 'leave the window open' paraphrases as 'I hereby command you to leave the window open'.[5] Give the intuitively right paraphrases for 'don't shut the door' and for 'shut the door or leave the window open'.

8    M *Extensions*: We saw in section 5 that many mixed-mood sentences – that is, sentences which appear to have parts with different moods – don't look like they make very much sense. Compare the following sentences to those in section 5, and try to explain the differences:

  1    It's freezing in here but leave the door open.
  2    Shut the door, for it's freezing in here.
  3    It's freezing in here, so shut the door.
  4    Shut the door or I'll hurt you.
  5    I'll hurt you or shut the door.

Why do you think that 'it's freezing in here but leave the door open' seems to make perfect sense, even though 'shut the door and I'm running late' doesn't seem to make any sense? What difference does the word 'but' make? Why? Does the fact that these sentences make sense increase your level of optimism that some noncognitivist theory must be able to work? Why or why not? Does the unacceptability of some mixed-mood sentences tell us about which sorts of meanings are possible, or just about English grammar? How can we tell?

9    D *Suggestions for progress*: Two kinds of mixed-mood sentence that appear to make perfect sense are conditional imperatives and conditional interrogatives, as follows:

  1    If you're going to the store, can I come with you?
  2    If you're going to the store, then pick up some milk.

It is sometimes said that conditional imperatives are not used to issue commands outright, but only to issue commands provided that a certain condition is satisfied. Similarly, conditional interrogatives are not used to ask questions outright, but only to ask questions provided that a certain condition is satisfied. First, check to see if this interpretation is correct by determining whether sentences 1 and 2 really cannot be interpreted as meaning the same as sentences 3 and 4:

3   Is it the case that if you're going to the store I can come with you?
4   Make it true that if you go to the store, then you pick up some milk.

10   D   *Suggestions for progress* (continuing from exercise 9): Compare sentences 1 and 2 from exercise 9 to sentence 5, sometimes called a 'biscuit' or 'sideboard' conditional:

5   If you want some biscuits, there are some on the sideboard.

It is sometimes said that a sentence like 5 is not used to make an outright assertion of a conditional, but rather to perform a *conditional assertion* that there are biscuits on the sideboard, provided that the condition that the addressee wants some is satisfied. Is sentence 5 more like sentences 1 and 2? Or more like ordinary conditional sentences? Why? Compare the answer given by DeRose and Grandy (1999).

11   D   *Suggestions for progress* (continuing from exercise 10): Compare sentence 5 from exercise 10 to the following, *faith-based* conditional:

6   If you believe McCain, then tax cuts increase revenues.

In what ways are faith-based conditionals like biscuit conditionals? In what ways are they not? Adequately understanding peripheral cases like these may be a way of gaining leverage on the question of how the previous sorts of conditionals work, which is an important step for understanding how mood interacts with composition, which is what we need to do in order to fully assess Hare's argument for license for optimism.[6]

12   D   *Branching out*: The clearest case of mixed-mood sentences that are totally unacceptable would seem to be the case of sentences with imperative antecedents, as in sentences 11 and 12 from section 5. But Hare seems to have believed that there *are* good examples from ordinary language of sentences with imperative antecedents. He believed that one such example was the following:

'If you want to go to Harlem, then take the A train.'

It is a famous problem that someone can offer this advice, and yet at the same time issue the apparently contrary advice, 'don't take the A train', even though she knows that her addressee wants to go to Harlem, as in the following dialogue:

*Clara:*    'If you want to go to Harlem, then take the A train.'
*John:*     'I do want to go to Harlem. So should I take the A train?'
*Clara:*    'No – I wouldn't do that, if I were you.'
*John:*     'I thought you just said that if I want to go to Harlem, then I should take the A train? I do want to go to Harlem.'
*Clara:*    'I know you want to go to Harlem. And if you *want* to go to Harlem you should take the A train, but you still shouldn't take it. You should go somewhere else, instead.'

Hare believed that this was because the sentence 'If you want to go to Harlem, then take the A train', on the interpretation that Clara intended, is not a conditional command with an *indicative* antecedent, but rather a conditional command with an *imperative* antecedent. He just believed that there was a purely grammatical problem – not one about meaning – with imperative sentences appearing in the antecedents of conditionals. Investigate Hare's view in more detail in Hare (1971) and evaluate whether it really is a promising proposal. Decide whether it increases or decreases your level of optimism that noncognitivists can carry out his promise of constructing recipes for the meanings of complex moral sentences.

13    D *New problem*: We observed in the main text that Geach assumed that noncognitivist theories must be offering a condition on what it takes for a particular instance or *token* of the string of words, 'stealing money is wrong' to mean that stealing money is wrong. (The distinction between *types* and *tokens* corresponds to two different ways of counting the letters in 'alphabet'. By the token way of counting, there are eight letters, but by the type way of counting, there are only seven, because the letter 'a' appears twice. So the letter 'a' in general is a *type*, but each appearance of the letter 'a' is a *token*.) Urmson's answer to Geach was that noncognitivism is not a theory about the meaning of *token*s of sentences – that is, individual utterances, but rather of *types* of sentences. That is why not every token needs to be used for the speech act, in order to have the same meaning. It has the meaning

that it does because of the *type* that it belongs to. However, in cases of ambiguity there are two ways of individuating sentence types. By one way of counting, 'I'll meet you at the bank' and 'I'll meet you at the bank' are the same sentence, because the same letters or sounds appear in each. But by another way of counting, these are really two different sentences, if 'bank' means *financial institution* in one, and *edge of a river* in the other. Explain why this potentially makes for a problem for the noncognitivist who wants to give a theory of meaning to sentence types, rather than to sentence tokens. Do truth-conditional semanticists face a similar problem?

14  D   *Branching out*: John Searle (1962) offered an argument that was very similar to that of Geach. Read Searle's argument, and then try to explain what Searle thinks the disanalogy is supposed to be between *performative* verbs like 'promise' and 'good'.

15  D   *Branching out*: In the main text, I've been emphasizing that noncognitivism is a view about the meaning of moral sentences. It is not always described in that way in the literature; for example, Stoljar (1993) explicitly says that the idea that moral sentences are used to perform speech acts is not a thesis about their meaning at all, but only a *pragmatic* thesis. Read Stoljar's article, and try to explain what Stoljar thinks the meaning of moral words *does* consist in. Does he think that they aren't meaningful at all? What problems can you raise for that idea?

## Partial answers

13  Hint: The meaning of complex sentences is a function of the *meanings* of their parts, so in order for the parts to input the right meanings into that function, the parts have to *have* the right meanings. If Geachian performativism is true, then the moral parts of a complex moral sentence have the meanings that they do because of the speech act they are used to perform. What makes the moral parts of complex moral sentences have the meaning that they do, if Geachian performativism is false?

## Morals

5  The truth table for 'if P, then Q' in section 4 is what is called the *material conditional* by philosophers. This truth-conditional account of the meaning of 'if P, then Q' is generally agreed to be adequate for mathematical

reasoning, but it is highly controversial whether this is an adequate account of what 'if P, then Q' means in ordinary English. Some philosophers advocate more complicated truth-conditional accounts which still preserve the advantages outlined in the main text. Others believe that there are domain-specific reasons to think that we need a non-truth-conditional account of the meaning of conditional sentences. Such philosophers offer nondescriptivist semantic theories in order to explain the meaning of 'if P, then Q'.

7    Compare the following pairs of paraphrases:

'I hereby command you to not shut the door.'
'I don't hereby command you to shut the door.'

'I hereby command you to shut the door or leave the window open.'
'I hereby command you to shut the door or I hereby command you to leave the window open.'

Which paraphrase in each pair is the right one? The difference in each pair is what philosophers call a difference in *scope*. In the first member of each pair, the command takes what is called *widest scope*. This means that it is a command to do a *negated* thing, in the first case, and a command to do a *disjunctive* thing, in the second case. ('Negated' just means 'having *not* in it' and 'disjunctive' just means 'having *or* in it'; the previous sentence would be a mouthful, if not for words like 'negated' and 'disjunctive', which make it easier to say.) In the second member of each pair, in contrast, the command takes what is called *narrow scope*. This means that it is the *lack* of a command, in the first case, and the *disjunction* of two commands, in the second case (that is, it is two potential commands joined by 'or'). If the command sometimes takes narrow scope, then Hare's argument from license for optimism is particularly powerful – for then there are literally sentences that are made up out of smaller imperative sentences as parts. But if the command always takes widest scope, then Hare's argument is less exciting. In that case, we can think of mood as something that applies only to *whole sentences*, sort of as a last step that we do to a sentence, after using ordinary truth-conditional semantics in order to assemble a sentence out of its parts. If that is right, then how much license for optimism does your answer to the exercise give you that Hare is right?

8    It is very puzzling why some mixed-mood sentences seem to be fine, though others are not fine. A complete assessment of Hare's argument

from license for optimism would need to take a careful look at the full range of such sentences in order to determine whether mixed-mood sentences really can be meaningful, and whether their kind of meaning could be extended to apply to complex sentences with both moral and non-moral parts. Do you have any ideas about what might explain why some mixed-mood sentences are OK and others seem not to make sense?

14   Searle's argument is more concessive than Geach's, because he grants that a noncognitivist does not need to accept Geachian performativism. This is because Searle himself accepts the view that to understand the meaning of 'I promise to do it', we need to understand that it is suited for being used to perform a certain speech act – but he recognizes that 'it is not the case that I promise to do it' is not used to perform that same speech act. Searle's argument is therefore somewhat more subtle than Geach's; it turns on the idea that the trick that Searle uses in order to provide an account of the meaning of complex sentences containing the word 'promise' won't in turn work for Hare. It is tricky, however, to understand exactly how these subtleties are supposed to work, which is what this exercise invites you to try to sort out for yourself.

# References

Dreier, James (2009). 'Practical Conditionals.' In David Sobel and Stephen Wall, eds., *Reasons for Action*. Cambridge: Cambridge University Press.

Geach, Peter (1965). 'Assertion.' *Philosophical Review* 74: 449–65.

Hare, R.M. (1952). *The Language of Morals*. Oxford: Oxford University Press, chapter 2.

—— (1970). 'Meaning and Speech Acts.' *Philosophical Review* 79(1): 3–24.

Karttunen, Lauri (1977). 'Syntax and Semantics of Questions.' *Linguistics and Philosophy* 1: 3–44.

Ross, W.D. (1939). *Foundations of Ethics*. Oxford: Clarendon Press, chapter 2.

Searle, John (1962). 'Meaning and Speech Acts.' *Philosophical Review* 71: 423–32.

Smart, J.J.C. (1984). *Ethics, Persuasion, and Truth*. Oxford: Oxford University Press.

Strawson, P.F. (1949). 'Truth.' *Analysis* 9: 83–97.

Urmson, J.O. (1968). *The Emotive Theory of Ethics*. New York: Oxford University Press.

Wittgenstein, Ludwig (2005). *Philosophical Grammar*. Rush Rhees, ed. Berkeley: University of California Press.

# 4

## EXPRESSIVISM

### 4.1 Speaker subjectivism

In Chapter 2, we saw that when Stevenson first introduced his view, he contrasted it explicitly with what he called 'traditional interest theories'. Traditional interest theories were a kind of predecessor to noncognitivism, and have been advocated by various philosophers for thousands of years. In this section we're going to encounter the most important kind of traditional interest theory, a view called *speaker subjectivism*, and see why it attracted philosophers for many of the same reasons that philosophers have been attracted to noncognitivist theories. Then in the remainder of the chapter we'll see why speaker subjectivism faces very serious problems, and how a certain kind of noncognitivist theory, *expressivism*, arises directly out of a simple idea about how to solve those problems. There are hints of the main ideas of expressivism in Ayer and Stevenson, but it really came into its own more recently, in the views of Simon Blackburn and Allan Gibbard. Expressivism is now the dominant version of noncognitivism − so dominant that people often write articles and books in which they define 'noncognitivism' to *mean* 'expressivism'. Our most important task in this chapter is therefore to find out what this view is, and why it has been thought to amount to such a big improvement on the earlier theories of Ayer, Stevenson, and Hare.

Recall from Chapter 1 that noncognitivist theories can be motivated in either of two ways. They can be motivated on the basis of domain-neutral considerations deriving from a certain strategy for avoiding the 'core questions' of metaethics. Or they can be motivated on the basis of providing an attractive solution to the *motivation problem* – to explain why there seems to be a more intimate connection between our views about moral questions and motivation than there is between our views about non-moral questions and motivation. Philosophers knew about all of these problems long before anyone came up with the idea of a noncognitivist metaethical theory. And there was a very common idea about how to solve them. Instead of denying that moral questions are about *anything*, this idea held that moral questions are merely about our own psychologies.

This theory is called *speaker subjectivism*. According to a very simple version of speaker subjectivism, the following two sentences have exactly the same meaning, and that fact suffices to explain the meaning of sentence 1:

1    'Stealing money is wrong.'
2    'I disapprove of stealing money.'

The main attractions of the theory are very clear: in general, people don't say, 'stealing money is wrong' unless they disapprove of it. This theory can explain why: if you don't disapprove of stealing money, then you don't speak truly by saying, 'stealing money is wrong'. So if you want to say only things that are true, you'll try not to say it unless you really do disapprove of stealing money.

We can now see why speaker subjectivism was thought to help answer the problem of motivation. If 'stealing money is wrong' just means, 'I disapprove of stealing money', then to think that stealing money is wrong will just be to think that you disapprove of stealing money. But in general, people are pretty good at knowing whether they disapprove of something or not – after all, who knows better what you disapprove of than you do? So most of the time, if you think that you disapprove of stealing money, that will be because you really do disapprove of stealing money. Hence, most of the time when you think that stealing is wrong, you really will disapprove of stealing. So if disapproving of stealing is the kind of mental state to motivate you not to steal, then there will be a close connection between thinking that stealing is wrong and being motivated not to steal. That is how speaker subjectivism can answer the problem of motivation.

We can also see why speaker subjectivism was thought to help escape the core questions of metaethics. It is for the same reason that Stevenson's view was able to do so. True, according to speaker subjectivism, moral questions really are about something – so we can't deny the presupposition of the core questions. But the thing that they are about is not unscientific or mysterious – it is just our own psychologies. Moreover, it is not puzzling how we find out about it – at least, no more puzzling than how we find out what we believe, what we desire, what we hope for, or what we intend. And it can't be *too* puzzling how we manage to talk or think about it, because we have other, non-moral, words for talking and thinking about the very same thing – words like 'I disapprove', for example.

So for all of these reasons, speaker subjectivism was the predecessor to noncognitivism: philosophers were attracted to it for very similar reasons. Historically, noncognitivism grew out of and replaced speaker subjectivism, which we can see most clearly in Stevenson, who still accepts *part* of the subjectivist view – in the form of his 'first pattern' of analysis – but simply insists that there is *more* to the meaning of moral words than is captured by speaker subjectivism alone. But to see why most philosophers have concluded that speaker subjectivism needed to be replaced by a kind of noncognitivism, we need to take a look at some of its biggest and most famous problems.

## 4.2 Two problems with speaker subjectivism

There are two important problems for speaker subjectivism that people have known about for a long time. These are the *modal problem* and the *disagreement problem*. The modal problem is simple, and asks us to compare the following two sentences:

3    'If I didn't disapprove of stealing money, then it wouldn't be the case that I disapprove of stealing money.'
4    'If I didn't disapprove of stealing money, then it wouldn't be the case that stealing money is wrong.'

Sentence 3 is clearly true. But sentence 4 is false unless, perhaps, God is the one who is saying it. If you are willing to accept sentence 4, then you seem to think that your attitudes can change what is right or wrong – and that is a strong thing to think! Similarly, compare sentences 5 and 6:

5    'If I stop disapproving of stealing money before tomorrow, then tomorrow it won't be the case that I disapprove of stealing money.'

6    'If I stop disapproving of stealing money before tomorrow, then tomorrow it won't be the case that stealing money is wrong.'

Sentence 5 is clearly true. But sentence 6 is, like sentence 4, false unless, perhaps, God is the one who is saying it. If you are willing to accept sentence 6, then you seem to think that your attitudes can change what is right or wrong.

The clear differences between sentences 3 and 4, and between sentences 5 and 6, lead to a problem for speaker subjectivism because according to speaker subjectivism, 'stealing money is wrong' is true under exactly the same conditions as 'I disapprove of stealing money' is true. But if these two sentences are true under the same conditions, then one couldn't be true without the other being true. So if one *could* have failed to be true, then the other would fail to be true under the same circumstances. And similarly, if one *will* fail to be true, then the other will fail to be true under the same circumstances. A fancier way of saying this is to say that these sentences behave differently under *modals* and *tense*. Modals are words like 'could have', 'would have', and 'necessarily', and sentences 3 and 4 are called 'subjunctive conditionals' because they are 'if ... then' sentences about what *could have* or *would have* been the case, if something else *had* been the case. Tense is just the temporal aspect of how we evaluate a sentence – present, past, or future. For short, I'll just call this the *modal problem*.

The modal problem is often characterized by saying that it follows from speaker subjectivism that morality is not a very *objective* thing. There is something intuitive about the idea that some things are more objective, and other things are more subjective – so for example, the nature of the laws of physics or of arithmetic might be thought to be 'more objective' than the value of the dollar, and the value of the dollar might in turn be 'more objective' than judgments of taste – for example, the claim that chocolate ice cream is tastier than vanilla, or that beer is preferable to wine. This is a vague idea, but given this vague idea, morality as speaker subjectivism characterizes it certainly does seem to be toward the 'subjective' end of this spectrum.

I am not personally a fan of talking about 'how objective' things are; I suspect that there are many differences between arithmetic and judgments of taste, and that calling them all a difference in 'objectivity' obscures their important differences. I prefer to spend time focusing on more precise questions, and the modal problem is one such more precise question. According to the modal problem, sentences 3 and 5 should turn out to be true, but sentences 4 and 6 should turn out to be false. But it follows from speaker subjectivism that sentences 4 and 6 are always true. This is part of what people often get at by saying that according to speaker subjectivism, morality is less objective. They mean that if you accept speaker subjectivism, you think that 'If I didn't disapprove of stealing, then it wouldn't be wrong' is true, and hence think that if you didn't disapprove of stealing, then it wouldn't be wrong. But to think that is to think that you have a certain amount of control over whether stealing is wrong, which makes it, intuitively, a less objective matter than the truths of arithmetic.

The other important problem for speaker subjectivism is the *disagreement problem*. To get an intuitive sense for what the disagreement problem is, imagine the following telephone conversation taking place between Phil, who is in Seattle, and Sally, who is in New York:

*Phil:*    'Hi, Sally. This is Phil. I'm in Seattle.'
*Sally:*    'That's false – I'm not in Seattle! I'm in New York.'

Something is obviously going wrong here. When Phil says, 'I'm in Seattle', he does not disagree with Sally when she says, 'I'm not in Seattle', even though one has added the word 'not' to what the other has said. On the contrary; what they say is completely compatible.

The same holds for the following conversations between Phil, who disapproves of stealing money, and Sally, who does not disapprove of stealing money:

*Phil:*    'I disapprove of stealing money.'
*Sally:*    'That's false – I don't disapprove of stealing money!'

Again, something is going wrong. What is going wrong is the same thing that was going wrong in the first case. What Phil says and what Sally says are completely compatible, so they are not really in disagreement. But now compare this to one more conversation:

*Phil:*    'Stealing money is wrong.'
*Sally:*    'That's false – stealing money is not wrong!'

On the face of it, nothing is going wrong with this conversation. In this conversation, Phil and Sally really *do* disagree, because they are saying incompatible things. But this is a big problem for speaker subjectivism, according to which the third conversation is merely a different way of having the second conversation.

Here is the flip side of the same problem. According to speaker subjectivism, the following two conversations should both make perfect sense:

*Phil:*   'I disapprove of stealing money.'
*Sally:.*  'When you say, "I disapprove of stealing money", what you say is true. Nevertheless, I do not disapprove of stealing money.'

*Phil:*   'Stealing money is wrong.'
*Sally:*  'When you say, "Stealing is wrong", what you say is true. Nevertheless stealing is not wrong.'

The first conversation makes perfect sense, because when Phil says, 'I disapprove of stealing money', he says something *different* from what Sally denies, when she says, 'I do not disapprove of stealing money'. Because speaker subjectivists believe that 'stealing money is wrong' has the same meaning as 'I disapprove of stealing money', they are committed to the result that the second conversation should make sense, as well. But on the contrary, Sally's contribution to the second conversation is quite bizarre.

I'll call this problem the *disagreement problem*. Stevenson knew about the disagreement problem, and it was apparently the main problem that convinced him to prefer his noncognitivist theory to speaker subjectivism. Let's turn now to look at how the modal and disagreement problems serve to motivate expressivism, the next generation of noncognitivist theory.

## 4.3 The basic expressivist maneuver

Expressivism, as I understand it, is motivated by an attempt to solve these two problems for speaker subjectivism – the modal and disagreement problems. The key ingredient in the expressivist's solution to these two problems is a diagnosis of the *source* of these two problems. That is, it is an answer to what feature of speaker subjectivism created the problems. To solve the problems, you need to give that feature up. To see what feature this is, imagine a theorist who comes along and says that the following two sentences have the same meaning, and that suffices to explain the meaning of the former:

7   'Grass is green.'
8   'I believe that grass is green.'

Now, there are a number of reasons why this is a bad theory about the meaning of 'grass is green' – not the least that the compositionality constraint tells us that we need to know the meaning of 'grass is green' in order to determine the meaning of 'I believe that grass is green' in the first place. So this theory is so clearly false as to be uninteresting in most respects. But one respect in which it is interesting is that it leads to both the modal problem and the disagreement problem.

To see how it leads to the modal problem, compare the following pairs of sentences:

9     'If I didn't believe that grass is green, then it wouldn't have been the case that I believe that grass is green.'
10    'If I didn't believe that grass is green, then it wouldn't be the case that grass is green.'
11    'If I stop believing that grass is green before tomorrow, then tomorrow it won't be the case that I believe that grass is green.'
12    'If I stop believing that grass is green before tomorrow, then tomorrow it won't be the case that grass is green.'

Again, sentences 9 and 11 are clearly true, but sentences 10 and 12 are clearly false. The only person who would accept such things would be someone who thought that her beliefs had some kind of effect on the color of grass. This is not a new problem – it is just the old modal problem that we are already familiar with, raised for a new view.

To see how this view leads to the disagreement problem, compare the following two conversations between Phil, who believes that grass is green, and Sally, who for reasons that I won't here explain, does not believe that grass is green:

Phil:    'I believe that grass is green.'
Sally:   'That's false! I don't believe that grass is green.'

Phil:    'Grass is green.'
Sally:   'That's false! Grass is not green.'

The theory about the meaning of 'grass is green' that we are considering predicts that these conversations should make equal sense, since they are simply two different ways of having the same conversation. But obviously these conversations do not make equal sense; the former makes no sense at all: Sally is obviously confused to respond to what Phil says in that way. Again, this is not a new problem – it is just the old disagreement problem that we are already familiar with, simply raised for a new view.

Now we can say how to make the expressivist move. Notice that the sentences 'grass is green' and 'I believe that grass is green' bear some interesting relationship to one another. This relationship cannot be that of having the same meaning, because as we've seen, that leads to the modal and disagreement problems. But since there are not really modal or disagreement problems for 'grass is green', that means that whatever relationship 'grass is green' and 'I believe that grass is green' really bear to one another would not create the modal problem or the disagreement problem.

So where speaker subjectivism goes wrong, the expressivist concludes, is by saying that the relationship between 'stealing money is wrong' and 'I disapprove of stealing money' is that they have the same meaning. That, after all, is what leads to the modal and disagreement problems. So, the expressivist concludes, we should say something else about the relationship between those two sentences, instead. In fact – and this is the fundamental idea of expressivism – we should say the same thing about the relationship between 'stealing is wrong' and 'I disapprove of stealing' as we say about the relationship between 'grass is green' and 'I believe that grass is green'. This is a brilliant idea, because we know that whatever this relationship is, it does not lead to either the modal or the disagreement problem. And we know that because we know that there is not really a modal or disagreement problem for 'grass is green'.

To reiterate: the fundamental idea of expressivism can be put terms of the following analogy (read 'A:B::C:D' as 'A is to B as C is to D'):

> 'stealing is wrong' : 'I disapprove of stealing' :: 'grass is green' : 'I believe that grass is green'

If we note that 'I disapprove of stealing' says that the speaker is in a certain mental state – disapproval of stealing – and that 'I believe that grass is green' says that the speaker is in another kind of mental state – the belief that grass is green – then we can put the same idea in terms of the following, equivalent, analogy:

> 'stealing is wrong' : disapproving of stealing :: 'grass is green' : believing that grass is green

Expressivism is the theory that this analogy suffices to tell us the meaning of 'stealing is wrong'. Hence, it is the minimal departure from speaker subjectivism required in order to solve the modal and disagreement problems. The expressivist turn began with Simon Blackburn, but became clearer and more explicit in the writings of Allan Gibbard. Terry Horgan and Mark Timmons have also advocated a paradigm expressivist theory in recent years. It is by far the dominant kind of noncognitivist theory in the literature, and has received the most attention.

The difference between 'grass is green' and 'I believe that grass is green' is often called the *expressing–reporting* distinction, on the grounds that we say that 'I believe that grass is green' *reports* the belief that grass is green, whereas 'grass is green' *expresses* that belief. Using this terminology, speaker subjectivism was the view that the meaning of moral sentences consists in their *reporting* states of mind like disapproval, whereas expressivism is the view that the meaning of moral sentences consists in their *expressing* states of mind like disapproval. That is why the view is called *expressivism*.

To understand the fundamental idea of expressivism, it is important not to become distracted by this word, 'express'. We all have pre-theoretical ideas about what the word 'express' means. We talk about things like freedom of *expression*, and work on being able to *express* our feelings to our loved ones, and become anxious while traveling in foreign countries with different languages when we are unable to *express* ourselves. This has tempted many philosophers to think that they can discern what follows from expressivism by thinking about the meaning of the word 'express', as we use it in ordinary English. Ayer used the word 'express' in such an intuitive sense. But be careful not to fall into this trap; according to *expressivism*, 'express' is just a placeholder term for whatever the relationship between 'grass is green' and the belief that grass is green turns out to be. It is a theoretical term, within the theory of expressivism.

The distinction between the ordinary sense of 'express' and the expressivist's use of 'express' as a theoretical term for the relationship between 'grass is green' and the belief that grass is green – whatever that relationship turns out to be – is useful for helping us to understand why even though some of the early emotivist theories *anticipated* expressivism in important ways, none of them really fully appreciated the fundamental idea of expressivism. For example, even Ayer, who had one of the earliest and simplest noncognitivist theories, described his view by saying that moral sentences 'express' states of mind. So if we were to classify his view casually, simply on the basis of these words, then we might be tempted to call Ayer an expressivist.

But Ayer did not yet understand the fundamental idea of expressivism, and his suggestions about the meaning of 'stealing is wrong', though colorful and suggestive, therefore do not take the form of an expressivist theory of meaning.

## 4.4 Expressivism contrasted with earlier views

Though expressivism is clearly anticipated in important ways by both Ayer and Stevenson, it is better to think of it as a significant departure from the earlier generations of noncognitivist theories. Ayer, Stevenson, and Hare all aspired to tell us the meaning of moral words like 'good' and 'wrong' by telling us what they are used to do – at least, what *simple* or *atomic* sentences containing them, such as 'stealing money is wrong' are used to do. Such theories can be thought of as essentially *speech act* theories, and if we followed Hare's suggestion and developed such theories into complete theories of meaning, they would work by assigning each sentence to some speech act which it is suited to perform. First, they would give us recipes to determine which speech acts atomic sentences are suited to perform, and then they would give us recipes to determine which speech acts bigger and more complex *molecular* sentences are suited to perform, on the basis of which speech acts their parts are suited to perform. According to such a theory, meanings are speech acts. Not the speech acts that we do perform with a given sentence, necessarily, but the speech acts that they are primarily suited to perform.

Some versions of expressivism are also speech act theories. They hold that expressing a mental state is performing a certain kind of speech act. But not all versions of expressivism are speech act theories, because to accept the fundamental idea of expressivism, you don't have to think that expressing an attitude is a speech act. You don't have to think that it is anything that you *do* at all. You might just think that it is a special kind of relationship between a sentence and a mental state – one in virtue of which the sentence means what it does. So in general, expressivist theories of meaning need not associate sentences with speech acts that they are suited to perform. What an expressivist theory of meaning does instead is to associate each sentence with a mental state.[1]

For each sentence, 'P', an expressivist theory says what 'P' means by saying what it is to think that P. To think that grass is green, the expressivist will say, is to be in a state of mind with mind-to-world direction of fit – one which is like part of a map to the world we live in. But to think that stealing money is wrong, the expressivist will say, is to be in a different sort of state of mind – one with world-to-mind direction of fit, like the destination for which we are headed – pointing away from stealing money. Then a complete expressivist theory of meaning which follows Hare's suggestion will provide us with recipes which tell us how to determine, for complex sentences 'P', what it is to think that P, on the basis of what it is to think that Q, that R, and so on, for each of the parts of 'P'.

Once we characterize the differences between expressivism and earlier noncognitivist views in this way, we can immediately see two important reasons why expressivism has been taken to be more promising. The first is that we need to have some theory of the nature of moral thought. Noncognitivists avoided the 'core questions' of metaethics by denying the presupposition that there is something that moral questions are about. And that left noncognitivists with an important task: to say what we are doing when we use moral language, if there is nothing that it is about. They sought to fulfill this task by offering us an alternative account of the kind of meaning that moral words have. But on the face of it, that is only half of the task that we incur if we deny the presupposition that moral questions are really about anything. For just as there are moral sentences which we were presupposing to be about something, there are also moral thoughts which we were presupposing to be about something. If you want to deny that presupposition, then you are left with the puzzle of what on earth I am thinking when I think that stealing money is wrong, if there is nothing that I am thinking about.

In a natural sense, explaining what we are doing with moral language, if it is not really about anything, and explaining what we are doing with moral thought, if it is not really about anything, are two sides of the same coin. If we give up the presupposition that moral language is about something, that doesn't help to avoid the core questions unless we also give up the presupposition that moral thought is about something. So these two tasks come hand in hand. But early noncognitivist theories only accomplish half of this task. Ayer, Stevenson, and Hare all give some hints as to what is involved in moral thought, but there is no direct way to read it off their views, which are really primarily about language. Expressivism, in contrast, is explicitly a view about both moral language and moral thought. In fact, its accounts of moral language and moral thought are intertwined. An expressivist theory gives an account of the meaning of moral sentences by giving an account of the nature of the corresponding moral thoughts. So it is natural to think that this is a significant leg up for expressivism.

The second main advantage in expressivism's corner, is that insofar as noncognitivist theories are motivated, at least in part, by the aspiration to solve the motivation problem, from Chapter 1, expressivism looks most neatly poised to do so. The motivation problem, after all, arose from the following observation about the nature of moral thought: that if you convince your friend that she ought to donate money to CARE, then you will expect her to be motivated to do so, in a way that you would expect no similar thing on the basis of convincing your friend that the Alcove serves doughnut-sized onion rings. This was an observation about what happens when your friend *thinks* that she ought to donate money to CARE, not an observation about what happens when she *says* any particular thing. So it really needs to be explained by an account of the nature of moral thought. Since expressivism directly provides such an account and earlier versions of noncognitivism do not, expressivism is more directly poised to answer the motivation problem.

It is hard to overstate the significance of the first of these advantages. If moral thoughts are not about anything, then what kind of thoughts are they, and why do they seem to work so much like non-moral thoughts do? Every noncognitivist theory needs to answer this question eventually, and expressivists are simply more upfront about it. In Chapter 5 we'll look in detail at the kinds of difficulties that arise in the process of trying to do so.

## Chapter summary

In this chapter we introduced the theory of speaker subjectivism, and observed that it falls prey to two difficult problems, the *modal* problem and the *disagreement* problem. We saw how the noncognitivist theory of *expressivism* avoids those problems, and that it has the added advantage of giving a unified account of moral language and moral thought.

## Further reading

This chapter is designed to be read along with Stevenson (1937) and chapter 1 of Gibbard (1990), and another appropriate supplement is Gibbard (2003, 1–13). Schroeder (2008a) is a general discussion of what expressivists mean by 'express'. For sophisticated contemporary variants on speaker subjectivism, see Dreier (1990) and Finlay (2004).

# Exercises

1    E *Comprehension*: Indexicals are words like 'I', 'you', 'here', and 'now', which refer to different things in different conversations. Speaker subjectivism is the view that 'wrong' is a certain kind of indexical. Pick out the indexical words in the following sentences (there may be more than one indexical per sentence):

1    My dog ate my homework.
2    This is the last straw.
3    You aren't listening well enough to us.
4    He is tall.
5    Today is the first day of the rest of your life.
6    The stapler is empty.

2    E *Extensions*: What is it to express a mental state? Suppose that Max is a child pretending to be sick in order to stay home from school. Max moans and grimaces, but he is neither uncomfortable nor in pain. Do Max's groans and grimaces express pain? Or is he merely pretending to express pain? Now suppose that Max tells an explicit lie: he says, 'I feel miserable'. Is he expressing a belief that he feels miserable? Or is he just pretending to express a belief that he is miserable? In answering, provide your own judgments, given what you think 'express' intuitively means.

3    M *Extensions*: Some people find it intuitive to think that expression is a *causal* relation (see exercise 2). When you express a mental state by uttering some sentence, that is because your utterance is *caused*, in part, by your being in that mental state. For example, in normal cases people who say, 'grass is green' say it, in part, because they believe that grass really is green. Consider the following two sentences:

1    Being friendly is wrong.
2    If being friendly is wrong, then being friendly to strangers is wrong.

Is 'being friendly is wrong' caused by the same mental state, for ordinary speakers who might utter each of these two sentences? Or not? According to expressivism, what makes 'being friendly is wrong' mean what it does is the mental state that it expresses. Should expressivists say that expression is a causal relation? Why or why not?

4    M *Extensions*: The Open Question argument. In addition to the modal and disagreement problems, one of the main arguments that led most philosophers to reject speaker subjectivism was Moore's Open Question argument (see exercises 3–4 from Chapter 1). But in fact, for many years philosophers were not very clear about the differences between Moore's Open Question argument and the modal problem – in fact, as late as 1968, Urmson describes the modal problem when he is trying to explain Moore's argument! Suppose that someone argues that speaker subjectivism can't be true, because it is possible to recognize that you disapprove of something, but still wonder whether it is wrong, but it is not possible to recognize that you disapprove of something, but still wonder whether you disapprove of it. How would you respond to this objection, if you wanted to defend speaker subjectivism?

5    M *Comprehension*: Ayer wrote the following about expression:

Thus I may simultaneously express boredom and say that I am bored, and in that case my utterance of the words, 'I am bored,' is one of the circumstances which make it true to say that I am expressing or evincing boredom. (1936, 109)

Should expressivists agree with Ayer that 'I am bored' may express boredom? Why or why not?

6    D *New problem*: The fundamental idea of expressivism is given by the analogy at the bottom of page 72. It says that no matter what the relationship is between 'grass is green' and the ordinary descriptive belief that grass is green, that same relationship holds between 'stealing is wrong' and disapproval of stealing, and that suffices to explain why 'stealing is wrong' has the meaning that it does. Now consider the theory that the relationship between 'grass is green' and the ordinary descriptive belief that grass is green is that they have the same *content*: that is, that the conditions under which 'grass is green' would be true, given what it means, are the same as the conditions that the ordinary descriptive belief that grass is green represents as being the case. Try to put this view together with expressivism. Do they fit together well, or poorly? Why?

7    D *Qualifications*: Some contemporary theorists have defended speaker subjectivism against the disagreement problem, by proposing that instead

of having the same meaning as 'I disapprove of stealing money', 'stealing money is wrong' has a meaning that is more like that of 'those of us around here disapprove of stealing money'. Others have said that it means something more like 'local people disapprove of stealing money'. Call the former the *plural indexical* view and the latter the *flexible* view. To test how these adjustments change the dialectic surrounding the disagreement problem, construct analogues of the dialogues from section 2 for both the plural indexical view and the flexible view. How do things change? Do these views make disagreements easier to explain? Do they leave any problem remaining? Is either better than the other?

8   D *Extensions*: Suppose that Jeremy and Immanuel have the following conversation:

Immanuel:   'It is always wrong to lie, no matter what.'
Jeremy:     'You just said that it is always wrong to lie, no matter what. But it is not always wrong to lie, no matter what. So what you said is false.'

Translate Immanuel and Jeremy's conversation as speaker subjectivists must understand it. Do you have any choices about how the translation works? Is anything weird about this conversation? If so, what?

9   A *Qualifications*: According to a relatively recent idea, speaker subjectivism can be saved from the modal problem by amending it to hold that 'stealing money is wrong' has the same meaning as 'I *actually* disapprove of stealing money', rather than the same meaning as 'I disapprove of stealing money'. This view, known as *actually rigidified speaker subjectivism*, avoids the problem, because if you really do disapprove of stealing money, then the following sentence is *false*:

1   If I didn't disapprove of stealing money, then it wouldn't be the case that I actually disapprove of stealing money.

The reason why this sentence is false, is that in the way that philosophers ordinarily interpret 'actually', the word 'actually' always refers back to the actual world, even if we are considering what might happen in other possible situations. But on the other hand, actually rigidified speaker subjectivism appears to have its own problems. Compare the following two sentences:

2    If there was one extra grain of sand in the rings of Saturn but everything else was the same, then I would still think that stealing money is wrong.

3    If there was one extra grain of sand in the rings of Saturn but everything else was the same, then I would still think that I actually disapprove of stealing money.

The problem is this: according to actually rigidified speaker subjectivism sentences 2 and 3 mean the same thing. So since 2 is true, 3 must be true as well. But now we face a dilemma: which world does 'actually' refer to, in sentence 3? To the real actual world? Or to the way that things would be, if there were an extra grain of sand in the rings of Saturn. There is something troubling about both of these choices: explain what.

10  A  *Qualifications*: According to speaker subjectivism as described in the main text, 'stealing money is wrong' has the same meaning as 'I disapprove of stealing money', and so it appears to be about the speaker. Speaker subjectivism has contemporary, sophisticated cousins which say instead that 'stealing money is wrong' has the same meaning as 'stealing money instantiates dthat (the property I disapprove of things for instantiating)'. (If you're unfamiliar with 'dthat', see Kaplan [1987].) Call this alternative view 'neo-subjectivism', and the traditional view 'traditional subjectivism'. Evaluate how neo-subjectivism and traditional subjectivism compare with respect to the modal problem and the disagreement problem. Is neo-subjectivism progress? If so, in what ways? If not, why not?

## Partial answers

9  Hint: 'Actually' refers to the actual world. So if things had been different – even so slightly as for there to be one extra grain of sand in the rings of Saturn – then that would not have been the actual world. Why is it strange to think that thinking that stealing money is wrong is having a belief about the actual world?

## Morals

2  Some people are inclined to think that Max isn't really expressing pain, or the belief that he feels miserable, but only pretending to. If so, that

would be a problem for expressivism, because when Max lies and says that he feels miserable, he *means* the same thing as he would have meant if he weren't lying. But according to expressivism, the meaning of Max's sentence is given by the mental state that it expresses, so if he expresses a belief when he is not lying, but doesn't express that belief when he is lying, then the lie must not mean the same thing. This is why it's important to keep in mind that expressivists might not be using the word 'express' in the way that you or I would. Even if you or I wouldn't say that Max expresses the belief that he feels miserable when he lies, expressivists will say that he does.

3    This exercise illustrates the *composition problem*. In order for the meaning of a complex sentence to be determined by the meanings of its parts, its parts must *really have* that meaning. So expressivists need to be careful about what they mean by 'express'.

5    If 'I am bored' expresses boredom, then by analogy, 'I disapprove of murder' should express disapproval of murder. But according to expressivism, 'Murder is wrong' also expresses disapproval of murder, and what makes a sentence mean what it does is the mental state that it expresses. What problem does this create for expressivism? (Hint: What assumption led to speaker subjectivists' problems?)

6    The fundamental idea of expressivism is that *whatever* explains why the modal and disagreement problems don't arise for 'grass is green' will suffice to show that they don't arise for 'murder is wrong', either. This exercise shows that this is false – some theories about why those problems don't arise for 'grass is green' cannot be appealed to by expressivism. For further discussion see Schroeder (2008a).

## References

Ayer, A.J. (1936). *Language, Truth, and Logic*. New York: Dover.

Dreier, James (1990). 'Internalism and Speaker Relativism.' *Ethics* 101(1): 6–25.

Finlay, Stephen (2004). 'The Conversational Practicality of Value Judgment.' *Journal of Ethics* 8: 205–23.

Gibbard, Allan (1990). *Wise Choices, Apt Feelings*. Cambridge, MA: Harvard University Press, chapter 1.

—— (2003). *Thinking How to Live*. Cambridge, MA: Harvard University Press.

Kaplan, David (1989). 'Demonstratives.' In John Perry, Joseph Almog, and Howard Wettstein, eds., *Themes from Kaplan*. Oxford: Oxford University Press.

Schroeder, Mark (2008a). 'Expression for Expressivists.' *Philosophy and Phenomenological Research* 76(1): 86–116.

Stevenson, C.L. (1937). 'The Emotive Meaning of Ethical Terms.' Reprinted in Stevenson (1963), *Facts and Values*. Westport, CT: Greenwood Press.

Urmson, J.O. (1968). *The Emotive Theory of Ethics*. New York: Oxford University Press.

# 5

---

# MORAL THOUGHT

## 5.1 The variety of attitudes

At the end of Chapter 4, we saw that just as noncognitivists need to give us a special answer to the question, 'if moral *words* aren't about anything, then what kind of meaning do they have?', they also need to give us a special answer to the question, 'if moral *thoughts* aren't about anything, then what kind of thoughts are they?'. It is to that second question that we turn in this chapter. Our main goal is to understand not only what kind of thoughts moral thoughts are, but to understand why they seem so much like non-moral thoughts in so many respects.

The first thing to notice about this question is that there are many different kinds of moral thoughts. Not only do we have *beliefs* about what is good or wrong, we *want* the actions which benefit us to not be wrong, we *hope* that we haven't acted wrongly, we *wonder* whether early-term abortion is wrong, we *assume* that some things are wrong for the sake of argument, we are *proud* that we have been good or *afraid* that we won't be as good as is expected of us. Each of these − believing, wanting, hoping, wondering, assuming, being proud of, and being afraid of − is a kind of *attitude*, and there are many, many more. These are all attitudes that we appear to be able to have either toward moral contents or toward non-moral contents. For example, we can also believe that Colorado is rectangular, want to go there, hope that it votes Republican, wonder whether it is faster to fly or drive there, assume for the sake of argument that it votes Democrat, be proud that we have seen more of it than the airport in Denver, or be afraid that our plane will crash on the way there. These are all non-moral thoughts – the very same sorts of attitudes with non-moral contents.

If I wonder whether Colorado will vote Republican in the next election, and you hope that Colorado will vote Republican in the next election, then there is something that you hope, and about which I wonder. It is the same thing that Phil anticipates, if he anticipates that Colorado will vote Republican in the next election, and the same thing that Howard dreads, if he dreads that Colorado will vote Republican in the next election. Philosophers have a name for such things – which are the objects of wonder, hope, anticipation, and dread. They are called *propositions*. According to the theory of propositions, propositions are the objects of the attitudes and bearers of truth and falsity. Your belief is true, according to this theory, when it is a belief in a proposition which is true. Similarly, your wish comes true when it is a wish whose propositional object turns out to be true.

Propositions tell us what each of these attitudes is *about*. When you believe that Colorado is rectangular, you have a belief that is about Colorado, and about the similarity demarcated by 'rectangular'. Similarly, when you hope that Colorado will vote Republican in the next election, your hope is about Colorado, voting, the next election, and the Republican Party. So if noncognitivism is to let us off of the hook for the presupposition of the 'core questions' of metaethics, then noncognitivists are going to have to explain what moral beliefs, wants, hopes, wonderings, and so on are, if they are not just beliefs, wants, hopes, and wonderings with moral propositions as their objects. For to have moral propositions as their objects, they would have to be *about* something moral.

So noncognitivists need a story not only about what it is to believe that something is good or wrong, but also a story about what it is to want something to be good or wrong, of what it is to hope for something to be good or wrong, and so on, for each and every attitude there is. This is a very big task, because there are very many attitudes, and belief is just one of them. So I will call it the *Many Attitudes* problem. It turns out that noncognitivist theories have not had very much to say, so far, about any of the attitudes other than belief, so in this chapter we'll focus mostly on belief. But as we'll see, that will be more than enough to keep us busy.

## 5.2  A putative problem

Some philosophers have worried that the project of trying to give a noncognitivist account of what it is to believe that stealing money is wrong is
doomed from the start. Their argument goes like this:

> **premise one**  Noncognitivism is, by definition, the view that where 'P'
> is a moral sentence, there is no such thing as the belief that P. Instead,
> according to noncognitivism, to think that P is to be in a non-belief state,
> a desire-like attitude.
> **premise two**  'Stealing money is wrong' is a moral sentence.
> **conclusion**  Noncognitivists hold that there is no such thing as the belief
> that stealing money is wrong.

It is easy to see where this argument goes wrong. It tries to define noncognitivism into being unable to give an account of what it is to believe that
stealing money is wrong. Such arguments are always easy to escape, because
they are 'merely semantic' in the pejorative sense. Interesting philosophical
issues don't turn on how we define theoretical terms like 'noncognitivism'.
On the contrary, it is easy to grant the philosopher who offers this argument
his use of the term, and make up a new name for the view that is shared by
Ayer, Stevenson, Hare, and the expressivists. It is not possible to define this
view out of existence, or to define it into being unable to give an account of
what it is to believe that stealing money is wrong.

It is true, and you will see this as soon as you begin to do further
reading on noncognitivism or expressivism, that many noncognitivists have
described their theories as holding that thinking that stealing is wrong is
not a matter of believing that stealing money is wrong. Such theorists say
things like the following:

> There are two kinds of ways in which it can be true that someone thinks
> that P, for some sentence, 'P'. When 'P' is a non-moral sentence, someone
> thinks that P just in case she believes that P. Belief has mind-to-world
> direction of fit. But when 'P' is a moral sentence, someone thinks that P
> just in case she is in a certain desire-like attitude – for example, a state of
> disapproval. Disapproval has world-to-mind direction of fit.

But again, this looks like just one choice about how to describe things. Here
is what a different theorist might say:

There are two kinds of ways in which it can be true that someone believes that P, for some sentence, 'P'. When 'P' is a non-moral sentence, someone believes that P just in case she bears a certain attitude toward the proposition that P, which we can call 'ordinary descriptive belief'. This attitude has mind-to-world direction of fit. But when 'P' is a moral sentence, someone believes that P just in case she is in a different sort of attitude, which we can call 'moral belief'. This attitude has world-to-mind direction of fit.

The first theorist says that there are two kinds of 'thinking' – one kind 'belief' and the other not. The second theorist says that there are two kinds of 'belief' – one kind with mind-to-world direction of fit and the other with world-to-mind direction of fit.

There is not a big difference between these two views; they are merely using different words to say the same thing. But one of these ways of speaking is better. Someone who says things in the first way cannot then go on to say what it is to believe that stealing money is wrong. She is forced to say things like, 'there is no such thing as the belief that stealing money is wrong'. This may be one way of speaking, but it is not an intuitive way of speaking; in ordinary English we certainly do allow that there is such a thing as the belief that stealing money is wrong – it is certainly something that I believe, and I hope you do, too. So the second way of speaking is a better choice from the point of view of noncognitivism. It preserves more of common sense.

Still, it is a funny thing to use the same words, 'believes that', to say two such apparently different things. If we really use the words 'believes that' in this way, then sometimes when we say that Jones believes that P, we are ascribing to Jones a state of mind with mind-to-world direction of fit. Whereas other times, when we say that Jones believes that P, we are ascribing to Jones a state of mind with world-to-mind direction of fit. What a funny phenomenon! Ordinary non-moral words, as we saw in Chapter 2, serve to demarcate some kind of similarities among things in the world. But here are some words, 'believes that', which we apparently use, on this view, to pick out things that are strikingly dissimilar. Any noncognitivist who wants to talk in this way therefore has an explanatory debt: she owes us not only an account of what it is to believe that stealing money is wrong, but also an account of the meaning of 'believes that' which explains why a word with one and the same meaning can be used to talk about two such different things. I'll call this the One Word problem.

Existing noncognitivist views mostly do not say how to solve the One Word problem. Sometimes people say that they are going to use the words 'believes that' in a *deflationary* way. This means essentially that they are going to use the words in such a way that they can be used to talk about very different things. But that isn't an account of *what* 'believes that' means, or of *how* it lets us talk about such very different things. But we can do better. In the remainder of this section, I'm going to provide a sketch of how this problem can be approached by an expressivist theorist. Then in later sections we'll return to the question of what it is to believe that stealing money is wrong.

Recall that an expressivist theory of meaning tells us what each sentence, 'P', means, by telling us what it is to believe that P. (I'll use the words 'believe' and 'think' interchangeably.) So each sentence is associated with some kind of mental state, which we can say is the mental state *expressed* by the sentence. So now consider the following principle:

> **believes**   For any sentence, 'P', and person, 'S', 'S believes that P' is true just in case 'S' is in the mental state expressed by 'P'.

This principle gives us a unified account of what 'believes that' might mean, from which it falls out that we might use sentences like 'S believes that P' in order to say very different things. For it follows from this principle, together with the assumption that 'Colorado is rectangular' expresses a certain state of mind with mind-to-world direction of fit, that 'Max believes that Colorado is rectangular' is true just in case Max is in a certain state of mind with mind-to-world direction of fit. Similarly, it follows from this same principle, together with the assumption that 'stealing money is wrong' expresses a state of disapproval of stealing money, with world-to-mind direction of fit, that 'Max believes that stealing money is wrong' is true just in case Max disapproves of stealing money, a state with world-to-mind direction of fit.

The principle is *not* flawless, and one of the exercises will get you started on seeing why not. But it is the kind of thing that expressivists should want. It gives us a single story about the meaning of 'believes that' which still makes sense of how we could use those words to say such different things, as of course any noncognitivist who wants to say that there are such things as moral beliefs needs to think that we are able to do. It is not, however, an *expressivist* account of the meaning of 'believes that', because it explains the meaning of 'believes that' by saying what it takes for sentences involving 'believes that' to be true. But we can fix that as well. Let's call the attitude with mind-to-world direction of fit that non-moral sentences express *ordinary descriptive belief*. Given that stipulation, we can reframe our principle as an expressivist account of the meaning of 'believes that':

> **expressivist believes**   For any sentence, 'P', and person, 'S', 'S believes that P' expresses the ordinary descriptive belief whose object is the proposition that 'S' is in the mental state expressed by 'P'.

This account is an expressivist account, because it tells us what the sentence, 'S believes that P' means, by telling us what it is to believe that S believes that P.

Here is where we are so far: we have answered the putative problem by showing how 'believes that' could have a meaning that would allow us to talk about both ordinary descriptive beliefs, with mind-to-world direction of fit, and about states like disapproval, with world-to-mind direction of fit. If 'believes that' really does have such a meaning, then it is not doomed from the start to think that there are two very different kinds of belief – that moral beliefs are very different in kind from ordinary descriptive beliefs. It gives us, for the attitude of belief, an answer to the One Word problem. But that still leaves open the question of just what it *is* to believe that stealing money is wrong, and why in so many respects, it seems to be so much like ordinary descriptive belief.

## 5.3  Disagreement

It's not just that we use the word 'belief' for both the belief that Colorado is rectangular and the belief that stealing money is wrong. These states of mind also resemble each other in many important respects. One important example is that if you believe that Colorado is rectangular and I believe that Colorado is not rectangular, then we disagree with one another. We are in disagreement about the shape of Colorado. Similarly, if you believe that stealing money is wrong and I believe that stealing money is not wrong, then we disagree with one another. We are in disagreement about the moral status of stealing money. In general, where 'P' is some sentence, someone who believes that P disagrees with someone who believes that it is not the case that P. And this is true no matter whether 'P' is a moral sentence or a non-moral sentence. We may call this the *interpersonal disagreement property* of belief.

But if believing that Colorado is rectangular and believing that stealing money is wrong are quite different kinds of mental states – because one has mind-to-world direction of fit and the other has world-to-mind direction of fit – then this looks like a big coincidence. For when we say that for any sentence 'P', someone who believes that P disagrees with someone who believes that it is not the case that P, we are really saying two things – one about ordinary descriptive belief, and one about moral belief. Since ordinary descriptive belief and moral belief are not, after all, a single kind of thing, it looks like a coincidence for it to turn out that they both have the interpersonal disagreement property. After all, many other kinds of mental states don't have that property. For example, someone who wonders whether Colorado is rectangular does not thereby disagree with someone who wonders whether Colorado is not rectangular. And someone who is afraid that the monsters are coming does not thereby disagree with someone who is afraid that the monsters are not coming. So if both ordinary descriptive belief and moral belief have this property, that is something that needs to be explained.

There is a simple argument that noncognitivists cannot give a totally happy account of the nature of moral belief, and it goes like this:

**P1**   According to noncognitivism, to believe that stealing money is wrong is to be in a certain desire-like attitude – that is, a state of mind with world-to-mind direction of fit.

**P2**   According to noncognitivism, to believe that stealing money is not wrong is to be in a certain desire-like attitude – that is, a state of mind with world-to-mind direction of fit.

**P3**   People cannot disagree with one another simply by having different desire-like attitudes – that is, simply by having different states of mind with world-to-mind direction of fit.

**C**   So it follows from noncognitivism that people who believe that stealing money is wrong do not necessarily disagree with people who believe that stealing money is not wrong.

Stevenson knew about this objection in the 1930s. But he argued that premise P3 is false. People *do* sometimes disagree with one another by having different desire-like attitudes. For example, if we are planning to spend the evening together, you might intend for us to go to the symphony, but I might intend for us to go to the cinema. If those are our respective intentions, then it seems like we *do* disagree with one another. We disagree about what to do this evening. So if intentions are desire-like attitudes, with world-to-mind direction of fit, then we have a counterexample to premise P3.

Allan Gibbard takes Stevenson's reasoning one step further. If moral belief is a desire-like attitude – as noncognitivists claim – and if belief has the interpersonal disagreement property – as it clearly does – then to understand the nature of moral belief, we should look to the best examples that we have of desire-like attitudes with the interpersonal disagreement property. Moral belief must be *more like* those kinds of attitudes, and *less like* desire-like attitudes which lack the interpersonal disagreement property. So far, what we've seen is that intentions – our plans about what to do tonight – are plausibly a good example of desire-like attitudes which may have this property. Gibbard (2003) makes a big deal out of this idea. Just as Hare (1952) argued that we *need* a non-truth-conditional theory of meaning in order to make sense of the meaning of imperative sentences, Gibbard argues that we *need* to understand how people can disagree with one another by having different desire-like attitudes, because that happens with intentions. Similarly, just as Hare proposed to take advantage of whatever account of meaning would go for imperative sentences, Gibbard proposes to take advantage of whatever account of disagreement goes for ordinary intentions. Intentions are *planning states*, according to Gibbard, and moral beliefs are a kind of plan. That is why, Gibbard holds, they have the interpersonal disagreement property.

This doesn't exactly give Gibbard an *explanation* of why ordinary descriptive belief and moral belief share the feature that they have the interpersonal disagreement property. This is because he doesn't, in fact, go on to explain *why* people disagree with one another when they have conflicting plans. But what it does give him is, like Hare, an argument for *license for optimism*. Gibbard argues that we should be *optimistic* that we will be able to explain why moral beliefs have the interpersonal disagreement property, provided that we model them on plans or intentions. We should be so optimistic because people *do* sometimes disagree with one another by having conflicting plans. In the next section we're going to look more closely at how optimistic Gibbard's argument should make us that this is so, and similarly at whether we should be convinced by Stevenson's counterexample to premise P3. But first, let's look at a second respect in which ordinary descriptive belief and moral belief are strikingly similar.

If you believe that Colorado is rectangular, but also believe that Colorado is not rectangular, then you are being inconsistent. Just as when one person believes that Colorado is rectangular and another believes that Colorado is not rectangular, the first disagrees with the second, when you believe both, you are disagreeing with yourself. This is a special kind of rational clash among your beliefs. This special kind of rational clash does not happen if you both wonder whether Colorado is rectangular and wonder whether Colorado is not rectangular, and it does not happen if you both suppose for the sake of argument that Colorado is rectangular and suppose for the sake of argument that Colorado is not rectangular. So the fact that belief has this property – that for any sentence 'P', believing that P clashes in this way with believing that it is not the case that P – is a special property of belief. We may call it the *intrapersonal disagreement property*, to contrast it with the *interpersonal disagreement property*.

Again, it is a striking fact that moral belief shares this feature with ordinary descriptive belief. Your moral beliefs clash outrageously if you both believe that stealing money is wrong and also believe that stealing money is not wrong. But this is something that requires explanation, if moral beliefs and ordinary descriptive beliefs are simply two different kinds of attitude. For as we saw in the last paragraph, many attitudes don't have the intrapersonal disagreement property. In particular, wondering and supposing don't have this property. So if moral belief and ordinary descriptive belief both have it, even though they are, at bottom, quite different kinds of attitude, then that looks like a coincidence. It is certainly something that an adequate noncognitivist account of the nature of moral belief will need to explain.

Furthermore, some philosophers have argued that no desire-like attitude could have the intrapersonal disagreement property, and hence that noncognitivists are committed to denying the obvious fact that moral beliefs have this property. But again, Allan Gibbard has argued that plans, or intentions, are a perfectly good example of a kind of desire-like attitude with the intrapersonal disagreement property. If you intend to meet me at the symphony tonight and also plan to not meet me at the symphony tonight, then your plans clash in a very uncomfortable sort of way – it is generally irrational to have such plans, in plausibly the same sort of way that it is generally irrational to both believe that Colorado is rectangular and believe that Colorado is not rectangular.

In fact, Gibbard believes that the *interpersonal disagreement property* and the *intrapersonal disagreement property* go hand in hand. He believes that mental states which interpersonally disagree with one another, in the sense that if one person has one and the other has the other, then those two people disagree, are just the same as mental states which intrapersonally disagree with one another, in the sense that you are undergoing our special kind of rational clash, if you have both. One of the exercises will ask you to look at whether Gibbard is right about this.

## 5.4 The challenge from CAIR

So far, we've noted two similarities between moral belief and ordinary descriptive belief – similarities that would be striking if, as noncognitivists claim, moral belief and ordinary descriptive belief are really two fundamentally different kinds of mental state. Stevenson and Gibbard suggest that we look to intentions, or plans, as an example of a kind of desire-like attitude which has these features. In order to explain why moral belief has these features, they advocate, all that we need to do is to develop a theory according to which moral belief is a lot like intention or planning.

But this strategy faces an important obstacle. The obstacle is that it turns out that some philosophers have argued that intention is *not* just a desire-like attitude, with world-to-mind direction of fit, after all. On the contrary, these philosophers claim, the reason why intending to meet me at the symphony tonight and intending to not meet me at the symphony tonight clash in the special way that we've been talking about is that in order to intend something, you have to have an ordinary descriptive belief that it will happen. After all, these philosophers say, you and I do not necessarily disagree, just because you *want* us to go to the symphony and I want us to go to the cinema; it is only when we *intend* conflicting things that we disagree.

So according to this theory, to intend to meet me at the symphony tonight you must have the ordinary descriptive belief that you will meet me at the symphony tonight, and similarly, to intend to not meet me at the symphony tonight you must have the ordinary descriptive belief that you will not meet me at the symphony tonight. But then it turns out that the clash that you undergo by having both intentions can turn out to be just a clash in ordinary descriptive belief. The theory that this is how the clash among your intentions is explained is called *Cognitivism about Instrumental Reason*, which I'll simply abbreviate as CAIR. (Don't get distracted by the fact that 'Cognitivism' means something different in the name of this view than it does in 'noncognitivism'! Philosophers are nothing if not egregious about recycling old terms.)

CAIR is an obstacle to Stevenson's and Gibbard's idea that there really are disagreements in attitude – disagreements between mental states that do not involve belief, but are rather solely among attitudes from the world-to-mind side of the direction of fit dichotomy. If CAIR is right, then Stevenson and Gibbard have not really given us a very good argument for license for optimism that they will be able to give an account of the nature of moral belief that explains why moral beliefs have the interpersonal and intrapersonal disagreement properties. So we would do well to evaluate whether CAIR is right.

The primary assumption made by CAIR is the strong belief thesis:

**strong belief thesis**    Necessarily, if X intends to do A, X believes that she will do A.

So one way to evaluate CAIR is to try to evaluate the strong belief thesis directly. Unfortunately, the intuitive evidence on this score is mixed. In support of the strong belief thesis, it seems unintuitive to say, of someone who knows that she has little hand–eye coordination but who throws a dart at a dartboard attempting to hit the bull's-eye, that she intends to hit the bull's-eye. This seems to support the idea that trying to do something is not sufficient for intending to do it – and hence that to intend to do it, you must, further, be confident that you will be successful.

But on the other hand, Michael Bratman (1987) has introduced cases in which it does seem intuitive that someone intends to do something, even though she does not believe that she will do it. One such case is the following: Michael forms an intention to stop at the bookstore on his way home, even though he is aware that once he leaves work, he tends to go into autopilot, and there is a significant chance that if that happens, he'll end up at home without having first stopped at the bookstore. Bratman claims that Michael intends to stop at the bookstore, even though he doesn't believe that he will. He therefore claims that this is a counterexample to the strong belief thesis.

Unfortunately, it's hard to know who is right – CAIR or Bratman. Some people find it obvious that Michael really does intend to stop at the bookstore on the way home. But others find it obvious that he doesn't really intend to stop – only to try to stop, if he does not go into autopilot. Since intuitions clash, relying on these intuitions does not look like a particularly promising way to resolve this problem. It starts to look like merely a matter of how we choose to use the word, 'intention'. So what we need is some other way of figuring out whether the strong belief thesis is correct.

A more promising strategy to evaluate CAIR is to ignore how we use the word, 'intention'. Let us grant for the sake of argument that the strong belief thesis is true. Still, Bratman's bookstore example is a case of someone who has a state of mind that is very much like an intention, except for the part about believing that it will be carried out. Let's call such states of mind quasi-intentions, because we are granting, for the sake of argument, that they are not really intentions. According to CAIR, what explains *why* intentions to do inconsistent things clash in the way we have been talking about, is the fact that such intentions involve beliefs, and the beliefs clash. So CAIR seems to make a prediction: the prediction is that since quasi-intentions *don't* involve such beliefs, quasi-intentions to do inconsistent things will not clash.

Let's test this idea: suppose that Michael quasi-intends to stop at the bookstore on his way home. So despite knowing that he tends to go into autopilot, he decides in a way that is otherwise very much like forming an intention, except that he is not terribly confident that he will carry it out, to stop at the bookstore on the way home. And then suppose that, without changing his mind about this quasi-intention, Michael also forms a quasi-intention to *not* stop at the bookstore on the way home. He admits that this might not be successful, either, given his quasi-intention *to* stop at the bookstore, but that's no problem, since this is only a quasi-intention, and so doesn't require the belief that it will be successful. I trust you'll agree with me that this situation is patently weird. The clash between quasi-intending to stop at the bookstore and quasi-intending to not stop at the bookstore does not appear to depend on how confident Michael is in his success at either. The same thing goes in the dartboard example: no matter how confident Linda is of her own talents at darts, she is undergoing a quite significant clash, if she is both trying to hit the bull's-eye and trying to not hit the bull's-eye.

These examples make it look like the phenomenon to be explained – the clash between intentions to do inconsistent things – is independent of whether intention involves belief. This kind of clash seems to happen even between mere quasi-intentions that do not involve beliefs. This means that it is unpromising to hold, as CAIR does, that the clash is to be explained in terms of the clash between the involved beliefs. And it also means that Stevenson and Gibbard appear to be right, that we *can* find examples of interpersonal and intrapersonal disagreement wholly between mental states from the world-to-mind side of the direction of fit dichotomy.

This is an important, though defensive, victory for noncognitivists. If *some* attitudes from the world-to-mind side of the direction of fit dichotomy can underwrite interpersonal and intrapersonal disagreements, then that licenses tentative optimism that noncognitivists can explain why moral belief shares with ordinary descriptive belief the interpersonal and intrapersonal disagreement properties. To do so, they must assign each moral sentence and its negation to a pair of attitudes which disagree in the way that the intention to meet me at the symphony and the intention to not meet me at the symphony disagree.

So, for example, suppose that *disapproval*, like intention, is a kind of desire-like attitude which has the property that two states of disapproval disagree whenever they are disapproval of two inconsistent things. Then it follows that disapproval of stealing money will disagree with disapproval of not stealing money, since stealing money and not stealing money are inconsistent. So if believing that stealing money is wrong is disapproving of stealing money, and believing that stealing money is not wrong is disapproving of not stealing money, then these two beliefs really do disagree with one another, even though they are different in kind from ordinary descriptive belief.

We'll see in Chapter 7 that there is still a major problem with the idea in the last paragraph. But for now, it at least gives us a picture of how a noncognitivist theory of moral thought can explain how moral beliefs have some of the same properties as ordinary descriptive beliefs, even though they come from different sides of the direction of fit dichotomy.

## 5.5 Other challenges

The interpersonal and intrapersonal disagreement properties are only two of many interesting properties that moral beliefs share with non-moral beliefs. For example, belief has a certain kind of *phenomenology*. That means roughly that it *feels* a certain kind of way to believe something – different from what it feels like to merely assume it, or to want it to be true. This is sometimes put more carefully by saying that there is something it is *like* to have a belief. Belief also interacts causally with desire in a certain kind of predictable way. If you desire to go to the beach, and believe that the beach is to your left, that is the kind of thing to motivate you to go to your left. Similarly, if you desire to do something wrong, and believe that stealing money is wrong, that is the kind of thing to motivate you to steal money. Philosophers call this the *functional role* of belief. Moreover, beliefs can vary in their level of *confidence*. About some of our beliefs we are more confident than others – for example, I am more confident that Colorado is rectangular than I am that it will vote Republican in the next election. Similarly, I am more confident that stealing money is wrong than I am that early-term abortion is not wrong. So variation in confidence is one more dimension along with moral and ordinary descriptive beliefs are the same.

Since moral beliefs are similar to ordinary descriptive beliefs in all of these ways, a noncognitivist account of moral belief needs to explain, for each of these ways, how that comes to be so. In the last two sections we looked at Stevenson's and Gibbard's arguments for license for optimism that they will be able to do this for the cases of the interpersonal and intrapersonal disagreement properties; the next step would be to explore similar arguments for the phenomenology, functional role, and variation in confidence of moral beliefs. Then, once we have arguments for optimism about all of these things in hand, the next step would be to provide an account of what moral beliefs *are* that predicts and explains why they have each of these properties.

This is clearly a difficult project, but part of the difficulty derives from the fact that it is not well understood why ordinary descriptive belief has each of these properties. Since that is not well understood, that makes it even harder to see whether a different kind of attitude, from the opposite side of the direction of fit dichotomy, could turn out to have all of these properties, as well. So in that respect, it is unfair to expect noncognitivist theories to be able to explain more than their competing theories, according to which there is only one kind of belief, are able to explain.

Still, the hypothesis that there is only one underlying kind of attitude that is picked out by the words 'believes that' clearly has an explanatory advantage. The noncognitivist view is that there are two kinds of attitude which share a remarkably long list of features in common:

| Moral belief | Ordinary descriptive belief |
| --- | --- |
| interpersonal disagreement | interpersonal disagreement |
| intrapersonal disagreement | intrapersonal disagreement |
| phenomenology | phenomenology |
| functional role | functional role |
| variation in confidence | variation in confidence |

The cognitivist view, in contrast, allows that there is only one kind of attitude which has all of these features. That means that the noncognitivist view has much *more* to explain than the cognitivist view. It needs to not just give us an account of the nature of moral belief, it must also explain the large coincidence between the properties of moral belief and ordinary descriptive belief. According to noncognitivism, this really is a coincidence, because even though we use the word 'belief' for both of these attitudes, they are really, at bottom, different kinds of attitudes. Whereas according to cognitivism, there is no coincidence, because there is really only one kind of attitude. We can call this the *Multiple Kinds* problem, because it stems from the fact that noncognitivists posit multiple kinds of belief, and hence must explain why these different kinds of belief have so much in common.

Moreover, even once the noncognitivist has explained all of these things, her work in the philosophy of mind is not done. Far from it! We saw at the beginning of the chapter that belief is only one kind of attitude. In addition to belief, there is desire, wondering, hope, anticipation, dread, and more. So in addition to a distinction between moral beliefs and ordinary descriptive beliefs, noncognitivists must distinguish between moral desires and ordinary descriptive desires, between moral wonderings and ordinary descriptive wonderings, between moral hopes and ordinary descriptive hopes, and so on. For each and every one of these attitudes, noncognitivists will say that there are really two kinds of attitude. For each and every one, they will need to explain how we manage to use one and the same word in order to talk about both. And for each one, they will need to tell us *what* the moral attitude is, and to explain why despite the fact that it is different from its ordinary descriptive counterpart, it is nevertheless similar to it in so many ways.

What is more, things get even worse. As we'll see in Chapter 7, until very recently the most promising expressivist solutions to the Frege–Geach problem postulate not just two different kinds of belief – moral belief and ordinary descriptive belief – but *infinitely many* different kinds of belief, corresponding to the infinite range of possible sentence structures in a language like English. Views like this face a particularly acute version of the Multiple Kinds problem. They need to explain not only how there could be two kinds of attitude which coincidentally have so many of the same properties, but how there could be *infinitely many* different kinds of attitude which coincidentally have so many of the same properties. And one of the exercises in Chapter 7 will ask you to show how the same reasoning would lead to the conclusion that there are infinitely many different kinds of desire, infinitely many different kinds of anticipation, and so on.

Just to sum up: in this chapter we've seen both limited progress for noncognitivism and grounds for ultimate pessimism about it. We saw that noncognitivists are not committed to denying that there are such things as moral beliefs, and we saw how an expressivist could answer the One Word problem, and explain how we manage to use the words 'believes that' to talk about two totally different kinds of attitude, even though 'believes that' is not ambiguous. We also saw that, contrary to CAIR, Stevenson and Gibbard have good grounds for licensed optimism that they will be able to explain the interpersonal and intrapersonal disagreement properties for moral belief. But we saw that these are only two out of many properties of moral belief that noncognitivists will need to explain as part of solving the Multiple Kinds problem. Moreover, we saw that they will need to do similar things for each and every other kind of attitude – and that was the Many Attitudes problem. The coincidences between the properties of moral belief and ordinary descriptive belief, and similarly for each of the other attitudes, make noncognitivism look like an extraordinarily elaborate hypothesis about the mind.

## Chapter summary

In this chapter we encountered three main kinds of problems for noncognitivist accounts of the nature of moral thought. The first problem, the *Many Attitudes* problem, was that noncognitivists need to account not only for the nature of moral *belief*, but also the nature of many other moral attitudes. The second problem, the *One Word* problem, was that even though noncognitivists hold that moral belief is a deeply different kind of thing from ordinary descriptive belief, we still manage to refer to both using a single word, 'belief'. The third problem, the *Multiple Kinds* problem, was that moral belief and ordinary descriptive belief have much in common – things like being subject to interpersonal and intrapersonal disagreement – which noncognitivists must explain, including explaining the coincidence between the properties of moral and ordinary descriptive belief.

## Further reading

It is suggested that this chapter be read along with supplementary material on the norm of inconsistency on intention. I suggest Harman (1976) or Davis (1984) for introductory audiences, and some combination of Bratman (2009), Setiya (2007), and Ross (2008) for philosophically more experienced readers. Stevenson (1937) makes the case for disagreement in attitude, and Horgan and Timmons (2006) is the most extensive discussion by proponents of expressivism of the task of explaining the nature of moral belief.

## Exercises

1    E *Comprehension*: Illustrate the size of the Many Attitudes problem by naming twenty attitudes not mentioned in this chapter.

2    E *Comprehension*: Illustrate the intrapersonal disagreement property by listing three attitudes not mentioned in the chapter which have it and three attitudes not mentioned which do not.

3    E *Extensions*: What kinds of behavior do you expect from someone who hopes that it will rain tomorrow? What kinds of inferences might you make about her? What do you expect from someone who wonders whether it will rain tomorrow? Or from someone who dreads that it will rain tomorrow? Show that the Multiple Kinds problem comes up for non-belief attitudes by listing three important properties of hoping, three important properties of wondering, and three important properties of dreading. Show that you expect the same things from people who hope for, wonder about, or dread moral things.

4    M *Extensions*: We saw in the text that Gibbard assumes that interpersonal and intrapersonal disagreement go hand in hand. But here is a putative counterexample. I intend to go to the cinema, and you intend to not go to the cinema. Now if *I* intended what you intend – namely, to not go to the cinema – then I would exhibit intrapersonal disagreement. I would be being irrational to both intend to go to the cinema and also intend to not go to the cinema. But when I intend to go to the cinema and you intend to not go to the cinema, we do not seem to be disagreeing about anything. So this example makes it look like there can sometimes be *intrapersonal* disagreement without *interpersonal* disagreement. That is, there are mental states, M and N, such that a person who is simultaneously in both suffers from intrapersonal disagreement, but a person who is in one does not necessarily interpersonally disagree with someone who is in the other. (Notice that Stevenson's examples were carefully chosen to avoid this potential problem, by being intentions about what *we* are to do together.) But what about the other way around? Does interpersonal disagreement guarantee intrapersonal disagreement? If not, why not? If you think it must, explain your reasoning.

5    M *Extensions* (continued from exercise 4): The counterexample in exercise 4 assumes that if you intend to not go to the cinema and I intend to not go to the cinema, then we intend the same thing. But that turns out to be controversial. Many philosophers believe that when you intend to not go to the cinema, what you intend is *that you not go*, whereas when I intend to not go to the cinema, what I intend is *that I not go*, and these

are different things – one is about you, and one is about me. This is the view that intention takes *propositional objects*. On this view, the right inter-personal analogue of the intrapersonal disagreement that I have if I both intend to go and intend to not go, arises if I intend to go and you intend *me* not to go. But it does seem like if I intend to go to the cinema, and you intend for me not to go, then we are in some kind of disagreement. And that supports Gibbard's thesis that interpersonal and intrapersonal disagreement go hand in hand after all. Evaluate the view that intention takes propositional objects by discussing whether it is possible to intend another person to do something.

6   M *Qualifications*: Some people believe that it is *impossible* to both believe that P and believe that ~P at the very same time, not just irrational to do so. What do you think? Even if it is impossible, the reason why it is impossible might simply be that it is so obviously irrational. A more general thesis about intrapersonal disagreement is the claim that if someone believes two or more things which can't all be true, she suffers from intrapersonal disagreement. So, for example, you suffer from intrapersonal disagree-ment if you believe that everyone from Wisconsin has a funny accent, and you believe that I am from Wisconsin, but you also believe that I don't have a funny accent. Evaluate whether intentions are analogous, by first considering whether it is possible or impossible to intend to do something and not intend to do it at one and the same time, and then considering whether it is irrational (but possible) to intend two or more things which it is impossible for you to do all of. Is intention similar to belief when it comes to intrapersonal disagreement, or not?

7   M *Extensions*: Philosophers who accept CAIR sometimes make the obser-vation that there are three apparent parallels between the norms governing ordinary descriptive belief and those governing intention. The first parallel is between the norm of *inconsistency* on intention and the norm of *inconsist-ency* on belief – intending inconsistent things involves intrapersonal disa-greement in the same sort of way that believing inconsistent things does. The second parallel is between the norm of *means–end coherence* on inten-tion, and the norm of *deductive closure* on belief. The norm of means–end coherence on intention says that if you intend that P, and believe that Q is a necessary means to P, then you are committed to intending that Q, and the norm of deductive closure on belief says that if you believe that P and believe that if P, then Q, then you are committed to believing that Q. One

way of drawing out this similarity looks like this (treat 'P→Q' as an abbreviation for 'if P, then Q'):

INTEND(P)                 BELIEVE(P)
BELIEVE(P→Q)              BELIEVE(P→Q)
INTEND(Q)                 BELIEVE(Q)

Philosophers who notice the striking parallels between these two cases sometimes take this as evidence that they should receive a common explanation, and further, that the norm of means–end coherence, on the left, can be explained in terms of the norm of deductive closure on belief. And this, in turn, supports CAIR's idea that disagreements among intentions can be explained in terms of disagreements among ordinary descriptive beliefs. But there is something misleading about the way I gave of drawing the similarity between means–end coherence and deductive closure, just above. What is it? Why is it significant?

8    M *Extensions*: The third parallel sometimes drawn between the norms on intention and the norms on belief is between their respective norms of *conglomeration*. The norm of conglomeration on belief says that if you believe that P and you believe that Q, then you are committed to believing that P and Q – that is, you are committed to putting your beliefs together into a single picture of the world. The norm of conglomeration on intention says that if you intend that P and you intend that Q, then you are committed to intending that P and Q – that is, you are committed to putting your intentions together into a single plan for what to do. If there really is a norm of conglomeration on intention, then this is further support for the CAIR idea that given the striking similarities to the norms on belief, we should be able to use the norms on belief to explain the norms on intention. Evaluate whether the norm of conglomeration on intention is really plausible, by constructing one example of two intentions such that it seems like one would be rationally required to put them together into a single intention, and one example of two intentions for which it seems weird to require that someone with those intentions would need to put them together into a single plan. What do you think? Is the norm of conglomeration really true?

9    M *Extensions*: As we noted in section 2, expressivism is sometimes *defined* as the thesis that moral thoughts are not beliefs. Some philosophers worry

that expressivism *needs* to be defined in this way, or else we will not be able to say what makes it different from cognitivism. For this exercise, give a characterization of the difference between cognitivism and expressivism that does not build in the assumption that moral thoughts are not beliefs.

10  D  *Qualifications*: The expressivist account of the meaning of 'believes that' in section 2 is flawed in at least one important way. Show that it is subject to a problem that is exactly analogous to the modal problem for speaker subjectivism, from Chapter 4.

11  D  *New problem*: Return to the third paragraph of section 1 and replace each appearance of 'Colorado will vote Republican in the next election' with 'abortion is wrong'. Can you detect any asymmetries between the usual philosophical arguments in favor of propositions like the proposition that Colorado will vote Republican in the next election, and analogous arguments in favor of moral propositions like the proposition that abortion is wrong? Why or why not? Is this a problem for noncognitivism or not, and why or why not?

12  D  *Branching out*: Terry Horgan and Mark Timmons have defended an expressivist theory which takes seriously all of the problems discussed in this chapter. Horgan and Timmons distinguish between (at least) two kinds of belief – moral belief and ordinary descriptive belief. The former they call *ought*-belief and the latter they call *is*-belief. According to Horgan and Timmons, both *is*-belief and *ought*-belief take propositional objects. The belief that Max ought not to murder, according to their theory, is the *ought*-belief whose content is the proposition that Max does not murder, whereas the belief that Max does not murder is the *is*-belief whose content is the proposition that Max does not murder. It appears to follow from this way of describing Horgan and Timmons' view that if you believe that Max ought not to murder and I believe that Max does not murder, then we are both believing the same thing, albeit in different ways. You are *ought*-believing it, and I am *is*-believing it. But it does not seem plausible to say that there is something that we both believe in such a situation. How would you respond to this problem, if you were Horgan and Timmons? Look through Horgan and Timmons (2006) in order to see what they might say. Can you find a satisfactory answer?

13  A  *Qualifications*: Another problem with the expressivist account of the meaning of 'believes that' in section 2 is that it doesn't make room for

*quantified* belief reports as in, for example, the most natural reading of 'Whenever Max asks a girl out, he believes that she'll say yes'. The problem, is that only *closed* sentences express mental states – for an open sentence like '*x* is tall', there is no such thing as believing that *x* is tall. Try to construct an expressivist account of 'believes that' which gets around this problem. What kinds of resources do you need to develop in order to do so? Are there other problems that you need to solve, first? If so, what are they?

## Partial answers

3    Someone who hopes that it will rain tomorrow does not, normally, believe that it won't rain tomorrow. If she did, then there would be no sense in hoping that it will. Similarly, someone who hopes that she is doing the right thing does not, normally, believe that she is not doing the right thing. If she did, then there would be no sense in hoping that she is. So that is one important feature of hoping, and it is true of both hopes for non-moral things and hopes for moral things. Complete your answer by giving two more similar examples for hoping and three each for wondering and dreading.

7    Hint: Strategic Bomber intends to bomb the enemy's ammunition factory. She believes, however, that since the ammunition factory is next to an elementary school, any way of bombing the ammunition factory will have the side effect of killing some children. Is Strategic Bomber committed to intending to kill some children?

## Morals

7–8 It is important not to exaggerate the similarities between means–end coherence and deductive closure. Means–end coherence doesn't apply to beliefs about necessary side effects, only to beliefs about necessary means. The importance of this for noncognitivism is that if means–end coherence doesn't need to be explained in terms of the norm of deductive closure on ordinary descriptive belief, then there is less pressure to think that the disagreement properties of intention must be explained in terms of the disagreement properties of ordinary descriptive belief. And if so, then Stevenson's and Gibbard's argument for license for optimism is in better shape.

9    The worry that it becomes harder to tell the difference between expressivism and cognitivism if the expressivist gets to say that moral thoughts are beliefs is part of a larger problem sometimes called the problem of *creeping minimalism*.

# References

Bratman, Michael (1987). *Intention, Plans, and Practical Reason*. Cambridge, MA: Harvard University Press.

—— (2009). 'Intention, Belief, Theoretical, Practical.' In Simon Robertson, ed., *Spheres of Reason: New Essays in the Philosophy of Normativity*. Oxford: Oxford University Press, 29–61.

Davis, Wayne (1984). 'A Causal Theory of Intending.' *American Philosophical Quarterly* 21: 43–54.

Gibbard, Allan (2003). *Thinking How to Live*. Cambridge, MA: Harvard University Press.

Hare, R.M. (1952). *The Language of Morals*. Oxford: Oxford University Press.

Harman, Gilbert (1976). 'Practical Reasoning.' Reprinted in Harman (1999), *Reasoning, Meaning, and Mind*. Oxford: Oxford University Press.

Horgan, Terry, and Mark Timmons (2006). 'Cognitivist Expressivism.' In Horgan and Timmons, eds., *Metaethics after Moore*. Oxford: Oxford University Press.

Ross, Jacob (2008). 'How to Be a Cognitivist about Practical Reason.' *Oxford Studies in Metaethics* 4: 243–82.

Setiya, Kieran (2007). 'Cognitivism about Instrumental Reason.' *Ethics* 117(4): 649–73.

Stevenson, C.L. (1937). 'The Emotive Meaning of Ethical Terms.' Reprinted in Stevenson (1963), *Facts and Values*. Westport, CT: Greenwood Press.

# 6

# THE FREGE–GEACH
# PROBLEM, 1973–88

## 6.1 The Frege–Geach challenge

Noncognitivism, recall, is a view about the meaning of moral language. It is the view that moral words have a different kind of meaning from ordinary non-moral words like 'rectangular' and 'aluminum', usually accompanied by the idea that this allows us to evade the 'core questions' of metaethics or to solve the motivation problem. But moral words don't *appear* to have a different kind of meaning from non-moral words. In fact, moral words seem to work in all of the same ways as non-moral words. We can put together moral words to make complex sentences in the same kinds of ways that we can put together non-moral words to make complex sentences, and the resulting complex sentences behave in all of the same ways. The Frege–Geach problem for noncognitivism is the problem of how this could be so: how moral words could have meanings that behave so much like the meanings of non-moral words, in terms of their contribution to the meanings of complex sentences in which they appear, if they really have, at bottom, a quite different kind of meaning.

In Chapter 3 we saw a different way of putting the same problem. One of the main achievements of the truth-conditional approach to understanding the meanings of words and sentences is that it has been very successful at explaining how meaning could be compositional – that is, how the meanings of complex sentences could be determined by the meanings of their parts and how they are put together. Every adequate theory of meaning must respect this constraint, we saw, because we have the ability to understand the meanings of new and novel complex sentences – and this must be something that we somehow manage to do by means of our understanding of their parts and how those parts are put together. So since noncognitivist theories claim that moral words have a very different kind of meaning from what a truth-conditional theory of meaning would assign to them, they need to explain how the compositional constraint can be satisfied. They need to show us how to understand the meanings of complex sentences in terms of the meanings of their parts.

We also saw that Hare (1970) outlined exactly what noncognitivists need to do in order to answer this challenge. They need to provide us with recipes for determining the meanings of complex sentences from the meanings of their parts. So a noncognitivist like Hare, who thinks that the meaning of a sentence is the speech act that it is suited to perform, needs to give us recipes which tell us how to determine, on the basis of the speech acts that simpler sentences are suited to perform, the speech acts that complex sentences made up out of those simpler sentences are suited to perform. Similarly, expressivists, who think that the meaning of a sentence is the mental state that it *expresses*, need to give us recipes which tell us how to determine, on the basis of the mental states that simpler sentences express, the mental states that are expressed by complex sentences made up out of those simpler sentences.

Hare didn't actually *give* any such recipes, but since 1970, many noncognitivists have tried to do so, almost all of them working within the expressivist framework. In this chapter and the next we're going to take a critical look at these attempts from a developmental point of view. First we'll look at the very earliest attempt by Simon Blackburn and then at a new sort of view that Blackburn offered in the 1980s, which appealed to *higher-order attitudes*. Each particular version of these earlier generations of views was subject to its own particular kinds of problem, but they were also subject to a set of *endemic* problems, and so our main goal will be to learn what those endemic problems were and why they ultimately gave rise to a newer generation of expressivist views, starting in the late 1980s. We'll turn to look at these more recent expressivist theories in Chapter 7.

Since all of these approaches arise within the expressivist tradition, I'll assume throughout this chapter that we are talking only about expressivism, though some of the exercises will then invite you to generalize the main conclusions of the chapter to speech-act-oriented noncognitivist theories. Through essentially a historical accident, for a long period most of constructive theorizing about the Frege–Geach problem was done solely about conditional sentences (that is, 'if … then' sentences). So for most of this chapter, we'll be looking at the special problem of how to give an expressivist recipe for the meaning of conditional sentences. Keep in mind, however, that this is just a special case of the general problem, which is to give an expressivist recipe for the meanings of *every* kind of complex sentence.

## 6.2 What do we need from an account of the meaning of conditional sentences?

In Chapter 3 we noted that one of the most important semantic properties of conditional sentences is that they validate *modus ponens*.[1] That is, for any sentences 'P' and 'Q', the argument from 'P' and 'P→Q' to 'Q' is a valid argument. (Philosophers sometimes write 'P→Q' as an abbreviation for 'if P, then Q', just as '~P' was an abbreviation for 'it is not the case that P'. From here forward I'll follow both of these conventions, as well as writing 'P&Q' as an abbreviation for 'P and Q'.)

Now 'valid' is usually defined to mean that an argument is valid just in case the truth of the premises guarantees the truth of the conclusion – so if 'P' and 'P→Q' are both true, it follows that 'Q' in some sense *has* to be true. This turns out to be an important complication. Many theorists like to define 'noncognitivism' to mean 'the view that moral sentences can't be true or false'. People who define 'noncognitivism' in this way infer that 'noncognitivists' cannot explain how moral arguments can be valid, no matter what they do.

But this is, just as in Chapter 5, semantics in the pejorative sense. If someone wishes to define 'noncognitivism' in that way, we can let them and use some other word for the interesting strand of ideas that runs through Ayer, Stevenson, Hare, Blackburn, and Gibbard. The kind of noncognitivism that we are interested in does not explain the meaning of moral sentences by saying what it takes for them to be true, but that doesn't mean that it must deny that moral sentences *can* be true or false. It is helpful to compare truth-conditional semantics to the somewhat odd thesis called *occasionalism*, defended by the seventeenth-century philosopher Malebranche. Occasionalism was the view, essentially, that nothing ever causes anything else without God personally stepping in to make it happen. So in Malebranche's theory, God does an awful lot of work. It is possible, however, to believe in God without believing that He does so much work. One might believe, for example, that God got everything started, but now He only steps in from time to time to set things right.

Truth-conditional semantics is like Malebranchean occasionalism. It is the view not only that moral sentences can be true or false, but that this does a lot of work in explaining their meaning. Theists can deny Malebranchean occasionalism but still believe in God – simply by believing that God exists but does less work. Similarly, noncognitivists can deny truth-conditional semantics but still believe that moral sentences can be true or false – simply by believing that they can be true or false, but by thinking that this fact does less work in explaining their meanings. Since we routinely talk about moral sentences being true or false, and we routinely think of moral arguments as being valid or invalid, I will assume that the most interesting versions of noncognitivism take the second route, and agree that moral sentences can be true or false, but simply disagree with truth-conditional semantics over how much work that does, in explaining their meaning.

Still, for the remainder of this chapter and the next, I'm going to set aside the question of whether moral sentences can be true or false, and the question of whether moral arguments can be valid or invalid, in the sense that the truth of their premises guarantees the truth of their conclusion. We'll return and settle this question in Chapter 8. The reason for doing this is that the expressivist strategy for explaining how moral arguments can be valid is *indirect*. Instead of appealing directly to the meanings of moral sentences in order to draw conclusions about which arguments are valid and which are not, expressivist theories first appeal to the meanings of sentences in order to establish that moral arguments have a *different* sort of property that is *closely related* to validity, and is coextensive with validity. Normal truth-conditional theories would explain this property *in terms of* validity, but expressivists work backwards, and explain validity in terms of this other property.

Actually, there are two such properties of arguments that expressivist accounts of conditionals attempt directly to explain. The first is what I call the *inconsistency property*. Someone who accepts the premises of a valid argument but denies its conclusion is being inconsistent. It is generally *irrational* to accept the premises of a valid argument but deny its conclusion. It may not *always* be irrational – for example, some philosophical paradoxes are cases which are so puzzling that it's hard to figure out how to *avoid* both accepting the premises and denying the conclusion of a valid argument. But in general, and other things being equal, it is irrational to accept the premises of a valid argument but deny its conclusion. If you do so, then your states of mind *clash* in the same way that they do if you both believe that Colorado is rectangular and believe that Colorado is not rectangular.

It is not hard, in fact, to see that the way in which you are being inconsistent when you accept the premises of a valid argument but deny its conclusion is just a *generalization* of the kind of clash that we called 'intrapersonal disagreement' in Chapter 5. That is because the following is an example of a valid argument:

> **premise**  Colorado is rectangular.
> **conclusion**  Colorado is rectangular.

Arguments like this one clearly don't help us to find anything out that we don't already know. But this is a set of premises and a conclusion, and the truth of the premises guarantees the truth of the conclusion, so it is a valid argument. Moreover, to accept the premises is to believe that Colorado is rectangular. And to deny the conclusion is to believe that Colorado is not rectangular. So the kind of clash that you have when you both believe that Colorado is rectangular and believe that Colorado is not rectangular is just a special case of the kind of rational inconsistency involved in accepting the premises of a valid argument and denying its conclusion. It is what we have been calling 'intrapersonal disagreement'. This observation will be important later, when we will use it in order to take advantage of some of the progress we made in Chapter 5.

The second important property of valid arguments that expressivist theories attempt directly to explain is what I'll call the *inference-licensing* property. To see what this property is, imagine that your friend started out accepting both premises of the following argument, but denying its conclusion:

**P1**  Being friendly is wrong.
**P2**  If being friendly is wrong, then being friendly to strangers is wrong.
**C**  Being friendly to strangers is wrong.

That is, she accepted both P1 and P2, but also accepted ~C:

**~C**  Being friendly to strangers is not wrong.

So she was being rationally inconsistent. Fortunately, you came along and pointed out the error of her ways. 'Can't you see,' you pointed out, 'it is rationally inconsistent to accept all three of P1, P2, and ~C?' Persuaded, your friend gives up ~C. She says: 'Oh – I see that I was being irrational to accept all three of P1, P2, and ~C. So I'll just accept P1 and P2 instead, and avoid irrationality that way.' You say, 'So you agree that being friendly to strangers is wrong?' 'No!' she says – 'why ever would I agree to that? I mean, I don't deny it, of course, because that would be irrational, since I agree that being friendly is wrong, and that if being friendly is wrong, then being friendly to strangers is wrong. But I just haven't made up my mind one way or the other about whether being friendly to strangers is wrong.'

Something is obviously going wrong here. Your friend is right that she has escaped the inconsistency that is involved in accepting the premises of the valid argument but denying its conclusion. But she is not right that she is therefore off of the hook for needing to go on to *accept* the argument's conclusion. Indeed, one of the most useful purposes for arguments is to get people to see that they are committed to accepting conclusions which follow validly from premises which they accept. This is what I call the inference-licensing property of valid arguments: accepting the premises of a valid argument *commits* you, in some sense, to accepting its conclusions, should the matter come up. If you aren't going to follow through on this commitment, then you need to give up one of the premises. The inference-licensing property of valid arguments is one of the things that expressivists will want to explain.

## 6.3  Recipes and explanations

It will be helpful to take two final steps before we look at any expressivist accounts of the meaning of complex sentences, and pause to develop some notation for talking about expressivist views and to compare how an ordinary, non-expressivist view would explain the inconsistency and inference-licensing properties.

In order to describe expressivist recipes for the mental states expressed by complex sentences in a simpler way, I'm going to introduce a new piece of technical notation. It is just that – notation – so it doesn't let us say anything that we can't say using other words. But like truth tables did, it will let us say some of these things in a simpler way. So what I'll do, is to use square brackets around a sentence, as in '[P]', as a name for the mental state expressed by 'P' – that is, for the state of thinking that P – for any sentence 'P'. So, for example, [stealing is wrong] is the state of thinking that stealing is wrong, and [P→Q] is the state of thinking that P→Q – that is, that if P, then Q.

This terminology lets us say in a simpler way what we need out of an expressivist account of the meaning of 'P→Q'. What we need is a recipe which tells us what [P→Q] is, given [P] and [Q] as inputs. It also lets us say more concisely what the inconsistency property and the inference-licensing properties consist in. The inconsistency property is the fact that to be in all three of [P], [P→Q], and [~Q] at the same time is to suffer from intrapersonal disagreement. The inference-licensing property is the fact that the states [P] and [P→Q] together commit one to the state [Q]. So the expressivist project is to give a recipe for [P→Q] given [P] and [Q] as inputs, which allows us to explain these two things.

We can now say how a non-expressivist theory would explain the inconsistency and inference-licensing properties. A non-expressivist theory would explain these by appeal to the assumption that an argument is valid. The explanation of the inconsistency property would go something like this. First, notice that the attitude of belief satisfies a generalized version of the intrapersonal inconsistency property from Chapter 5 – namely, that it is rationally inconsistent to believe three things which can't all be true. Second, notice that since the argument is valid, if the premises are true, then the conclusion *has* to be true as well. But third, notice that the truth table for 'not' guarantees that if C is true, then ~C is *not* true. Together, the second and third observations entail that if P1 and P2 are both true, then ~C is not true. But someone who accepts both premises of the argument and denies its conclusion believes P1, believes P2, and believes ~C. So she believes three things that can't all be true – if the first two are true, then the last one is not! Hence, by the generalized intrapersonal inconsistency property of belief, it is rationally inconsistent to accept the premises of this argument and deny its conclusion.

Similarly, a non-expressivist explanation of the inference-licensing property might go something like this. First, notice that belief is an attitude with the following property: that you are committed to believing whatever is guaranteed to be true by the truth of other things that you believe. And second, notice that since this argument is valid, the truth of the premises guarantees the truth of the conclusion. Putting these two observations together, we get the conclusion that if you accept P1 and P2, then you are committed to accepting C, as well. And that is the inference-licensing property.

So much for the ordinary, truth-conditional way of explaining the inconsistency property and the inference-licensing property. Expressivist theories are going to work backwards. First, they are going to give a recipe for

[P→Q] given [P] and [Q] as inputs that makes it possible to explain the inconsistency and inference-licensing properties of the argument. Only then they are going to use the fact that the argument has one or both of these properties in order to explain why the truth of the premises guarantees the truth of the conclusion (i.e., why it is valid). In the remainder of this chapter and the next we'll be focusing on the first part of this explanation, which turns out to be the hard part. Then in Chapter 8 we'll look at the second part of the explanation, which turns out to be somewhat easier.

## 6.4  The involvement account

The first attempt to give an expressivist recipe for the meaning of 'P→Q' in terms of the meanings of 'P' and of 'Q' was due to Blackburn (1973), and it is what I'll call an *involvement* account, for reasons that will become clear in a moment. Blackburn's involvement account is somewhat obscure, but it appears to be inspired by the idea that sentence P2 is plausible because someone who has said that being friendly is wrong has already, in some way, committed to the view that being friendly to strangers is wrong – after all, being friendly to strangers is just a special case of being friendly. So, Blackburn said, what P2 says is that making claim P1 somehow *involves* making claim C. That is, P2 means that [P1] involves [C]. On this account, the argument goes as follows:

P1    Being friendly is wrong.
P2    [Being friendly is wrong] involves [being friendly to strangers is wrong].
C     Being friendly to strangers is wrong.

What seems initially nice about this account is that it explains why this argument has the inference-licensing property. Someone who accepts P1 and P2 is rationally committed to accepting C, because by her own lights (P2) her acceptance of P1 *involves* already being committed to accepting C.

It is hard to overstate, however, how problematic this account is. It appears to be motivated, for example, on the basis of a paucity of cases. Compare, for example, the following argument:

P1'    Lying is wrong.
P2'    If lying is wrong, then murder is wrong.
C'     Murder is wrong.

This argument is valid, but its major premise does not appear to say that accepting P1' *involves* accepting C'. Murder, after all, is *much worse* than lying. So if lying is wrong, then murder has to be. So premise P2' is plausible. But it is not plausible that accepting P1' *involves* accepting C', at least on any intuitive reading of 'involves'. Murder is not a special case of lying, in the way that being friendly to strangers is a special case of being friendly. Conditionals with the feature that accepting their consequent is in some natural sense *involved* in accepting their antecedent are what philosophers call *analytic*. But not all conditionals – not even all true conditionals – are analytic. So Blackburn's idea about involvement seems not to have the right structure to explain the validity of *modus ponens* arguments with non-analytic conditional premises.

The involvement account also does not generalize in any natural way to Moral–Descriptive, Descriptive–Moral, or Descriptive–Descriptive conditionals. Compare, for example, each of the following conditional sentences:

**MD**   If being friendly is wrong, then my parents lied to me.
**DM**   If the Bible says not to be friendly, then being friendly is wrong.
**DD**   If the Bible says not to be friendly, then my parents lied to me.

An adequate recipe for the meanings of conditional sentences needs to apply to these sentences, too, and to explain why *modus ponens* arguments involving them have the inconsistency and inference-licensing properties. But take just the second, Descriptive–Moral case. Presumably, Blackburn accepts some Descriptive–Moral conditionals. But he does not really think that accepting any descriptive sentence really *involves* accepting any normative sentence, because descriptive sentences express ordinary descriptive beliefs, and normative sentences express desire-like attitudes, and Blackburn thinks, in accordance with the Humean Theory of Motivation, from Chapter 1, that it is possible to have any belief without having any particular desire-like attitude. So by his own lights, his recipe doesn't work for sentences like DM.

We can also test the involvement account by its treatment of our two key properties of valid arguments: their licensing inference and the inconsistency condition. So long as we take the 'involvement' thesis literally, it would seem to follow that as long as the conditional premise of a *modus ponens* argument is true, anyone who accepts the other premise *already* accepts the conclusion – independently of whether she even accepts the conditional premise. That seems both to give the wrong role in the argument to the conditional premise, and to fail to license genuine inference, except in cases in which the conditional premise is false. And it is not possible to assess whether the view passes the test of explaining the inconsistency condition. If we grant the literalness of the claim of 'involvement', then so long as the conditional premise is true, someone who accepts the premises accepts the conclusion. So now suppose that she also accepts the negation of the conclusion. Does she accept inconsistent things? This follows on the condition that the conclusion and its negation are inconsistent. But nothing in this view so far explains why a sentence and its negation are inconsistent, so nothing in the view explains why the *modus ponens* argument satisfies the inconsistency condition.

Moreover, since arguments of the form of *modus ponens* are not the only valid arguments, they are not the only arguments for which we should want to be able to explain the inference-licensing property. But the involvement account's explanation of the inference-licensing property, such as it is, does not lend itself in any natural way to explaining the inference-licensing property of arguments that don't have conditional premises. Consider, for example, arguments of the form, 'A&B' ; 'A' (philosophers call arguments with this form 'conjunction elimination'). What makes these arguments valid? What gives them the inference-licensing property?

If Blackburn's answer needs to appeal to any claim about involvement, then we need to know whether that is required as an extra premise. For in the *modus ponens* cases, the thesis about involvement is required as a separate premise, for the argument from 'being friendly is wrong' to 'being friendly to strangers is wrong' was not supposed to have been explained as valid – it doesn't even have the form of *modus ponens*. So in that case the conditional was a necessary further premise. But then if we make a claim about involvement in this case, for example, by saying that accepting 'A&B' involves accepting 'A', then it would seem that we must need it as a further premise in this argument. But in that case we would not have explained the validity of conjunction elimination at all, but only the validity of a distinct argument form, 'A&B', '(A&B)→A' ; 'A', which is only a special case of *modus ponens*. So the involvement account can't generalize in any clear way to help explain the validity of other kinds of arguments.

In short, there is not much to be said for any version of the view on which conditionals make claims about 'involvement' in any literal sense, and many considerations tell against this idea. But it is illustrative, in that it let us test out various criteria to which we should expect an adequate account to be responsive. We should expect an account to give us a plausible story about the meanings not only of analytic conditionals, but of *any* conditional sentence. We should expect an adequate account to explain both the inference-licensing and inconsistency properties. We should expect an adequate account to generalize to MD, DM, and DD conditionals in addition to MM conditionals, and we should expect the general considerations about validity to generalize to arguments of other forms than *modus ponens*. These are some of the key basic kinds of tests that we will want to apply to more sophisticated views. They are a good start on a list of criteria that we should expect a satisfactory expressivist theory to satisfy.

## 6.5  Higher-Order Attitudes

The next important improvement in expressivist attempts to solve the Frege–Geach problem came in 1984, when Blackburn tried to fix his 'involvement' account by developing some ideas that were implicit in his 1973 article. The expressivist treatment of conditional sentences in Blackburn (1984) is both historically important and representative of an important *general* kind of idea about how expressivists can provide recipes for the meanings of complex sentences. It was a major step forward from the involvement account. The general idea is what I'll call the *Higher-Order Attitude* approach, or HOA, for short. I'll first explain a slightly streamlined version of how Blackburn's view actually worked, and then comment on what makes it an HOA view. Then we'll look at how well suited HOA views are to account for the inconsistency and inference-licensing properties, before taking a look at some of the deep problems which eventually led to their rejection.

Blackburn starts by imagining that something like Ayer's view is right, and that what we mean by the sentence, 'Being friendly is wrong' could just as well have been meant by the sentence, 'Boo!!(being friendly)'. We may imagine that 'Boo!!(being friendly)' is a sentence which wears, on its sleeve, everything that we need to know about the mental state that it expresses. Someone who accepts this sentence 'boos' being friendly. I'll just say that she *disapproves* of being friendly and write:

[being friendly is wrong] = DIS(being friendly)

to mean that the state of mind expressed by 'being friendly is wrong' is disapproval of being friendly ('DIS' for disapproval). Similarly, what we mean by the sentence, 'Being friendly to strangers is wrong' could just as well have been meant by the sentence, 'Boo!!(being friendly to strangers)'.

So someone who accepts this sentence 'boos' or *disapproves* of being friendly to strangers:

[being friendly to strangers is wrong] = DIS(being friendly to strangers)

So what Blackburn needs to do is to give us a recipe which allows us to determine, from these two lines, how to fill in the following line:

[being friendly is wrong→being friendly to strangers is wrong] = ???

Blackburn's answer is simple. It is that the conditional sentence should express the state of disapproval of both disapproving of being friendly and not disapproving of being friendly to strangers. Blackburn's notation is a little bit different, but we can write this as follows:

[being friendly is wrong→being friendly to strangers is wrong] =
DIS(DIS(being friendly)&~DIS(being friendly to strangers))[2]

His idea is that just as thinking that being friendly is wrong is having a certain kind of attitude from the world-to-mind side of the direction of fit dichotomy, so is thinking that if being friendly is wrong, then being friendly to strangers is wrong. But the latter, Blackburn thinks, is an attitude *about what to think*. Instead of being a negative attitude directly toward being friendly, it is a negative attitude toward thinking that being friendly is wrong and failing to draw the conclusion that being friendly to strangers is wrong. That is what makes this account a HOA account: because it says the complex sentence expresses a 'higher-order' attitude *toward* the attitudes expressed by the smaller sentences which build it up.

HOA accounts like Blackburn's are *constructive*, in the sense that they give us a real, genuine recipe for determining [P→Q] given [P] and [Q] as inputs. As long as lacking the mental state [Q] always itself counts as a mental state, as long as the conjunction of two mental states always counts as a mental state, and as long as disapproval is an attitude that it makes sense to hold toward mental states, Blackburn's recipe is always guaranteed to yield an output. This guarantee is what qualifies Blackburn's account as *constructive*. (In Chapter 7 we'll encounter some expressivist theories that are not constructive.) The very general recipe behind Blackburn's account can be put as follows:

$$[P{\rightarrow}Q] = \text{\small DIS}([P]\&{\sim}[Q])$$

This recipe tells us, for any sentences 'P' and 'Q', how to determine [P→Q] on the basis of [P] and [Q]. It says that [P→Q] is the state of disapproving of being in [P] but not being in [Q]. So this account has the structure that an expressivist account needs to have. The only question remaining is whether it succeeds in explaining the semantic properties of conditional sentences – whether it explains why *modus ponens* arguments have the inconsistency and inference-licensing properties.

Fortunately, Blackburn designed his HOA account specifically in order to be able to explain the inference-licensing property of *modus ponens*. On an expressivist theory, to accept a sentence is to be in the mental state expressed by that sentence. So on Blackburn's account, someone who accepts the premises of our moral *modus ponens* argument but does not accept its conclusion is in the first of these two states of disapproval, but not in the third: DIS(being friendly), DIS(DIS(being friendly)&~DIS(being friendly to strangers)), DIS(being friendly to strangers). But since she is in the first of these states but not the third, she is in the state, DIS(being friendly)&~DIS(being friendly to strangers). And that is precisely the state that she disapproves of! Hence, Blackburn concludes, accepting the premises of this argument and not accepting its conclusion is irrational – it involves being in a state of mind that you yourself disapprove of being in. That is the sense in which you are rationally committed to accepting the conclusion, so long as you don't give up one of the premises.

Now, unfortunately it is less obvious how Blackburn's account explains the inconsistency property. It shows, after all, why there is something irrational about accepting the premises of the argument and not accepting the conclusion. But so far as Blackburn's theory goes, maybe there is nothing irrational about both accepting and denying the conclusion of the argument. Because Blackburn (1984) gave a recipe only for the meaning of conditional sentences – and didn't give any recipe for the meaning of sentences containing the word 'not' – we can't fully evaluate this question. Still, there is a different sort of Higher-Order Attitude theory which can explain the inconsistency property. Its general recipe for [P→Q] assumes that we already have a recipe for [~Q], given [Q] as input. But assuming that we have such a recipe in hand, the recipe for [P→Q] looks like this:

$$[P{\rightarrow}Q] = \text{\small DIS}([P]\&[{\sim}Q])$$

This theory can explain the inconsistency property, on the grounds that someone who accepts the premises and denies the conclusion is in the following three states: [P], DIS([P]&[~Q]), and [~Q]. But since she is in the first and third states, she is in precisely the state that she disapproves of, by being in the second state. So there seems to be something irrational about being in all three of these states. Hence we get an explanation of the inconsistency property.

Unfortunately, though this HOA theory does better at explaining the inconsistency property, it does not do as well at explaining the inference-licensing property. As far as this theory goes, it is not clear why accepting the premises commits you to actually accepting the conclusion of the argument, as opposed to merely not denying it. Still, the resources of HOA accounts have not been exhausted; one might combine both of the HOA accounts so far considered and say that conditional sentences express two states of disapproval – each one that was postulated by each of the other theories. Then we could explain both the inconsistency and the inference-licensing properties.

## 6.6 Problems with Higher-Order Attitude accounts

Still, you are likely to have noticed something odd about these explanations of the inconsistency and inference-licensing properties. In both cases, the specific kind of irrationality involved is that you are doing something that you yourself disapprove of. And this is exactly the same kind of irrationality involved, according to this view, in telling lies, even though you think that telling lies is wrong (that is, even though you disapprove of telling lies). There is something funny about equating these two kinds of irrationality. In fact, it's not even clear that the latter is necessarily irrational, which should make us wonder whether the former is irrational.

Moreover, although there is something problematic about both thinking that telling lies is wrong and telling lies anyway, it does not seem like changing your mind about whether it is wrong is an equally good way of resolving this problem – on the contrary, changing your mind about what is wrong in order to fit your actions is a distinctive moral vice. Yet in contrast, it seems like giving up the conditional premise of a valid argument is a perfectly good way of resolving the tension involved in believing inconsistent things. After all, if you accept the premises of a valid argument and also deny the conclusion, nothing says which way you have to fix things: you could fix things by changing your mind about the conclusion, but you could also fix things by changing your mind about either of the premises.

I think that these are good worries, but there are a couple of important problems for HOA accounts that are even sharper. The first of these is due, essentially, to Bob Hale. As we noted in section 3, a good recipe for the meaning of conditional sentences needs to work for all of the following kinds of sentence:

**MM**  If being friendly is wrong, then being friendly to strangers is wrong.
**MD**  If being friendly is wrong, then my parents lied to me.
**DM**  If the Bible says not to be friendly, then being friendly is wrong.
**DD**  If the Bible says not to be friendly, then my parents lied to me.

But whereas 'being friendly is wrong' and 'being friendly to strangers is wrong' are both moral sentences, expressing the desire-like attitude of disapproval, 'the Bible says not to be friendly' and 'my parents lied to me' are not moral sentences – they are ordinary non-moral sentences, expressing ordinary descriptive beliefs.

The good thing about Blackburn's account, is that it *does* give us a recipe to understand the meaning of sentences MD, DM, and DD, as well as the meaning of sentence MM. That is because Blackburn's recipe works *no matter* what kinds of mental states [P] and [Q] turn out to be, whether they are states of disapproval or ordinary descriptive beliefs. What is good about this, is that Blackburn's account *tells* us what mental states are expressed by these conditional sentences, and how to determine this from the mental states expressed by its parts. The recipe is very simple: $[P \rightarrow Q]$ = DIS$([P] \& \sim [Q])$.

Unfortunately, what is *bad* about this is that it tells us the *wrong thing*. Thinking that if the Bible says not to be friendly, then my parents lied to me, should turn out to be a matter of having an ordinary descriptive belief that the world is a certain way – namely, that if the Bible says not to be friendly, then my parents lied to me. But Blackburn's account tells us that it is something else, instead. According to Blackburn's account, to think that if the Bible says not to be friendly, then my parents lied to me is just to disapprove of being in a certain state of mind. It turns out that this is a very general problem for any sort of Higher-Order Attitude account. Any theory which tells us that complex sentences express desire-like attitudes *towards* the attitudes expressed by their parts will generalize to complex descriptive sentences, but instead of allowing that they express ordinary descriptive beliefs, it will tell us that they express desire-like attitudes, too. This seems like a very strong conclusion to have to draw.

But the biggest and most important problem for HOA attempts to solve the Frege–Geach problem is due essentially to Mark van Roojen (1996). What van Roojen pointed out was that every HOA account shows too much. Any HOA account will attribute to obviously non-valid arguments exactly the same properties that it attributes to valid arguments. So no HOA account can distinguish between the genuinely valid arguments and these other, obviously non-valid arguments. (My presentation of this point is going to be somewhat different from van Roojen's, but the basic point is the same.) To see why this is so, compare the following two arguments:

**P1**   Murder is wrong.
**P2a**  If murder is wrong, then stealing is wrong.
**C**    Stealing is wrong.

**P1**   Murder is wrong.
**P2b**  It is wrong to think that murder is wrong but not think that stealing is wrong.
**C**    Stealing is wrong.

The first of these two arguments is valid. The truth of its premises guarantees the truth of its conclusion. The second is obviously not valid. Yet Blackburn's expressivist recipe for the meaning of P2a assigns it the same meaning as his recipe for the meaning of 'wrong' assigns to P2b. So everything that Blackburn can explain about the first argument, given the meaning that he assigns to P2a, he can also explain about the second argument, given the meaning that he assigns to P2b. But this is very, very bad, since the first argument is valid, but the second argument is not. Since everything Blackburn manages to explain will go for both arguments, it follows that either he can't explain why the first argument is valid, or he will go wrong by explaining (contrary to fact) why the second argument is valid, too. But it is a bad thing to have a theory which explains things that are false.

You might think that the problem is only that Blackburn appealed to the same attitude in his HOA account of conditional sentences that he appealed to in his account of the meaning of 'wrong' itself. Perhaps he should have appealed to a different attitude instead – perhaps one expressed not by 'wrong' sentences but by 'irrational' sentences. On this new account,

Blackburn can avoid equating sentence P2a with sentence P2b. But now he equates it with sentence P2c:

**P1**    Murder is wrong.
**P2c**   It is irrational to think that murder is wrong but not think that stealing is wrong.
**C**     Stealing is wrong.

So this is no progress at all; this argument is no more valid than the last.

A better idea might be to respond to this problem by saying that conditional sentences express higher-order attitudes that are not themselves expressed by *any* ordinary predicates. One might say, for example, that P2a expresses the attitude, AGAINST([P1]&~[P2]), where no simple sentences express the attitude of being against something. But that doesn't look like a very promising strategy, either. Even if there doesn't happen to be a predicate that expresses the attitude of being against, what could prevent us from introducing one? So let's make up a new word, 'againstisch'. We can offer the following expressivist recipe for the meaning of 'againstisch': for any gerundive phrase, 'X', 'X is againstisch' is a sentence that expresses the state, AGAINST(X) – that is, the state of being against X. That is, [X is againstisch] = AGAINST(X). Now with this new word in hand, we can construct a new invalid argument that even this new, sophisticated, HOA account will fail to distinguish from valid arguments:

**P1**    Murder is wrong.
**P2d**   Thinking that murder is wrong but not thinking that stealing is wrong is againstisch.
**C**     Stealing is wrong.

The only way for the HOA account to block this problem is to have some story about why we are not allowed to introduce a new word, 'againstisch', in this sort of way. But it is very hard to see what that story could be, for the attitude of being against needs to be in every other way very much the same kind of thing as other kinds of attitudes that *can* be expressed by sentences – for example, it will need to turn out to share the same characteristics as every other kind of belief, as we discussed in Chapter 5. Given that the attitude of being against is so much like other kinds of belief, why couldn't we introduce a predicate, 'againstisch', to express this attitude?

So van Roojen's overgeneralization problem for HOA accounts is very, very general. It looks like a serious obstacle to any HOA account whatsoever, no matter how its details were spelled out, and no matter how much better than Blackburn's original theory it looked on other counts. These are the main reasons why HOA attempts to solve the Frege–Geach problem have been generally concluded to be unsuccessful.

## 6.7  The challenge remaining

Now, van Roojen offered a diagnosis of where this problem comes from. His diagnosis was that though Blackburn may have explained why there is something irrational about accepting the premises of an argument and denying its conclusion, irrationality is too easy to come by in order to suffice for an account of validity. Lots of combinations of mental states are irrational. Not only is it irrational to be in a mental state that you disapprove of being in, it is also irrational to believe that you are not in a mental state, even though you really are. So there is something irrational about accepting both 'Colorado is rectangular' and 'I don't believe that Colorado is rectangular.' Yet these two sentences are not, for all that, actually inconsistent.

The kind of irrationality involved in accepting both 'Colorado is rectangular' and 'I don't believe that Colorado is rectangular' is often called *Moorean inconsistency*, because G.E. Moore was originally responsible for pointing out that there is something paradoxical about saying, 'Colorado is rectangular but I don't believe that it is.' Moorean inconsistency contrasts with the *genuine* inconsistency between 'P' and '~P'.

So the moral of the failure of HOA approaches is that if expressivists are going to explain a version of the inconsistency property or the inference-licensing property that suffices to distinguish valid argument from invalid arguments, then they can't appeal to just any old kind of rational conflict between mental states – they need to appeal to the very kind of clash that obtains between beliefs with inconsistent contents. Fortunately, however, we've already put some thought, in Chapter 5, into whether desire-like attitudes can clash with each other in precisely this way. It was what we called 'intrapersonal disagreement'. The idea that we might use what we learned in Chapter 5 about intrapersonal disagreement in order to overcome van Roojen's problem is an important one, and was one of the major developments in expressivist thinking about the Frege–Geach problem. It takes us to the next stage in the development of expressivist theories, which we'll consider in Chapter 7.

## Chapter summary

In this chapter we explored an early generation of approaches to providing expressivist recipes for the meanings of complex sentences, in order to answer the Frege–Geach problem. We distinguished between different *semantic properties* that we might hope to explain, including the *inconsistency* and *inference-licensing* properties of *modus ponens*. We evaluated Blackburn's very early 'involvement' account, and then more thoroughly explored his *Higher-Order Attitude* theory from the 1980s. The main problem for this account was the *van Roojen problem*, which pointed out that it makes too many arguments turn out to be valid.

## Further reading

This chapter is designed to be read along with chapter 6 of Blackburn (1984). van Roojen's argument comes from van Roojen (1996), which is also an excellent comparative discussion of several different expressivist theories. Blackburn's original account appears in Blackburn (1973), which is necessary reading for enthusiasts but now of mostly historical interest. Blackburn (1988) and Hale (1993) are much more difficult papers than these others, but should also be read in this connection by serious students of noncognitivism. It may be helpful to read Schueler (1988) before Blackburn (1988), which responds to it.

## Exercises

1   E *Comprehension*: Translate the attitude expressed by 'If tax cuts raise revenue, then if it is wrong to not raise revenue, then it is wrong to not cut taxes' into our notation using '[]' and '→'. If you have trouble, try replacing each sentence with a letter ('P', 'Q', etc.) to help you see things more clearly.

2   E *Comprehension*: Explain the difference between the inconsistency property and the inference-licensing property.

3   E *Extensions*: In classical logic, it is assumed that the inference from any sentence, 'P', to an 'or' sentence made up of 'P' with any other sentence, such as 'P or Q', is a valid inference. Let 'P' be the sentence, 'Max is short' and 'Q' be the sentence, 'Max is tall but fat'. First write out the sentences

'P' and 'P or Q'. Then test whether the argument from 'P' to 'P or Q' has the inconsistency property and whether it has the inference-licensing property. Do you get the same answer?

4   E *Comprehension*: Explain the difference between the following two HOA accounts:

1   $[P{\rightarrow}Q] = \text{DIS}([P]\&{\sim}[Q])$
2   $[P{\rightarrow}Q] = \text{DIS}([P]\&[{\sim}Q])$

Which one provides a better explanation of the inconsistency property of *modus ponens*? Why?

5   M *Comprehension*: Consider the HOA account according to which conditional sentences express an attitude called 'scorn', and which follows the following recipe:
$[P{\rightarrow}Q] = \text{SCORN}([P]\&[{\sim}Q])$

Explain why this view faces the van Roojen problem, by constructing an invalid argument that this account cannot distinguish from a valid argument. If you get stuck, see the hint in the partial solutions.

6   M *Extensions*: Show that Blackburn's earlier involvement account also falls prey to the van Roojen problem by constructing an invalid argument that the involvement account cannot distinguish from a valid argument. (Hint: Choosing premise 1 and the conclusion should be easy; the trick is to choose premise 2 in the right way.)

7   M *New problem*: Structurally, Blackburn's HOA recipe, $[P{\rightarrow}Q] = \text{DIS}([P]\&{\sim}[Q])$, is reminiscent of the fact that 'A$\rightarrow$B' is sometimes defined to be equivalent to '${\sim}(A\&{\sim}B)$'. In fact, it is natural to think that it should be a constraint of adequacy on a semantic account of 'A$\rightarrow$B' that it turns out to be equivalent to, or at least to entail, '${\sim}(A\&{\sim}B)$'. In this exercise, show that Blackburn's account fails this constraint, by showing that there is no natural pair of recipes for 'and' and 'not' which results in this equivalence. Work with the possible accounts provided below, and add any others that you can think of:

If $[A] = \text{DIS}(\alpha)$ and $[B] = \text{DIS}(\beta)$, then ...

&: [A&B] = ...                      ~: [~A] = ...

(&1) DIS(α&β)                        (~1) DIS(~α)

(&2) DIS(α)&DIS(β)                   (~2) ~DIS(α)

                                    (~3) dis(DIS(α))

Explain why there seem to be no expressivist accounts of the meanings of 'and' and 'not' that will work for Blackburn to get this equivalence right.

8  M  *Extensions* (continuing from exercise 7): In the last exercise, the only account of the meaning of 'not' which itself looks like a Higher-Order Attitude account is the one labeled '(~3)'. This account predicts that if [A] = DIS(α), then [~~A] = DIS(DIS(DIS(α))). Now, for any sentence 'A', 'A' and '~~A' are equivalent. That is, if 'A' is true, then so is '~~A', and if '~~A' is true, then 'A' must be true as well. That means that if this account is to capture the inference-licensing property of the argument from 'A' to '~~A' and of the argument from '~~A' to 'A', then someone who disapproves of disapproving of disapproving of α must be committed to disapproving of α, and likewise someone who disapproves of α must be committed to disapproving of disapproving of disapproving of α. Are both of these theses plausible? If one is less plausible than the other, then which, and why?

9  D  *Branching out* (continuing from exercise 8): In chapter 1 of Blackburn (1998), Blackburn describes what he calls the staircase of 'emotional ascent'. You undergo emotional ascent when you don't just prefer something, but (at the first step) prefer that people prefer it, or (at the second step up) prefer that people prefer that people prefer it, and so on. Use the problem in exercise 8 to argue that an HOA account of the meaning of 'not' leads to the view that if an attitude is expressed by a sentence, then anyone who has that attitude is committed to going all of the way up Blackburn's ladder of emotional ascent. Blackburn suggests that when it comes to mere tastes, we don't ascend up this ladder. Use these observations to show that the HOA account of 'not' means that sentences can't express mere tastes – not even sentences like 'Vanilla is scrumptious.'

10  D  *Qualifications* (continuing from exercises 7, 8, and 9): Assume account (~3) of 'not' from exercise 7, and assume that the hypothesis of exercise 8 is correct, and DIS(DIS([P])) and [P] commit to each other. Show that if you define '&' in terms of '~' and '→', you can satisfy the constraint that [P→Q]

and [~(P&~Q)] are *very close* to committing to one another. Why are they only *very close*? Is this a good thing, or a bad thing, for the HOA account of 'not'? Why?

## Partial answers

5    Hint: To solve this problem, you may need to invent a new word and give an expressivist explanation of what it means. Look more closely at section 6.

7    Assume throughout that [A] = DIS($\alpha$) and [B] = DIS($\beta$). Suppose account (&1) for '&' and (~2) for '~'. By rule (~2), [B] = ~DIS($\beta$). But then rule (&1) doesn't tell us what [A&~B] is – it is defined only for conjuncts which express states of disapproval. So these rules give us no way of determining what [~(A&~B)] is. Now suppose account (&2) for '&' and account (~2) for '~'. By rule (~2), [B] is ~DIS($\beta$). So by rule (&2), [A&~B] is DIS($\alpha$)&~DIS($\beta$). So by rule (&2), [~(A&~B)] = ~(DIS($\alpha$)&~DIS($\beta$)). But according to Blackburn, [A→B] = DIS(DIS($\alpha$)&~DIS($\beta$)), and these are not equivalent, because disapproving of a mental state is not the same thing as not being in it. Show the same thing for each other pair of accounts of '&' and '~'.

## Morals

3    The inconsistency property and the inference-licensing property go hand in hand for *modus ponens*, but may not go hand in hand for every form of inference. Classical logic is good at capturing which inferences have the inconsistency property; an alternative kind of logic known as *relevance logic* is designed with the aim of capturing the inference-licensing property. It may turn out that all classically valid arguments have the inconsistency property, but that not all have the inference-licensing property – in which case that is something that an expressivist explanation of these two properties should explain.

7    Blackburn's account of '→' can be thought of as accepting account (&2) of '&' but having no consistent account of '~'. He needs account (~2) for the second '~' in '~(A&~B)', but account (~3) for the first. Although see exercise 10 for a possible qualification.[3]

# References

Blackburn, Simon (1973). 'Moral Realism.' Reprinted in Blackburn (1993), *Essays in Quasi-Realism*. Oxford: Oxford University Press.

—— (1984). *Spreading the Word*. Oxford: Oxford University Press.

—— (1988). 'Attitudes and Contents.' *Ethics* 98(3): 501–17.

—— (1998). *Ruling Passions*. Oxford: Oxford University Press.

Hale, Bob (1993). 'Can There Be a Logic of Attitudes?' In John Haldane and Crispin Wright, eds., *Reality, Representation, and Projection*. New York: Oxford University Press.

Hare, R.M. (1970). 'Meaning and Speech Acts.' *Philosophical Review* 79(1): 3–24.

Kolodny, Niko, and John MacFarlane (unpublished). 'Ifs and Oughts.' Unpublished manuscript.

Lycan, William (2001). *Real Conditionals*. Oxford: Oxford University Press.

McGee, Vann (1985). 'A Counterexample to Modus Ponens.' *Journal of Philosophy* 82(9): 462–71.

Schueler, G.F. (1988). 'Modus Ponens and Moral Realism.' *Ethics* 98(3): 492–500.

van Roojen, Mark (1996). 'Expressivism and Irrationality.' *Philosophical Review* 105(3): 311–35.

# 7

# THE FREGE–GEACH
# PROBLEM, 1988–2006

## 7.1 Where we are

In Chapter 6 we saw what constructive expressivist recipes for the meanings of complex sentence determined from the meanings of their parts might look like, and investigated the Higher-Order Attitude approach. The primary problem with Higher-Order Attitude accounts was that they *overgenerated* valid arguments, because they failed to be able to distinguish valid arguments from some invalid arguments. And that happened, as van Roojen noted, because they relied on too general a notion of 'irrational' in order to explain why it is irrational to both think that P and think that ~P. Consequently, in order to *avoid* overgenerating, an expressivist explanation of inconsistency needs to establish that [P] and [~P] – that is, the thought that P and the thought that ~P – clash with each other in the *very same way* as the ordinary descriptive belief that grass is green clashes with the ordinary descriptive belief that grass is not green.

More promising expressivist approaches to the Frege–Geach problem over the last twenty years seek to appeal to exactly this notion in order to provide recipes for the meanings of complex sentences. In this chapter we'll start by seeing how easy it is to give recipes for *descriptions* of the states expressed by complex sentences, if we appeal directly to concepts like that of disagreement. These descriptions have the advantage over HOA accounts that they do not run afoul of van Roojen's problem. They are, as I will put it, *formally adequate*. But unlike HOA accounts, we will see that this descriptive approach is *non-constructive*, and hence does not really answer the basic challenge posed by the Frege–Geach problem in the first place.

This is easily the most difficult chapter in this book, but it contains no material for which the previous chapters haven't prepared you. In order to make some of the ideas easier to express, I'll be introducing a few more technical abbreviations, and will use a few more logical and mathematical symbols. But at each point along the way, I'll explain what the new symbols mean. If you lose track of what something means, go back and look again.

## 7.2 Gibbardish semantics

In order to see how easy it is to construct descriptions of the mental states expressed by complex sentences if we allow ourselves to appeal directly to the notion of disagreement, start with the observation that for any sentence 'P', if you think that P, you land yourself in disagreements. For example, simply in virtue of thinking that P you will disagree with each and every person who thinks that ~P. Moreover, if you think that P or Q, you land yourself in *fewer* disagreements. Someone who thinks that P∨Q ('∨' for 'or') disagrees only with people who disagree with both someone who thinks that P and someone who thinks that Q. This simple observation suggests that we can characterize what it is to think that P∨Q in terms of the set of states of mind you land yourself in disagreement with, by having that thought.

Recall that we are using '[P]' to denote the thought that P – that is, the mental state expressed by 'P' – for any sentence 'P'. I'll now introduce a new piece of terminology: we'll use '|M|' to denote the set of states of mind that you land yourself in disagreement with by being in mental state M. So |M| is a set that contains all and only the mental states $x$ such that anyone who is in M disagrees with anyone who is in $x$. We may also refer to |M| as the *disagreement class* of M. (So given this terminology, we can write '|[P]|' to denote the disagreement class of thinking that P – that is, the set of states of mind you land yourself in disagreement with by thinking that P.) This notation lets us put the conclusion of the previous paragraph more concisely as follows: |[P∨Q]| = |[P]|∩|[Q]|.[1] That is, the set of mental states you land yourself in disagreement with by thinking that P&Q includes all of the same ones you land yourself in disagreement with by thinking that P, all of the same ones you land yourself in disagreement with by thinking that Q, and no others. (Symbol-check: '∩' is the mathematical symbol for the *intersection* of two sets — that is, the set that includes all and only the things that are in both of the other sets.)

Now, the project of giving a compositional expressivist semantics is the project of providing a recipe to determine [P∨Q], given [P] and [Q] as inputs. The observation in the previous two paragraphs doesn't tell us what [P∨Q] *is*, but it *does* tell us something very important about it. [P∨Q] is that mental state $x$, whatever it is, such that $|x| = |[P]| \cap |[Q]|$. The observation therefore allows us to specify what [P∨Q] is *by description*. It is that mental state whose disagreement class is the intersection of the disagreement classes of [P] and of [Q]. This sounds like progress — it allows us to say, at least by description, what [P∨Q] is, given [P] and [Q] as inputs. And it was *easy* to do. That is what I mean when I say that it is easy to specify the mental states expressed by complex sentences by description, if we allow ourselves to appeal to the notion of disagreement.

Moreover, it turns out that we can do a similar thing for [~P]. An expressivist semantics for '~P', recall, consists in a recipe for determining [~P], given [P] as input. So if we could provide a recipe for determining $|[\sim P]|$, given $|[P]|$ as input, then by the same reasoning as in the last paragraph, we could turn this into the recipe that we need. And it turns out that the latter recipe is not hard to give, though it is somewhat more complicated than the recipe for $|[P\lor Q]|$. Note that someone who thinks that ~P lands herself in disagreement with anyone who thinks that P. She also lands herself in disagreement with anyone who thinks anything *stronger* than P. But she doesn't land herself in disagreement with anyone else. But what *is* it to think something stronger than P? Well, it is this: thinking something at least as strong as P lands you in disagreement with all of the same people who you would land yourself in disagreement with by thinking that P. That is, any mental state, $y$, is at least as 'strong' as thinking that P just in case the disagreement class of thinking that P is a *subset* of the disagreement class of $y$, which we may write, using the standard mathematical symbol '⊆' for 'is a subset of', as: $|[P]| \subseteq |y|$. So, summarizing the foregoing remarks, $y \in |[\sim P]|$ just in case $|[P]| \subseteq |y|$. (Symbol-check: '∈' is the mathematical symbol for 'is a member of the set'.) This gives us a recipe for [~P], taking [P] as input. [~P] is that mental state $x$, whatever it is, such that $|x| = \{y : |[P]| \subseteq |y|\}$ (which just says, for those who have not seen this mathematical notation before, that $y$ is in the disagreement class of $x$ just in case $|[P]| \subseteq |y|$).

These recipes may not sound like much, but they allow us to prove many important and interesting things. For example, the recipe for [~P] makes it easy to prove that anyone who thinks that ~P thereby lands herself in disagreement with someone who thinks that P. This is because it is trivial that $|[P]|\subseteq|[P]|$, and so $[P]\in\{y:|[P]|\subseteq|y|\}$. Consequently, $[P]\in|[\sim P]|$, which is to say that thinking that P is in the disagreement class of thinking that ~P. And by the definition of 'disagreement class', that just means that anyone who thinks that ~P thereby lands herself in disagreement with anyone who thinks that P. Since that was precisely the important semantic property that we wanted to establish about 'not', that's an exciting result. Moreover, if we define 'P→Q' to mean '~P∨Q' (see exercise 5 from Chapter 3), an exactly analogous (though slightly more complicated) argument shows that *modus ponens* arguments satisfy the inconsistency property. You'll be asked to spell this proof out in the exercises.

In addition, we can prove not only that thoughts which intuitively *should* turn out to disagree with one another really do, but also that *no more* thoughts turn out to disagree with one another than intuitively should. That is, we can prove that this approach doesn't give rise to van Roojen's problem. The proof of that is slightly more complicated. The first step of the proof is to note that for a simple sentence like 'P', $|[P]|$ is simply *defined* to be the set of mental states that [P] lands you in disagreement with. Since this is true by definition, for simple sentences, it follows that for such sentences, [P] doesn't land you in disagreement with any more people than it intuitively should. The rest of the argument shows that once we know that simple sentences don't land you in any more disagreements than they intuitively should, it follows from the recipes for [~P] and [P∨Q] that complex sentences don't land you in any more disagreements than they intuitively should, either. Some of the exercises will walk you through the remainder of the proof.

I call the disagreement-class approach to expressivist semantics developed in this section *Gibbardish semantics*, because it is essentially the approach to the Frege–Geach problem advocated by Allan Gibbard in his two books on expressivism, as I understand that approach. My presentation here differs from Gibbard's own in two main respects, however, which is why it is only Gibbard-ish. These differences are explained and explored in the exercises.

## 7.3 Non-constructive and unexplanatory

All of this *sounds* like we're doing what an expressivist solution to the Frege–Geach problem is supposed to do: providing recipes for the mental states expressed by complex sentences, on the basis of the mental states expressed by their simpler parts – and then using those recipes in order to explain the semantic properties of the complex sentences. But really this is just an illusion. This approach doesn't *really* tell us what mental state is expressed by complex sentences, or even guarantee that there is one. And since it doesn't really tell us what mental states are expressed by complex sentences, it doesn't really explain their semantic properties, either.

The reason why the disagreement-class approach doesn't really tell us what mental states are expressed by complex sentences, or explain the semantic properties of those complex sentences, is that all it gives us is a *definite description* of [P∨Q], and of [~P]. It says that [P∨Q] is that state, x, whatever it is, such that $|x| = |[P]| \cap |[Q]|$, and that [~P] is that state, x, whatever it is, such that $|x| = \{y: |[P]| \subseteq |y|\}$. That's fine, if there really *are* such mental states. But what if there *is* no such mental state? This approach has no way of guaranteeing that there is — it just tells us what it would have to be like.

It is helpful to understand the limitations on this approach, to recognize that what it does is to work out the properties that an *adequate* expressivist account of [P∨Q] and [~P] would need to satisfy, and then to simply stipulate that there are mental states with those properties. That is why it is so easy for this approach to show that complex sentences have the right semantic properties. The approach simply works out what mental states [P∨Q] and [~P] would have to disagree with, in order for their semantic properties to turn out correctly, and then stipulates that those are the states that they disagree with. Certainly, if there do turn out to be such mental states, an expressivist with a view like this one can appeal to their properties, in order to explain things like why thinking that ~P lands you in disagreement with anyone who thinks that P. But the fact that we can come up with a wish list of the features that an expressivist account of [P∨Q] and [~P] would need to satisfy, in order to be adequate, should not thereby make us confident that expressivists can make good on that wish list.

We should not to be distracted by the fact that we all know that there *is* a state of thinking that P∨Q, which lands you in disagreement with all of the same people who you land yourself in disagreement with both by thinking that P and by thinking that Q. Of course there is such a state. It is the belief that P∨Q. The problem is not that there might not be such a state; the problem is that so far as expressivists have told us, there might not be such a state if *expressivism is true*. Now, if we already knew that expressivism has to be true, then we could use our confidence that there really is such a state in an argument that expressivism needs to be able to account for it. But the question that we are ultimately interested in is whether expressivism — or any form of noncognitivism, for that matter — is true. And so it is quite relevant that there is an alternative and very simple explanation of why there is such a state as thinking that P∨Q, with the right properties, even though expressivists can't tell us what it is, or explain why it has the right properties. The alternative explanation is that *expressivism is false*, and [P∨Q] exists and has the disagreement properties that it does because it is just an ordinary belief like any other.

It is helpful to contrast the strengths and weaknesses of Gibbardish semantics with the strengths and weaknesses of the HOA approach. The HOA approach was *constructive*, in the sense that it didn't merely give us descriptions of the mental states expressed by complex sentences – it actually told us what those states are, and guaranteed that there would always be such states. It also *explained* why these states clashed rationally with other mental states by appeal to more general assumptions about some of their properties. For example, Blackburn assumed that it is irrational to be in a mental state that you disapprove of being in, and that is how he *explained* why the mental states expressed by conditionals satisfy the inference-licensing property. In contrast, Gibbardish semantics only describes these states in terms of their disagreement classes. It doesn't really tell us which states of mind turn out to have those disagreement classes, nor does it explain why they disagree with the mental states that they disagree with, by appeal to independent facts about them. It merely hypothesizes that there are such states, and hopes that its hypothesis is fulfilled.

On the other hand, it is precisely the substantive explanations offered by the HOA approach which created its problems. In particular, they were *too* good, because they overgenerated and applied even in cases in which they should not have – that was the van Roojen problem. Gibbardish semantics avoids the van Roojen problem by not giving substantive explanations of disagreement relations. Since it gives no substantive explanation of disagreement relations, it *can't* overgenerate disagreement relations. So it purchases *formal correctness* at the expense of *constructiveness* and *explanatory power*.

It turns out that Gibbardish semantics is not alone in purchasing formal correctness at the expense of constructiveness and explanatory power. There is a whole new generation of expressivist theories which look very different from one another on the surface, but which are all, like Gibbardish semantics, non-constructive but formally correct. In fact, as we will see in the next two sections, there is a *reason* why all of these views are non-constructive. What we will see, is that no formally adequate expressivist theory satisfying a couple of very simple constraints *can* be constructive. And along the way, we will see in more detail why the failure to offer constructive recipes is so problematic for expressivism.

## 7.4 The negation problem

Since the 1980s, conditional sentences have received less direct attention, and gradually more attention has been paid to the case of *negation*. The reason for this is simple: explaining why *modus ponens* arguments have the inconsistency property is a matter of explaining why it is inconsistent to accept all three of the following sentences: {'P', 'P→Q', '~Q'}. But this problem has many moving pieces. In order to solve it, we need to have not only an expressivist account of the meaning of conditional sentences, but an expressivist account of the meaning of *negated* sentences (sentences like '~P'). So since it is a condition of adequacy for an account of the meaning of conditional sentences that *modus ponens* arguments turn out to have the inconsistency property, we need to know the meaning of 'not' in order to evaluate whether we have a satisfactory story about the meaning of 'if … then'.

However, on the flip side, we don't need to know anything about the meaning of 'if … then' in order to evaluate whether an account of the meaning of 'not' is successful. The most important semantic property of negated sentences is that they are inconsistent with the sentences that they negate. That is, for any sentence 'P', 'P' is inconsistent with '~P'. To evaluate whether this is so, we don't need to know anything about the meaning of 'if … then'. So that means that it is a more promising strategy to tackle the meaning of 'not' first, before the meaning of 'if … then'. This removes one degree of freedom on possible answers, and so it makes it easier to zero in on whether a promising solution will be possible.

'Inconsistent' is usually defined to mean 'can't both be true', but just as in Chapter 6 I put off explaining why *modus ponens* arguments are valid until Chapter 8, when we look at what noncognitivists should think about truth, I'm now going to put off explaining why 'P' and '~P' are always inconsistent, in this strict sense. Expressivists are going to explain that only indirectly, by first trying to explain why [P] and [~P] disagree with one another. Fortunately, we've already seen in Chapter 5 that Stevenson and Gibbard have begun the project of trying to explain how there could be attitudes from the mind-to-world side of the direction of fit dichotomy which admit of both interpersonal and intrapersonal disagreement. So just as in the last two sections, let's help ourselves to the idea that the attitude of disapproval is like that. In particular, let's suppose that disapproval is an attitude that we hold toward *actions*, and that it is like belief in the following way:

**inconsistency-transmitting**   Just as the belief that P disagrees with the belief that Q just in case P and Q are inconsistent, disapproving of A disagrees with disapproving of B just in case A and B are inconsistent.

It follows from these assumptions that the state of disapproving of stealing money disagrees with the state of disapproving of not stealing money. So if 'stealing money is wrong' expresses the former, and 'stealing money is not wrong' expresses the latter, then someone who accepts both of these sentences is being inconsistent, in the sense of having attitudes which disagree with one another. Moreover, by the account of 'believes that' from Chapter 5, section 2, it follows from this that someone who believes that stealing money is wrong disagrees with someone who believes that stealing money is not wrong. Since these are exactly the things that we have been hoping to explain, this looks very good.

Unfortunately, however, there is one itty-bitty snag. Actually, it turns out to be quite a large snag. It is known as the *negation problem*, and it received its clearest articulation from Nicholas Unwin (1999, 2001), who really brought the problem clearly into focus, though some had been aware of it previously. The problem is that if 'stealing money is wrong' expresses disapproval of stealing money, then 'not stealing money is wrong' should express disapproval of not stealing money. Yet 'not stealing money is wrong' means something very different from what 'stealing money is not wrong' means. The former means that stealing money is obligatory; the latter means that it is permissible. So even if disapproval of stealing money and disapproval of not stealing money disagree, that looks like it only explains the inconsistency of 'stealing money is wrong' and 'not stealing money is wrong' – it doesn't explain the inconsistency of 'stealing money is wrong' and 'stealing money is not wrong'.

This means not only that we have failed to give an account of what mental state is expressed by 'stealing money is not wrong', but also that there is no state that we can assign to it, such that we can explain all of the inconsistencies that we need to explain as cases of disapproving of inconsistent contents – which disagree in the same, non-Moorean way, as beliefs with inconsistent contents do: by being cases of the same attitude with inconsistent contents.

It turns out that this is easy to prove. Compare the following four sentences:

1   'Stealing is wrong.'
2   'Stealing is not wrong.'

3    'Not stealing is wrong.'

4    'Not stealing is not wrong.'

Sentences 1 and 2 are inconsistent, as are 3 and 4. So if their inconsistency is to be explained in terms of genuine disagreement between the mental states that they express – states which rationally conflict with each other in just the same way that beliefs with inconsistent contents do – and this is to be explained by the fact that disapproval, like belief and intention, is the sort of attitude that it rationally conflicts in this way to hold toward inconsistent contents, then 2 and 4 must express some states of disapproval:

1'    [Stealing is wrong] = DIS(stealing)

2'    [Stealing is not wrong] = DIS(x)

3'    [Not stealing is wrong] = DIS(not stealing)

4'    [Not stealing is not wrong] = DIS(y)

Sentence 2 must express disapproval of something inconsistent with stealing, in order to explain why 1 and 2 are inconsistent, and 4 must express disapproval of something inconsistent with not stealing, in order to explain why 3 and 4 are inconsistent. But if x is inconsistent with stealing, then x implies not stealing. Similarly, if y is inconsistent with not stealing, then not stealing implies not y. But from this it follows that x implies not y – i.e., that x and y are inconsistent with each other. But this yields the prediction that the states of mind expressed by 2 and 4 intrapersonally disagree, and hence are inconsistent. But 2 and 4 are not inconsistent sentences! It is perfectly consistent to think that stealing is not wrong, and also that not stealing is not wrong – on the grounds that it is permissible to do either.

So van Roojen's argument showed that if expressivists are not to explain why *too many* arguments are valid, they must be careful not to appeal to just any old rational conflict between mental states, but only to the special kind of conflict that we are calling *intrapersonal disagreement*, which holds between ordinary descriptive beliefs with inconsistent contents, and which holds between intentions with inconsistent contents. But this proof shows that if simple moral sentences like 'stealing is wrong' express a negative attitude toward their subjects, and disagreements between states of disapproval work *just like* disagreements among beliefs (which is just what Gibbard's and Stevenson's arguments from Chapter 5 were arguments for optimism in) then there *is no way* of making it turn out that 'stealing is not wrong' expresses the same kind of attitude as 'stealing is wrong' expresses.

Here is a helpful way of thinking about the dialectical structure of the negative proof in this section: rather than thinking of the disagreement-class approach of Gibbardish semantics as providing us with full-fledged recipes for the meanings of complex sentences, we can think of it as formalizing *conditions of adequacy* for any recipes for the states expressed by complex sentences. The idea is that it is necessary and sufficient for any expressivist recipe to explain, using their recipes, why [P∨Q] and [~P] have the disagreement classes that they do, relative to the disagreement classes of [P] and of [Q]. But what the argument of the last section shows is that given a limited set of assumptions shared by all expressivists so far, any constructive account whatsoever will yield the wrong disagreement classes. This is bad news for expressivism.

## 7.5 The hierarchy of attitudes

Nicholas Unwin (1999, 2001) used a simple example in order to illustrate where this problem comes from. He invited us to compare the following four sentences:

| | |
|---|---|
| **w** | Jon thinks that stealing is wrong. |
| **n1** | Jon doesn't think that stealing is wrong. |
| **n2** | Jon thinks that stealing is not wrong. |
| **n3** | Jon thinks that not stealing is wrong. |

The task of providing an expressivist semantics for 'not' is the task of giving content to n2 – for expressivism is the view that you give the meaning of 'P' by saying what it is to think that P. But the trouble is that we can't just read this off the expressivist account of the meaning of 'stealing is wrong', because w lacks sufficient structure. As n1–n3 illustrate, there are three places in which a 'not' can be inserted in w. But as n1\*–n3\* below illustrate, there are *not* three places in which a 'not' can be inserted in the schematic expressivist account of w:

| | |
|---|---|
| **w\*** | Jon disapproves of stealing. |
| **n1\*** | Jon doesn't disapprove of stealing. |
| **n2\*** | ??? |
| **n3\*** | Jon disapproves of not stealing. |

As Unwin's examples illustrate, there is not enough structure in expressivists' account of the attitudes expressed by the atomic sentences for any answer to fall out of expressivism as to what mental state is expressed by complex sentences. But this also suffices to show that the problem exists not only for negation, but for *every* complex-sentence-forming construction, as the following examples illustrate:

&1    Jon thinks that stealing is wrong and Jon thinks that murdering is wrong.
&2    Jon thinks that stealing is wrong and murdering is wrong.
&3    Jon thinks that stealing and murdering is wrong.

v1    Jon thinks that stealing is wrong or Jon thinks that murdering is wrong.
v2    Jon thinks that stealing is wrong or murdering is wrong.
v3    Jon thinks that stealing or murdering is wrong.

And it is easy to extend such examples indefinitely. For each case, all three sentences need to be distinguished. For each case, providing an expressivist recipe for that complex-sentence-forming construction is a matter of giving content to the second sentence. And for each case, there are one too few places in the structure of sentence w, for any account of the second sentence to fall out.

Because of the structure of this problem, contemporary expressivist theories don't try to analyze the mental states expressed by '~P' or by 'P&Q' or by 'P→Q' in terms of the attitudes involved in the states expressed by 'P' and by 'Q'. What the arguments of this section and the last establish is that given the assumptions that these theorists are making, they *can't*. So what they do, instead, is to postulate the existence of *new* attitudes to be expressed by complex sentences. So, for example, we might invent a new attitude called *tolerance* and say that n2 says that Jon *tolerates* stealing. Similarly, we might invent a new attitude called *double-disapproval*, which instead of taking one action for its object, takes two actions for its objects, and say that sentence &2 says that Jon is in a state of double-disapproval whose objects are stealing and murdering.

However, as you'll be asked to show in the exercises, the same kind of argument which shows that negations of atomic sentences can't express the same attitude as the atomic sentences do also shows that negations of conjunctions can't express the same kind of attitude either as negations or as conjunctions – so expressivists need to postulate a new kind of attitude to be expressed by sentence of the form '~(A&B)' in addition to the new attitudes expressed by '~A' and 'A&B'. But things don't stop there; expressivists also need to postulate a new attitude to be expressed by 'A&~B' and another for '~A&~B', and, in general, for any two sentences expressing different kinds of attitudes, they need to postulate a new kind of attitude to be expressed by their conjunction.

This means that once we go down this road, we end up postulating an infinite hierarchy of different kinds of attitude to be expressed by moral sentences – that is to say, we end up proposing not only that there are two kinds of belief, moral and non-moral, but that there are *infinitely many* different kinds of belief. And that, in turn, makes the problems in the philosophy of mind, from Chapter 5, all that much harder. Instead of merely needing to explain how there could be two different attitudes which coincidentally turn out to have as much in common as moral and ordinary descriptive belief seem to have in common, expressivists who accept the hierarchy of attitudes need to explain how there could be *infinitely many* different attitudes which coincidentally turn out to have as much in common as beliefs seem to have in common. Moreover, in the exercises you'll be asked to look at whether such expressivists will experience similar pressure to postulate infinite hierarchies of distinct kinds of desiring, distinct kinds of hoping, distinct kinds of wondering, distinct kinds of dreading, and so on, for each of the other kinds of attitude. It is easy to see that the hierarchy of attitudes is an extraordinarily elaborate hypothesis about the mind.

## 7.6 Inferential-commitment theories

Despite their apparent great diversity, expressivist approaches to the Frege–Geach problem developed since approximately 1988 all share the same essential feature that they tell us what mental states are expressed by complex sentences by telling us what those states have to be like. We may put such theories together into a single group and call them *inferential-commitment theories*. These theories do the same thing, but they do it in different ways.

For example, one theory might do this by inventing a new attitude called 'tolerance' and say that while 'stealing is wrong' expresses disapproval of stealing, 'stealing is not wrong' expresses tolerance of stealing, and disapproval and tolerance have the special feature that disapproval and tolerance of the same thing always disagree with one another. Such a theory describes the attitude of 'tolerance' in terms of the properties that it needs to have for the theory to work, and the theory does not work, unless there really is such an attitude. Moreover, as we saw in the last section, similar reasoning leads to postulating infinitely many more kinds of attitude. Terry Horgan and Mark Timmons' (2006) approach to expressivist semantics endorses the infinite hierarchy of attitudes approach explicitly.

An apparently quite different theory might do the same thing. But instead of telling us that 'stealing is not wrong' expresses a different kind of attitude than 'stealing is wrong' does, this theory might pick out the state of mind expressed by 'stealing is not wrong' by the same kind of description that it uses to pick out the states of mind expressed by any sentence. Gibbardish semantics, from sections 2 and 3, works like this. It has a uniform notation for describing the mental states expressed by sentences in terms of their disagreement classes. That uniform notation may make it seem like every sentence expresses, at some level, the same kind of mental state, but this is not the case. The same arguments, from sections 4 and 5, show that if we had to actually say what the mental states are that turn out to have these disagreement classes, it would turn out that they must be of infinitely many different kinds.

Yet a third kind of theory (as in Blackburn [1988]) might distinguish between the attitudes of *hooraying* and *tolerating*, and specify that hooraying A always disagrees with tolerating ~A, and then tell us that for any two states of mind [P] and [Q], there is a third state of mind of being *tied to a tree* between [P] and [Q], which has the property that anyone who is 'tied to a tree' between [P] and [Q] and comes to be in the state [~P] is rationally committed to being in the state [Q], and similarly anyone who is 'tied to a tree' between [P] and [Q] and comes to be in the state [~Q] is rationally committed to being in the state [P]. Such a view owes us some further clarification; if being 'tied to a tree' between [P] and [Q] is itself an attitude toward [P] and [Q], then this is just a version of the Higher-Order Attitude theory, but if being 'tied to a tree' is a description of the rational inferential properties of a state of mind, then this view is just another inferential-commitment theory, and the same arguments as before, from sections 4 and 5, lead to the conclusion that we can't stop here, with just three kinds of state – hooraying, tolerating, and being tied to a tree – but must also explain even more complex states of mind – for example, corresponding to the negation of states of being 'tied to a tree'.

So even though all of these views look very different, at bottom they are very similar. At bottom, they have the advantage of avoiding van Roojen's problem and achieving formal adequacy, precisely because they help them-selves to the very sorts of assumptions that they should be trying to explain. Instead of giving constructive recipes for the mental states expressed by

complex sentences, they merely describe those states, in terms of the properties that they need to have, and then assume that there really is a state that
has those properties. As we saw, there are strong reasons to think that this
means that they must postulate infinitely many kinds of belief.

Finally, since these theories are non-constructive, there is a natural sense
in which they don't explain the semantic properties of complex sentences,
as we originally set out to do, in the face of the Frege–Geach problem. To see
why, compare the following two explanations of why someone who thinks
that P and also thinks that ~P is undergoing the kind of clash of attitudes
that we have been calling 'intrapersonal disagreement':

- first, the cognitivist explanation. We start by noting that ordinary
  descriptive belief is, like intention but unlike wondering or supposing,
  the kind of mental state such that one disagrees with oneself if one
  holds it toward inconsistent contents. Next, we note that 'P' and '~P'
  are inconsistent – that is, they cannot both be true. That, moreover, is
  explained by the meaning of '~' – by its truth table, as in Chapter 3.
  Finally, we note that thinking that P is having a belief whose content is
  that P, and thinking that ~P is having a belief whose content is that ~P.
  It follows from these three assumptions that thinking that P disagrees
  with thinking that ~P;
- second, the inferential-commitment theorist's explanation. We start by
  assuming that given a mental state, [P], there is another mental state
  that disagrees with it. Our recipe for [~P] is to let [~P] be that mental
  state. By assumption, it disagrees with [P].

It is clear that the inferential-commitment theorist's explanation is no
explanation at all. It merely helps itself to what it should be trying to explain.
Is there really such a mental state as [~P]? Why does it disagree with [P]?
Inferential-commitment theories have unfortunately little to say about these
questions. So progress in actually anteing up to Hare's (1970) promise to
provide recipes for the meanings of complex sentences that would allow
noncognitivists to predict and explain all of the same sorts of things that
truth-conditional semantic theories can explain has still been quite limited.
The Frege–Geach problem remains a serious obstacle for noncognitivism,
and most of what we've learned so far is not encouraging.

## Chapter summary

In this chapter we explored more contemporary, *inferential-commitment*, approaches to the Frege–Geach problem, starting with Gibbardish semantics, a variant on the expressivist theory developed by Allan Gibbard. We saw how inferential-commitment theories trade off *constructiveness* for *formal adequacy*, and we proved why, given their assumptions, they are forced to do so. We also saw that inferential-commitment theories can take many different forms, and do not always wear their nature on their sleeve.

## Further reading

This chapter is designed to be read along with Gibbard – I recommend chapters 3 and 4 of Gibbard (2003), although some instructors will prefer to use chapter 5 of Gibbard (1990). Horgan and Timmons (2006) is the next piece of essential reading, and defends the inferential commitment strategy and the hierarchy of attitudes most explicitly. For the negation problem, see Unwin (1999 or 2001) (the former discusses Blackburn and the latter discusses Gibbard), and Dreier (2006). Some readers may also be interested in seeing how expressivists can avoid both forks of the dilemma of this chapter and offer recipes for the meanings of complex sentences that are both constructive and formally adequate – for the answer, and the further challenges that it leads to, see Schroeder (2008c).

## Exercises

1    E *Comprehension*: If [P] is in the disagreement class of M, i.e., [P]∈|M|, is [P&Q] in the disagreement class of M or not? Solve this problem by reasoning directly from what 'disagreement class' means, and from what you know about what it is to think that P&Q.

2    E *Comprehension*: Simon Blackburn has said that 'stealing is wrong' expresses a state of *booing* stealing. In 1990, Allan Gibbard said that 'crying is irrational' expresses a state of *accepting a norm that forbids crying*. In 2003, Gibbard said that 'being friendly is the thing to do' expresses a state of *planning to be friendly*. In 2006, Terry Horgan and Mark Timmons said that 'Jack ought to go' expresses the *ought-belief that Jack goes*. For each of these four views, write out the analogues of Unwin's four sentences, w* and n1*–n3*.

3   E *Extensions*: Show that Unwin's problem extends to conditional sentences by constructing the analogues of Unwin's n1–n3 for 'if ... then' sentences. Assume for the purposes of this exercise that 'murder is wrong' expresses disapproval of murder and 'stealing is wrong' expresses disapproval of stealing, and use that assumption to construct the analogues of Unwin's n1*–n3*. Compare these two groups of sentences, and point out where the problem comes from.

4   E *Extensions*: Show that Unwin's problem extends to *past tense* sentences by constructing the analogues of Unwin's n1–n3 for the past tense. Assume for the purposes of this exercise that 'murder is wrong' expresses disapproval of murder, and use that assumption to construct the analogues of Unwin's n1*–n3*. Compare the two groups of sentences, and point out where the problem comes from.

5   E *Extensions*: Show that Unwin's problem extends to *quantifier* words like 'every', 'some', and 'most' by constructing the analogues of Unwin's n1–n3 and n1*–n3* for each. Just to get you started, here is one of the sentences you need for each:

**every1**   Every action is something that Jon thinks is wrong.

**some2**   Jon thinks that some action is wrong.

**most3**   Jon thinks that the following thing is wrong: doing most things.

Compare the groups of sentences, and point out where the problem comes from.

6   M *Extensions*: 'Permissible' and 'obligatory' are said to be *duals*. This means that 'permissible' can be defined as 'not obligatory not', and 'obligatory' can likewise be defined as 'not permissible not'. So either one of these notions – permissibility or obligatoriness – can be used to define the other. Moreover, 'permissible' and 'impermissible' can be defined in terms of one another, because 'permissible' can be defined as 'not impermissible' or 'impermissible' can be defined as 'not permissible'. And similarly, 'obligatory' and 'unobligatory' can be defined in terms of one another in the same way. What this means is that any one of these four terms can be used to define all of the others. For expressivists, however, there is an important difference between the two occurrences of 'not' in the definition of permissible as 'not obligatory not'. The first of these two 'not's may be called *external* negation, because it appears to the left of and logically 'outside' the predicate, 'obligatory'. The

second may be called *internal* negation, because it appears logically 'inside' the predicate. One way to think of the inferential commitment solution to the negation problem is as defining external negation in terms of 'permissible' and 'obligatory', rather than defining 'obligatory' in terms of 'permissible' and external negation. First show how to define external negation in terms of 'permissible' and 'obligatory'. Can you define external negation in terms of 'permissible' and 'impermissible'? How about in terms of 'impermissible' and 'obligatory'? Count how many ways there are of defining external negation.

7   M *Extensions*: In section 4, we proved that if 'stealing is wrong' expresses an attitude toward stealing with the feature that two states involving that attitude disagree just in case they have inconsistent contents, then 'stealing is not wrong' must express a different kind of attitude. In this exercise, show the same thing for conjunctions like 'stealing is wrong and murder is wrong'. Proceed in the same way as we did in section 4, and make sure that you use our observation in section 2 that the state of mind expressed by a conjunctive sentence disagrees with all of the states that disagree with each conjunct – and no others.

8   M *Extensions* (continuing from exercise 7): Extend the previous exercise by explaining why 'murder is wrong and stealing is not wrong' must express a different kind of attitude from 'murder is wrong and stealing is wrong'. Use this kind of reasoning to argue that there must be infinitely many kinds of moral belief.

9   M *Extensions*: In sections 4–5 and in the last few exercises, we have focused on the need for inferential-commitment theorists to postulate an infinite hierarchy of different kinds of moral belief. This greatly aggravates the Multiple Kinds problem from Chapter 5, because that problem was formulated to explain how two such different states of mind as moral belief and ordinary descriptive belief could nevertheless have so many things in common. If two attitudes make a coincidence, however, infinitely many attitudes make a coincidence of colossal proportions. In this exercise show that the same problem will come up for attitudes other than belief, by showing how to construct an Unwin-style grid of sentences for the attitudes of hoping and dreading.

10  M *Qualifications*: In the statement of Gibbardish semantics in section 2, we characterized states of mind in terms of their *disagreement classes* – the

sets of states of mind that they land you in disagreement with. Explain why it is a prima facie problem for this approach that there are some states of mind that no one has ever been in. How would you fix this problem?

11    M    *Qualifications*: In sections 2 and 3 I characterized the descriptions generated by Gibbardish semantics as *definite* descriptions, which implies that there is only one mental state which they correctly describe. Was it right to characterize them in this way? Does Gibbard have any way of guaranteeing that there is not more than one mental state with the required disagreement properties? Compare the disagreement class of the state [P&Q] to the disagreement class of the state of simultaneously being in both the state [P] and the state [Q]. Compare sentences &1 and &2 from section 5.

12    M    *Branching out*: My presentation of Gibbardish semantics is intended to be a generalization of and more intuitive way of presenting the expressivist semantics advanced by Allan Gibbard in his two books on expressivism. There are two main differences between Gibbardish semantics as presented here and the way that Gibbard presents his own view. The first main difference is that the sets that Gibbard associates with sentences are their *non-*disagreement classes, rather than their disagreement classes. Since there is a 1:1 correspondence between every set and its complement, this difference is a non-substantive one. Gibbard uses non-disagreement classes rather than disagreement classes, which leads to some minor differences in how our recipes work. For example, in section 2, the recipe for the disagreement class of [P∨Q] told us that it was the *intersection* of the disagreement classes of [P] and of [Q]. Show that the recipe for non-disagreement classes will tell us that the non-disagreement class of [P∨Q] is the *union* of the non-disagreement classes of [P] and of [Q]. (Terminology-check: the *union* of two sets is the set of everything that is a member of either.)

13    D    *Branching out*: The other significant difference in detail from how Gibbard presents his own view is that rather than considering the sets of *any* possible mental state with which you land yourself in disagreement by thinking that P, Gibbard restricts the discussion to the complete mental states of *fully opinionated* thinkers – people who for each and every question 'P' either think that P or think that ~P. Gibbard calls such fully opinionated thinkers *hyperplanners*. The version of Gibbardish semantics that I've set up is able to dispense with the notion of hyperplanners, which in some ways makes it philosophically less problematic. But Gibbard's appeal to

hyperplanners simplifies his recipes for [~P] (and for [P&Q]) somewhat. Show that restricting to hyperplanners simplifies the recipe for [~P].

14   D *Extensions*: In section 2 we saw how Gibbardish semantics could be used to 'prove' that [P] is in the disagreement class of [~P]. Show that under Gibbardish semantics *modus ponens* has the inconsistency property, by first defining 'P→Q' to mean '~P∨Q', and then showing that [P&(P→Q)] is in the disagreement class of [~Q] – so someone who accepts the conjunction of the premises of a *modus ponens* argument disagrees with anyone who denies its conclusion. (Define 'P&(P→Q)' to mean '~(~P∨~(P→Q))'.)

15   D *Extensions*: At the end of section 2, we noted but did not finish proving that Gibbardish semantics avoids the van Roojen problem – that is, that the mental states expressed by two sentences disagree only if those two sentences are inconsistent. The overall strategy of the proof is to show that this is true for simple sentences, and then to show that *if* it is true for simple sentences, it is true for complex sentences made up out of them. In this exercise, prove that if ||[P]|| includes all and only the mental states that disagree with [P] and ||[Q]|| includes all and only the mental states that disagree with [Q], then ||[P∨Q]|| includes all and only the mental states that disagree with [P∨Q]. This will show that if you start with simpler sentences that don't disagree with more than they intuitively should, the recipe for '∨' will never result in sentences that disagree with more than they should.

16   D *Extensions* (continuing from exercise 15): In this exercise complete the argument that Gibbardish semantics doesn't suffer from the van Roojen problem by proving that if ||[P]|| includes all and only the mental states that disagree with [P], then ||[~P]|| includes all and only the mental states that disagree with [~P]. This will show that if you start with simpler sentences that don't disagree with more than they intuitively should, the recipe for '~' will never result in sentences that disagree with more than they should. Together with the last exercise, this shows that everything that we can define in terms of '∨' and '~' will avoid the van Roojen problem, as well (see exercise 14, for example).

17   D *Branching out*: Terry Horgan and Mark Timmons (2006) give a detailed version of inferential-commitment expressivist semantics in which they explicitly acknowledge that they believe in an infinite hierarchy of different kinds of moral belief. In some ways their article is one of the most

perspicuous statements of the philosophical commitments of the inferential-commitment strategy. Horgan and Timmons start by postulating
two basic kinds of belief – is-belief and ought-belief, for which they use
boldface, as 'I[ ]' and 'O[ ]'. Then they have a series of rules which postulate new and different kinds of belief. For example, they postulate that for
any kind of belief, $\Omega$, there is a further kind of belief, $\neg\Omega$, to be expressed
by the negations of sentences which express mental states involving $\Omega$.
Similarly, they postulate that for any kinds of belief, $\Omega$ and $\Psi$, there are
the following further kinds of belief: $\Omega\wedge\Psi$, $\Omega\vee\Psi$, $\Omega\to\Psi$, and $\Omega\leftrightarrow\Psi$, to be
expressed by sentences formed by conjunction, disjunction, conditionals,
and biconditionals. (I'll leave out quantifiers in this discussion just to keep
things simple, but Horgan and Timmons posit additional kinds of attitudes for those as well.) If we count simple or *atomic* sentences as having
complexity 0, and sentences that are formed from only sentences with
complexity of n or less, by being put together with one of 'not', 'and', 'or',
'if ... then', or 'if and only if' as having complexity n + 1, then how many
distinct kinds of belief do Horgan and Timmons need to postulate in order
to cover sentences with a complexity of up to 3?

18   D  *Branching out* (continuing from exercise 17): In Horgan and Timmons'
framework, a conjunction of two descriptive sentences – for example,
'Jon goes and Jan stays home' expresses the attitude I[ ]$\wedge$I[ ] – not itself
is-belief (ordinary descriptive belief), but a new and different attitude that
is postulated by one of their rules. So the state expressed by 'Jon goes and
Jan stays home' is I[G(jon)]$\wedge$I[S(jan)]. But on the other hand, in Horgan
and Timmons' system, 'it ought to be that Jon goes and Jan stays home'
expresses a simple *ought*-belief: O[G(jon)&S(jan)]. Is there anything about
this picture that is in tension with compositionality? If so, what? If not, why
not? Do Horgan and Timmons have anything to say about this?

19   A  *New problem* (continuing from exercise 17): Horgan and Timmons'
expressivist semantics treats 'ought' as the only moral word, and relies on
the premise that rather than being a predicate, it is a sentential operator.
But in ordinary language, there are moral words that function as adjectives:
'good', 'bad', 'right', and 'wrong', to name just a few. Presumably, Horgan
and Timmons must think that each of these words needs to be analyzed in
terms of 'ought'. For this exercise, look at Horgan and Timmons' article,
and try to analyze 'wrong' and 'good' in terms of 'ought'. Can you still
explain why the following argument is valid? 'Being friendly is good'; 'if

being friendly is good, then being friendly is not wrong'; 'being friendly is not wrong'?

20   A *Branching out* (continuing from exercise 19): Since in Horgan and Timmons' semantic framework, 'ought' corresponds to a kind of attitude that one bears toward non-moral contents, their expressivist language is unable to accommodate embedded 'oughts', as in 'it ought to be the case that he ought to give her the money.' If moral predicates like 'wrong' are really to be analyzed in terms of 'ought', then even a seemingly straightforward sentence like 'murder ought to be wrong' will express such a state. Look into what Horgan and Timmons have to say about this issue. Does it fit together with their philosophical interpretation of their formal language? Is it consistent with a way of trying to make sense of moral predicates within their view? Why or why not?

## Partial answers

13   Hint: First show that when we restrict to hyperplanners, the non-disagreement class is identical to the agreement class. Second, translate the recipe for $\|[\sim P]\|$ into a recipe for its non-disagreement class. Third, observe that if y is the complete state of mind of a hyperplanner, the class of complete states of mind of hyperplanners who agree with y is {y}. You should be able to show that the disagreement class of [∼P] is the complement of the disagreement class of [P] – which simplifies the recipe considerably.

## Morals

6   You can only define external negation out of two predicates if you would ordinarily use external negation in order to define one predicate in terms of the other. Compare chapter 6 of Blackburn (1984) to Blackburn (1988). Notice that in 1984, Blackburn discusses both 'Hooraying' and 'Booing', which sound like they are associated with 'obligatory' and 'impermissible'. Can you use these two attitudes to define external negation?

11   The idea that there is no distinction between &1 and &2 is called the thesis that belief *agglomerates* over conjunction. (Notice both the similarity to, and the differences from, the *norm of conglomeration* from exercise 8 in Chapter 5.) Despite the intuitive differences between &1 and &2, *possible-worlds semanticists* have an approach to semantic theorizing one of whose

consequences is that they are not distinct. Gibbard's (1990) approach to the Frege–Geach problem was modeled on possible-worlds semantics, and as a result it inherits some of that approach's intuitively implausible features. Note, however, that Gibbardish semantics doesn't need to accept agglomeration, if we give up the idea that the descriptions generated by the theory are *definite* descriptions and build in the hypothesis that [P&Q] is a distinct state from [P]&[Q], the state of simultaneously thinking that P and thinking that Q. You can see how this would be a first step, within Gibbardish semantics, to admitting an infinite hierarchy of attitudes. For more on the relationship between Gibbard's (1990) approach to the Frege–Geach problem and the drawbacks of possible-worlds semantics, see Dreier (1999).

12  Gibbard uses non-disagreement classes in order to emphasize the parallels with *possible-worlds semantics* (see the moral to exercise 11). I've done things the other way, because it makes the meaning of the formalism easier to unpack, and hence I think easier to keep in full view exactly how the view works and what its philosophical commitments are.

13  If we restrict ourselves to fully decided states of mind, then the recipe for $|[P\&Q]|$ mirrors the recipe for $|[P\lor Q]|$: $|[P\&Q]| = |[P]|\cup|[Q]|$ ('$\cup$' for 'union'). This is because every *fully decided* thinker disagrees with a conjunction only if they disagree with one of the conjuncts. Things are more complicated, however, for thinkers who are not fully decided – someone who is not fully decided may disagree with a conjunction without having a view about which conjunct is false. That is why my treatment of Gibbardish semantics needs to take '$\lor$' as a primitive, rather than '&'.

## References

Blackburn, Simon (1984). *Spreading the Word*. Oxford: Oxford University Press.
—— (1988). 'Attitudes and Contents.' *Ethics* 98(3): 501–17.
Dreier, James (1999). 'Transforming Expressivism.' *Noûs* 33(4): 558–72.
—— (2006). 'Negation for Expressivists: A Collection of Problems with a Suggestion for Their Solution.' In Russ Shafer-Landau, ed., *Oxford Studies in Metaethics*, vol. I. Oxford: Oxford University Press.
Gibbard, Allan (1990). *Wise Choices, Apt Feelings*. Cambridge, MA: Harvard University Press.

—— (2003). *Thinking How to Live*. Cambridge, MA: Harvard University Press.

Horgan, Terry, and Mark Timmons (2006). 'Cognitivist Expressivism.' In Horgan and Timmons, eds., *Metaethics after Moore*. Oxford: Oxford University Press.

Schroeder, Mark (2008c). *Being For: Evaluating the Semantic Program of Expressivism*. Oxford: Oxford University Press.

Unwin, Nicholas (1999). '*Quasi*-Realism, Negation and the Frege–Geach Problem.' *Philosophical Quarterly* 49(196): 337–52.

—— (2001). 'Norms and Negation: A Problem for Gibbard's Logic.' *Philosophical Quarterly* 51(202): 60–75.

# 8

## TRUTH AND OBJECTIVITY

### 8.1 The problem of truth

The earliest noncognitivists sometimes described their view as the view that moral sentences are incapable of being true or false. This idea can profitably be thought of as deriving from the analogies which they exploited. If 'murder is wrong' has a meaning similar to that of 'dammit, not murder!', we would expect that the former sentence, like the latter one, would not be the sort of thing that we would ordinarily call true or false. If your friend says 'dammit!', you wouldn't ordinarily describe her as having said something true or false; so if 'murder is wrong' is like 'dammit!', we wouldn't expect it to be the sort of thing to be true or false, either.

Unfortunately for this theory, we *do* ordinarily describe moral sentences as being true or false. When you agree with the moral view that someone has just expressed, you can say, 'that's true!' just as well as repeating what he said. And when you disagree, you can say, 'that's false!' just as well as denying it. That makes the claim that moral sentences really can't be true or false, after all, surprising and unintuitive. Moreover, it makes it sound as if morality is not very serious or 'objective'. If moral claims can't be true or false, then maybe they are, in some pejorative sense, 'just feelings' – matters of taste, about which we can feel whichever way we like, in contrast to questions of fact, about which it is important to get the right (true) answer.

After all, if no matter what your moral views are, they can't be false, that makes it sound like you can't go wrong, no matter what you think.

These are two reasons why it is worth seeing what noncognitivists can say about truth – because we really do, ordinarily, talk about moral claims being true or false, and because if moral claims *can't* be true or false, then it is hard to see why it shouldn't be the case that 'anything goes' when it comes to morality – perhaps, as in matters of taste, there should be no disputing moral questions. That, and other versions of the worry that 'anything goes', given noncognitivism, will be the focus of this chapter.

But first there is one more important reason why it is worth seeing what noncognitivists can say about truth, which it will be particularly important to address. In Chapter 6 we observed that the main semantic property of conditionals ('if … then' sentences) is that they make certain patterns of inference (*modus ponens*) valid. And 'valid' is usually defined in terms of truth – a pattern of inference is said to be 'valid' just in case when its premises are true, its conclusion is guaranteed to be true. Similarly, we saw that the main semantic property of 'not' is that 'P' and '~P' are inconsistent sentences. And 'inconsistent' is usually defined in terms of truth – two sentences are inconsistent if they are guaranteed not to both be true. In Chapters 6 and 7 we set aside these semantic properties of conditionals and of 'not', and explored how expressivist theories could explain some of their *other* semantic properties – the inconsistency and inference-licensing properties of *modus ponens* inferences, and the fact that accepting 'P' and '~P' involves intrapersonal inconsistency. As we noted earlier, ordinary truth-conditional theories explain these latter properties in terms of the fact that *modus ponens* is valid and the fact that 'P' and '~P' are inconsistent. In this chapter, one of our goals will be to see how expressivists can work backwards, and explain why *modus ponens* is valid and why 'P' and '~P' are inconsistent, in terms of the other semantic properties of conditionals and 'not' that we tried to account for in the last two chapters.

To return to an analogy from Chapter 6, if the truth-conditional seman-ticist is like the Malebranchean occasionalist, who not only believes in God, but requires God to do a lot of work, sophisticated noncognitivist theories are like an ordinary theist who denies occasionalism: who believes in God, but doesn't appeal directly to God in her explanations of everything. Like the dispute over occasionalism, which need not be a debate about theism itself but can be understood as an in-house debate among theists about how much work God does, the difference between truth-conditional and noncognitivist semantic theories need not be a debate about whether there are any moral truths, but can be understood as an in-house debate about how much work moral truths do. In Chapters 6 and 7 we looked at how expressivists hope to explain things without appealing to truth; now we get to see why they hope to count as believing that there are moral truths, anyway.

## 8.2  Correspondence vs. deflationism

According to *correspondence* theories of truth, a sentence is true just in case and because it *corresponds* to how the world is. Intuitively, what makes 'grass is green' true, the idea goes, is that it depicts the world as being a certain way – and that is how the world really is. If the world weren't the way that 'grass is green' depicts it as being, then the sentence wouldn't be true. This, according to the correspondence theory, is what truth is. Sentences are true only when the way they depict the world matches how the world actually is. Similarly, according to the correspondence theory a sentence is false only when it depicts the world as being a certain way and the world isn't that way. Truth, on the correspondence theory, is *match* between a sentence and the world, and falsity is *mismatch*.

It is a consequence of the correspondence theory that sentences which don't depict the world as being any particular way can't be true or false. Take, for example, the case of 'dammit!'. This sentence doesn't depict the world as being any particular way. So no matter how the world is, it can't match the way the sentence depicts it as being, and it can't mismatch the way the sentence depicts it as being. So the sentence can't be true or false, no matter how the world turns out to be. This is a good prediction of the correspondence theory, since 'dammit!' *doesn't* seem like the right kind of thing to be true or false. But it also means that the correspondence theory yields the prediction that if moral sentences don't depict the world as being some way, then moral sentences can't be true or false, either.

Noncognitivists hold that moral sentences don't depict the world as being a certain way – or at least, that moral words don't make any contribution to how they depict it as being. So to take Ayer's view, for example, 'you acted wrongly in stealing that money' depicts the world as being the same way as 'you stole that money' does – what the addition of 'wrongly' does is merely to affect *how* this is depicted, not *what* is depicted. Similarly, on Ayer's view, 'stealing money is wrong' depicts the world no differently from how 'stealing money' depicts it – which is to say, not at all. So if we assume the correspondence theory of truth, then it follows from Ayer's view that 'you acted wrongly in stealing that money' is true under the same conditions under which 'you stole that money' is true – and that 'stealing money is wrong' can't be true or false at all.

This means that to avoid these predictions, noncognitivists need to adopt a different kind of theory of truth from the correspondence theory. The usual alternative theory which noncognitivists propose is called *deflationism*. There are several different kinds of deflationist theory, but the basic idea which they share, very roughly, is that 'true' is a word that we use to agree with something, and 'false' is a word that we use to disagree with it. If your friend says, 'Colorado is rectangular' and you want to agree with her, you can repeat what she said, or you can just say, 'That's true.' On the other hand, if you want to disagree, you can say, 'Colorado is *not* rectangular', or you can just say, 'That's false.'

The word 'true' comes in handy, deflationists have noted, because it makes these things easier to say, and because it lets you agree with your friend, even if you don't know what she said. If you didn't catch what she said, but you trust her, you might confidently let someone else know, 'I didn't hear what she said, but it's definitely true.' But on the other hand, it's impossible just to repeat what your friend said, in order to agree with it, if you never heard what it was. This sounds like a trivial observation, but it is in fact a really big idea. Deflationists have argued that the reason we have the words 'true' and 'false' is so that we can agree or disagree, without having to repeat what we are agreeing or disagreeing with. This lets someone summarize agreement with everything in the Bible, for example, without repeating every word it says: all she needs to say is, 'Everything the Bible says is true.' According to deflationists, this is *all there is* to truth – that 'true' and 'false' are words we can use to agree or disagree, respectively, with other things people might say.

If deflationists are right and this is all that there is to truth, then it makes sense after all to call moral sentences 'true' or 'false', even if noncognitivism is true. You should call 'true' the ones that you agree with, and 'false' the ones that you disagree with. So as long as you think that female genital mutilation is wrong, for example, you will say that it is true that female genital mutilation is wrong, or that 'female genital mutilation is wrong' is true. On the other hand, if you think that female genital mutilation is not wrong, then you disagree with the thought that it is wrong. So you will say that it is false that female genital mutilation is wrong, or that 'female genital mutilation is wrong' is false. The only way that you would say that it is neither true nor false that female genital mutilation is wrong, or that 'female genital mutilation is wrong' is neither true nor false, would be if you didn't think that female genital mutilation is wrong, or that it is not wrong. Given deflationism, anyone who has a view about moral questions should say that their answers are true or false.

So what we've seen so far is that noncognitivism + correspondence theory leads to the thesis that moral sentences – at least, some of them – cannot be true or false. Whereas noncognitivism + deflationism leads to the view that moral sentences *can* be true or false. Except that the latter result is really a little bit more complicated; so far as we have said, even if noncognitivism and deflationism are both true, someone who doesn't have any moral views may think (and rightly so) that no moral sentences are true or false. The deflationist idea by itself only suffices to show that someone who *has* moral views will say (and properly, given the meanings of 'true' and 'false') that some moral sentences are true, and some are false.

Most noncognitivists' discussions of truth stop here, with the observation that given deflationism, it makes sense to think that moral sentences *can* be true or false. But a stronger sort of deflationist view would aspire to show not only that it is *possible* to think that moral sentences are true or false, but that moral sentences *are* true or false. In the next section, we'll look at an example of what an expressivist version of deflationism might look like, and we'll use it to explain why 'murder is wrong' has to be either true or false – and why this can't consistently be denied, even by someone who does not have any view about whether murder is wrong. We'll then see how this deflationist view can be used to explain why moral *modus ponens* arguments are valid, in the sense of being truth-preserving, and why 'murder is wrong' and 'murder is not wrong' are inconsistent, in the sense that they can't both be true.

## 8.3 Deflationism and truth-aptness

One thing that the correspondence theory of truth clearly gets right, is that sentences like 'dammit!' and 'Boo, stealing money!' cannot be true or false. The explanation of this provided by the correspondence theory is that these sentences do not represent the world as being any particular way. At first glance, deflationists say that to say that something is true is more or less equivalent to saying it in the first place – which is why it makes sense to say that it is true that stealing is wrong, if you are willing to say, 'stealing money is wrong', in the first place. But deflationism would show too much, if it also predicted that it makes sense to say that 'Boo, stealing money!' can be true or false. So it had better not turn out that deflationists are committed to holding that it makes just as much sense to say '"Boo, stealing money!" is true' as to say, 'Boo, stealing money!'. So deflationists must have some way of distinguishing between the sentences for which '"P"' is true' is just as acceptable as 'P', and the sentences for which it is not.

This problem is known the problem of providing an account of which sentences are truth-apt. Every deflationist theory of truth needs an account of truth-aptness, because every deflationist theory of truth needs an answer to which sentences it makes sense to say are true, just because it makes sense to say them – and this had better not apply to 'Boo, stealing money!' or to 'dammit!'. But noncognitivists who wish to make use of deflationism in order to explain why moral sentences can be true or false face an extra challenge in providing an account of truth-aptness that will do what they need of it: since noncognitivists frequently analogize the meaning of moral sentences to sentences that cannot be true or false, they need an account of truth-aptness which can explain why 'stealing money is wrong' is truth-apt even though 'Boo, stealing money!' is not, *and even though these two sentences have the same kind of meaning*. The fact that noncognitivists think these sentences have the very same kind of meaning – perhaps even the *same* meaning – is the principal challenge to any theory of truth-aptness being able to classify moral sentences as truth-apt, but not the others.

Now, there is a very simple way in which some philosophers have believed that this trick could be accomplished. According to these philosophers, the distinction between truth-apt and non-truth-apt sentences is not a semantic distinction at all. It is simply a *syntactic* distinction. The test for whether a sentence 'P' is truth-apt or not, they have said, is simply whether 'it is true that P' is grammatical (in the sense of being syntactically well formed) or not. Since on this view the distinction between truth-apt and non-truth-apt sentences is not a semantic one at all, but a purely syntactic one, it runs into no difficulty at all with the hypothesis that 'stealing money is wrong' and 'Boo, stealing money!' have *exactly* the same meaning, but the former is true and the latter is not.

This is because despite the fact that these two sentences are semantically identical, they are syntactically quite different. Indeed, the sentence 'it is true that stealing money is wrong' is grammatical, but the sentence 'it is true that Boo, stealing money!' is not. So this syntactic theory of truth-aptness not only tells us which sentences are truth-apt, and not only classifies this pair of sentences in the way that the noncognitivist hopes for, it does so in a way that is compatible with the very strongest sort of noncognitivism – with the view that these two sentences have exactly the same meaning.

Unfortunately, there are problems with the idea that truth-aptness is a merely syntactic property, rather than having any basis in semantics. This idea fares pretty well with how we actually classify existing sentences of English, sure enough, but it also predicts that all that we need to do in order to make a non-truth-apt sentence truth-apt is to change its grammar. Dreier (1996) tested this prediction by introducing a new predicate, 'hiyo'. According to Dreier, 'Bob is hiyo' is used in very much the same way as 'hey, Bob' is used – to accost Bob. But according to Dreier, 'hiyo' is grammatically an adjective, so 'Bob is hiyo' is an ordinary indicative sentence, and consequently 'it is true that Bob is hiyo' is syntactically well formed. Consequently, by the syntactic criterion, 'Bob is hiyo' is truth-apt, and so someone who is willing to accost Bob should be willing to admit that 'Bob is hiyo' is true. Dreier calls this view about 'hiyo' *accostivism*.

It is far from clear, however, whether this should really be so. In the case of moral sentences, we certainly do ordinarily say that they can be true or false. And they are certainly indicative. But what is at issue, here, is precisely whether it is their indicative syntax alone which suffices to guarantee that they can be true or false. And it isn't clear whether 'Bob is hiyo' really should be said to be true or false, simply because we are willing or unwilling to accost Bob.

Dreier sharpens the worry by noting that sentences like 'if Bob is hiyo, then I'm out of here' and 'everyone who isn't hiyo is boring' are *also* grammatically well formed, if 'hiyo' is an ordinary predicate – and indeed, are themselves truth-apt, by the syntactic criterion for truth-aptness. Moreover, since these sentences are formed truth-functionally on the basis of their parts, that tells us under what conditions these sentences *are* true. But as Dreier notes, even once we understand that 'Bob is hiyo' is used to accost Bob, so that we understand how to use *that* sentence, we *still* don't understand what sentences like 'everyone who isn't hiyo is boring' mean, or know how to use them. A theory which tells us that it is this easy to confer a meaning on these sentences makes too much out of syntax.

Dreier's discussion pushes the noncognitivist to explain the difference between 'stealing money is wrong' and 'Boo, stealing money!' on *semantic* grounds. The bare syntactic criterion on truth-aptness makes it too easy for sentences to turn out to be true or false, and consequently too easy to generate putatively meaningful complex sentences which are patently not meaningful at all. What noncognitivists need, in order to avoid the result that 'hiyo' is a perfectly intelligible predicate, is some kind of *semantic* constraint which, intuitively, goes hand in hand with indicative syntax in natural languages, but is violated when Dreier tries to simply stipulate indicative syntax for sentences involving 'hiyo'.

The best existing answer to Dreier's challenge that I know of comes from Allan Gibbard. Gibbard's idea is closely connected to our original characterization of deflationism as the idea that 'true' is used to agree, and 'false' is used to disagree. The rough idea is that some sentences do not express states of mind that it is possible to agree or disagree with – and that such sentences are not truth-apt. According to Gibbard, it is not possible to agree or disagree with an accosting, and so it is not possible to agree or disagree with 'Bob is hiyo'. Consequently, it does not make sense to say that 'Bob is hiyo' is true or false, even if you are willing or unwilling to accost Bob – and even though it is syntactically indicative.

Gibbard's account therefore leads to a semantic explanation of why 'Boo, stealing money!' and 'dammit!' cannot be true or false, but 'stealing money is wrong' can be. His explanation is that 'stealing money is wrong' expresses a state of mind that it is possible to agree or disagree with – and 'true' and 'false' are used to agree or disagree. Consequently it does not make sense to call 'Boo, stealing money!' or 'dammit!' true or false. This reduces the problem of explaining why moral sentences can be true or false to the problem of explaining why it is possible to disagree with moral thoughts – which was one of the problems for noncognitivism in the philosophy of mind that we already considered in Chapter 5. Of course, in order to offer this semantic explanation, Gibbard must reject Ayer's early emotivist view that 'Boo, stealing money!' and 'stealing money is wrong' have *exactly* the same sort of meaning, but as an expressivist, Gibbard never said that they did have exactly the same kind of meaning.

Gibbard's explanation of truth-aptness in terms of agreement and disagreement also has the virtue of making it quite straightforward to say what an expressivist version of deflationism about truth would look like, in terms of disagreement. In section 4 we'll therefore use our tools from Chapter 7 in order to give an example of what an expressivist version of deflationism might look like, and then in section 5 we'll apply it, in order to see how expressivists can argue not only that it *makes sense* to say that moral sentences can be true or false, but that moral sentences *must* be true or false – and how they can argue that moral *modus ponens* arguments are valid, in the traditional sense that the truth of their premises guarantees the truth of their conclusion.

## 8.4  Expressivist deflationism

Since the basic idea behind expressivist deflationism is that 'it is true that P' is used to agree with 'P' and 'it is false that P' is used to disagree with 'P', it turns out that disagreement classes – the tool that we used to explain Gibbardish semantics in section 2 of Chapter 7 – are the perfect tool to explain the commitments of expressivist deflationism. (Recall that in that chapter, we used square brackets around a sentence – [P] – to designate the mental state expressed by that sentence – what it is to think that P. And we used vertical lines around a term designating a mental state – |M| – to designate the *disagreement class* of M – that is, the set of states of mind that you land yourself in disagreement with by being in M.)

In terms of disagreement classes, then, the important fact about [it is true that P] is that it has the same disagreement class as [P] – that is, that |[it is true that P]| = |[P]| – and the important fact about [it is false that P] is that it has the same disagreement class as [~P] – that is, that |[it is false that P]| = |[~P]|. Since the disagreement classes of the mental states expressed by complex sentences formed by 'and', 'or', 'not', and 'if … then' are a function of the disagreement classes of the mental states expressed by their parts, these two assumptions are sufficient to guarantee the truth of Intersubstitutability:

> **Intersubstitutability**    For any sentences 'A' and 'B' which differ only in that some occurrence of the sentence 'P' in one is replaced by 'it is true that P' in the other or in that some occurrence of the sentence '~P' in one is replaced by 'it is false that P' in the other, |[A]| = |[B]|.

The exercises will invite you to prove Intersubstitutability and some closely related variations.

Intersubstitutability has the immediate consequence that [it is not true that stealing is wrong and it is not false that stealing is wrong] has the same disagreement class as [stealing is not wrong and stealing is not not wrong]. But it is rationally inconsistent to think that stealing is not wrong and stealing is not not wrong. So that means that it is rationally inconsistent to think that it is neither true nor false that stealing is wrong. But if it is rationally inconsistent to think that it is neither true nor false that stealing is wrong, then the only rationally consistent view would appear to be to think that it is either true or false that stealing is wrong. So since this is the only rationally consistent thing to think, we had better think it. And since we had better think it, we might as well say it: it is either true or false that stealing is wrong.

This is how expressivists can argue that it is either true or false that stealing is wrong. It is not a direct argument; in fact, it is a fairly unusual kind of argument. Rather than arguing directly that it is either true or false that stealing is wrong, what the expressivist does is to argue directly that it is *rationally undeniable* that it is either true or false that stealing is wrong, and then to make the *transcendental turn*, and, since this is rationally undeniable, go on to not deny it – and hence to affirm it, instead. After all, we might as well not deny things that it is rationally inconsistent to deny. Having argued that given her account, we *cannot but* think that P, the expressivist then goes on to assert that P. This counts as a 'transcendental' form of argument, because at no point does the expressivist directly prove that P. Instead, she indirectly proves that P is undeniable, or perhaps that it is something that we are all committed to accepting, no matter what else we accept. Since it is undeniable, or since we are committed to accepting it, we might as well accept it.

The very same style of argument can be used to argue that *modus ponens* arguments are truth-preserving. This argument works the very same way, by going back to Intersubstitutability. Another immediate consequence of Intersubstitutability is that [it is true that P and it is true that (if P, then Q) and it is not true that Q] has the same disagreement class as [P and (if P, then Q) and ~Q]. But it is rationally inconsistent to think that P and (if P, then Q) and ~Q (this was proved in exercise 14 of Chapter 7). So that means that it is rationally inconsistent to think that the premises of a *modus ponens* argument are true but its conclusion is not true.

Since it is rationally inconsistent to think this, the expressivist concludes, let's not think it. In fact, let's think the opposite. So, taking the transcendental turn, the expressivist concludes by accepting that if the premises of a *modus ponens* argument are true, then the conclusion is true as well. Since this is rationally inconsistent to deny, we might as well accept it. And since we accept it, we might as well say it: if the premises of a *modus ponens* argument are true, then the conclusion is, as well. That is, *modus ponens* arguments are truth-preserving.[1]

In this way, the same kind of transcendental argument leads to the conclusion that *modus ponens* arguments are valid in the ordinary sense of preserving truth – the expressivist has merely explained this the reverse way around from the ordinary explanation. The ordinary explanation, offered by the truth-conditional semanticist, explains the validity of *modus ponens* on the basis of the truth table for 'if ... then', and then explains why *modus ponens* has the inconsistency property by appeal to the fact that it preserves truth. Whereas the expressivist explains things the other way around – first explaining the inconsistency property of *modus ponens*, and then using this to drive the transcendental argument that it preserves truth. Like the theist who believes in God but denies Malebranchean occasionalism, the expressivist believes that there is a truth about moral questions, but denies that it plays an explanatory role in the meanings of complex sentences or their semantic properties (because she rejects truth-conditional semantics).

## 8.5 More transcendental arguments

In the last section we observed an expressivist strategy for arguing that there is a truth of the matter about whether stealing is wrong, and that *modus ponens* preserves truth. This style of argument is in some ways unconventional; nowhere does the expressivist lay out premises from which the conclusion follows. Instead, what the expressivist does is to lay out premises from which it follows that the conclusion is rationally undeniable, or that everyone is rationally committed to accepting it. That is what makes the arguments count as taking the *transcendental turn*. Arguments like this illustrate why the only rational course is to accept their conclusions, but they don't particularly illuminate why they would be true.

One helpful way to think about conclusions which are established in this way is as having a status akin to logical truths. It follows from the meanings of '~' and '&', for example, that any instance of '~(P&~P)' is rationally undeniable, no matter which sentence is substituted for 'P', according to the expressivist, and that is what makes it a logical truth. Similarly, it follows from the meanings of '→', '~', and 'it is true that', that every instance of '(it is true that P and it is true that P→Q)→(it is true that Q)' is rationally undeniable. So by analogy, that is a truth of the logic of 'true' – or as we would ordinarily say in philosophy, an *analytic* truth.

Expressivists have attempted to establish even more interesting results by this same sort of transcendental method – essentially, by trying to establish, given the meanings of words, that certain sentences are rationally undeniable. It is, in fact, a very general expressivist tool, which can be fit to many different purposes. Just take one very important example, Allan Gibbard (2003) has used this style of argument in order to argue that the moral *supervenes* on the non-moral.

The slogan of supervenience is, 'no moral difference without a non-moral difference'; the idea being that in order for two situations to differ in terms of what someone ought to do, or in terms of what is good or bad, they would also have to differ in some other way. The idea behind this thesis is incredibly compelling: how could two situations be exactly the same in every non-moral respect, but one is good, and the other one bad? Surely there would have to be some relevant difference between them, to explain why one is good and the other bad.

The basic idea behind supervenience is so compelling, in fact, that virtually everyone in moral philosophy accepts some version of the thesis. And as a result, it plays a very important role in metaethics, particularly in debates about moral metaphysics, because supervenience makes it look like how things are morally *depends* on how they are non-morally. So in trying to offer a transcendental argument for supervenience, Gibbard is trying to co-opt these debates about moral metaphysics, by showing that supervenience can be explained in an expressivist framework, without making any assumptions about moral metaphysics. Gibbard's interesting transcendental argument for supervenience is unfortunately too detailed to go into, here, but it is an excellent example of how the transcendental strategy can be taken further than we have gone with it, here, and it is important to understand that Gibbard's argument has this transcendental character.

## 8.6 Objectivity

One general worry that philosophers have about noncognitivism of any kind is that it makes it seem like anything goes, in the realm of moral thought. Since moral thoughts are not answerable to the world, moral judgment seems at bottom to be akin to judgments of taste. And in matters of taste, as the saying goes, there is no disputing. The expressivist account of truth mitigates the force of this worry somewhat, because it allows expressivists to say that moral questions have a right answer – even if we haven't made up our minds about whether stealing is wrong, we have to admit (on pain of rational inconsistency) that there is a truth of the matter about whether it is – either it is true that stealing is wrong and false that stealing is not wrong, or it is false that stealing is wrong and true that stealing is not wrong. So either way, there is something to be said against one of the possible views about whether stealing is wrong. So it's not the case that 'anything goes', because one of the answers is going to be *false*.

This mitigates the force of the worry that given expressivism anything goes, not just because it *lets* us say, if we think that stealing is wrong, that thinking that stealing is not wrong does not 'go', because it is false, but also because it *requires* us to admit, even if we don't know whether stealing is wrong, that one of the answers (though we don't know which) does not 'go', because it is false.

Some critics of expressivism have still complained, however, that according to expressivism, rightness and wrongness somehow depend on our attitudes, giving morality less objectivity and giving us too much control over its content. But it is hard to formulate a version of this objection that is not based on a confusion. It is true that expressivists explain the meanings of moral sentences in terms of the desire-like attitudes that they express. But they also explain the meanings of non-moral sentences in terms of the ordinary descriptive beliefs that they express. So right and wrong no more depend on our attitudes than rectangularity and aluminum do. That is the key idea, after all, that motivated expressivism in the first place, rising out of the ashes of speaker subjectivism. By claiming that 'stealing is wrong' bears exactly the same relationship to disapproval of stealing money that 'grass is green' bears to the ordinary descriptive belief that grass is green, the expressivist assures that wrongness cannot depend on our attitudes in any more objectionable a way than greenness does.

Even this, however, leaves many philosophers feeling unsatisfied, as if it failed to make the worry that 'anything goes' go away completely. It is still true that from the point of view of the semantic theory, there is no distinction between thinking that stealing is wrong (and that it is true that stealing is wrong), on the one hand, and thinking that stealing is not wrong (and that it is false that stealing is wrong), on the other. Nor, unlike the case with ordinary non-moral sentences like 'grass is green', does the contribution of the world help to create an asymmetry, either. From *within* moral thinking, it may be undeniable that there is a single correct answer to moral questions, but once we look at moral language from the *outside*, it looks like any answer to what this correct answer is, is as good as any other.

Of course, the expressivist will in turn answer this worry in the same way: by pointing out that one answer to what the correct answer is will be *false* – and that it is rationally undeniable that there is a correct answer to the question of what the correct answer is. And she will say that this in turn no more depends on our attitudes than the claim that we started with. But again the same question arises. Something fixes the rational undeniability, from within the moral point of view, of the existence of a correct answer, but apparently nothing fixes what it is.

It turns out that the possibility of interesting transcendental arguments points to one interesting way for an expressivist to escape this dialectic, and insist that with respect to at least *some* important moral questions, there *is* an asymmetry between possible answers. The idea behind this move is very simple; one of the most interesting things about transcendental arguments like the ones we have been considering in the last two sections is that they establish that even though expressivist semantics does not work by directly telling us which sentences are true and which are false, it is consistent with this that some sentences turn out to be rationally undeniable. These sentences — the *analytic truths* of the expressivist semantics — are ones that it is rationally inconsistent to deny, no matter what else you think. So the expressivist semantics does not treat them symmetrically, after all: one answer turns out to be rationally unacceptable.

It is true that the questions for which we have so far seen transcendental strategies to establish results like this one don't really help us to directly answer any interesting practical moral questions — they were things like the conclusion that there is a truth of the matter about whether stealing is wrong, that *modus ponens* preserves truth, and that the moral supervenes on the non-moral. But a small number of philosophers who have noncognitivist or related theories have believed that even more interesting conclusions can be established by this very same methodology. For example, one very natural way of understanding Immanuel Kant's moral theory is as espousing a strategy akin to this one. Certainly that is how Kant was understood by R.M. Hare, who is himself one of the best examples of a noncognitivist embracing this strategy. Christine Korsgaard's moral theory, another contemporary Kantian theory, can also be profitably understood as being a kind of expressivism according to which some interesting moral claims turn out to be rationally undeniable.[2]

Exploring whether any of these strategies work would unfortunately take us too far afield. But the important thing to observe is that it would take a *lot* for any of these strategies to work. It would have to turn out that there are interesting moral claims which essentially have the status of *logical* truths. This is an ambitious thesis, at best, and noncognitivists who are not able to establish anything like this will be forced to admit that their semantic theory does not distinguish between the view that stealing is wrong and the view that stealing is not wrong. The only way to decide whether stealing is wrong or not, such views will say, is to think about things from the moral point of view. Metaethical inquiry into the meanings of words can't decide the answer for you.

# Chapter summary

In this chapter we explored whether and how noncognitivist theories can account for the assumption that there is a truth of the matter about moral questions. We saw that this conflicts with correspondence theories of truth, but not with deflationist theories. We also saw that a deflationist theory which focuses on the notion of *disagreement* can solve problems about what makes a sentence truth-*apt*. Then we saw how an expressivist version of deflationism can lead to transcendental-style arguments that there is a truth of the matter about moral questions, and that moral *modus ponens* arguments are truth-preserving, and finally closed by briefly exploring the limits of such transcendental-style arguments, for noncognitivists, as well as how much can be said in favor of the view that moral truths are objective.

# Further reading

This chapter is suited to be read alongside chapter 6 of Blackburn (1984). For a look at the relationship between noncognitivism and deflationism, see Smith (1994b). Section 3 is suited to be read along with Dreier (1996). For Gibbard's transcendental argument for supervenience, see chapter 5 of Gibbard (2003), and for Korsgaard's view, see Korsgaard (1996), especially lecture 4.

# Exercises

1   E *Comprehension*: Gibbard (2003) considers the example of a predicate, 'yowee', whose meaning is as follows: 'I am yowee' has the same kind of meaning as 'ouch!': 'To say "I am yowee" is not to *say that* I have a head-ache; it is to *express* my headache' (65). Assuming that is the meaning of 'yowee', which of the following sentences are truth-apt:

    1   I am yowee.
    2   Ouch.
    3   You are yowee.
    4   If I am yowee, then ouch.
    5   I drank too much last night.
    6   If I am yowee, then I drank too much last night.
    7   If ouch, then I drank too much last night.

    (a) according to the correspondence theory of truth? (b) according to deflationism about truth plus the syntactic theory of truth-aptness? (c) according to deflationism about truth plus Gibbard's theory of truth-aptness? If there is something else that you need to know in order to classify some of the sentences, say what it is.

2    E *Comprehension*: The following sentence is the only sentence written on the door of Professor Kripke's office, who happens to currently be away at lunch: 'Professor Kripke is not in.' First use the correspondence theory of truth to decide whether this sentence is true. Then use the deflationary theory of truth to decide whether it is true. Do you get the same results? Explain why or why not.

3    M *Comprehension*: The following sentence is the only sentence written on the whiteboard in Professor Kripke's office: 'No sentence written on the whiteboard in Professor Kripke's office is true.' As in the last exercise, first use the correspondence theory of truth to decide whether this sentence is true. Then use the deflationary theory of truth to decide whether it is true. (Hint: This exercise is harder than the last.) Is either theory harder to apply than the other? Do they lead you to the same answer? Why or why not?

4    M *Extensions*: Recall that according to Ayer, just as 'stealing money is wrong' has the same significance as 'stealing money', 'you acted wrongly in stealing that money' has the same significance as 'you stole that money'. So if 'stealing money is wrong' lacks a truth-value because 'stealing money' lacks a truth-value, then we would expect 'you acted wrongly in stealing that money' to *have* a truth-value, because 'you stole that money' does. Explain why this conclusion would lead to the *wrong* truth-value for 'you acted wrongly in stealing that money'. (Hint: Look for an invalid argument involving this sentence which would be truth-preserving, if it had the same truth-value as 'you stole that money'.)

5    M *Extensions*: Consider the theory according to which 'what he said is true' just means 'I agree with what he said.' Show that this theory gives rise to each of the modal and disagreement problems, from Chapter 4. Should deflationism be understood as the view that 'true' sentences are used to *say* that we agree, or that they are used to *express* agreement?

6    M *Extensions*: In the terms of Chapter 7, the expressivist theory of truth stated in this chapter is *non-constructive*, which means that it doesn't really tell us what mental states are expressed by complex sentences; it just

describes them in terms of their disagreement properties. But there is an obvious candidate for what mental state [it is true that P] could be, such that |[it is true that P]| = |[P]|. What is it? Can you foresee any problems for this candidate answer?

7    M *New problem*: Transcendental proofs like the ones considered in this chapter are an unusual way of arguing. The mere fact that it is irrational not to think something doesn't seem to suffice to show that it is true – perhaps there are some truths which it is irrational to acknowledge. For example, as Moore pointed out, it is irrational to think, 'P, but I don't believe that P.' But this can quite easily be true. What grounds might there be for thinking that the transcendental arguments considered in this chapter are at least on better grounds than the argument from 'It is irrational for me to think that P but I don't believe that P' to 'If P, then I believe that P.' Discuss whether the form of argument is still problematic.

8    M *Extensions*: In the main text, we showed how expressivists can argue that conditionals validate *modus ponens*. We also mentioned that it is important for expressivists to show that 'P' and '~P' are guaranteed to be inconsistent – that is, that they can't both be true. Use Intersubstitutability in order to argue, in the same manner as the arguments in the main text, that 'P' and '~P' can't both be true.

9    D *New problem*: In Chapter 4 we saw how expressivists can claim that moral thoughts are beliefs, and in this chapter, we've seen how expressivists can claim that there are moral truths. Noncognitivism used to be *defined* as the view that moral sentences cannot be true or false, and when people began to see how the sorts of views which had been called 'noncognitivism' actually *could*, by appealing to deflationism, say that moral sentences can be true or false, many philosophers switched to defining 'noncognitivism' to mean the view that moral thoughts are not beliefs. If we say both that moral thoughts are beliefs and that moral sentences can be true, then we need yet a third way of characterizing noncognitivism. According to the *problem of creeping minimalism*, any third way we have of characterizing noncognitivism will use words that noncognitivists will also want to reclaim, just as they have sought to reclaim 'true' and 'believes'. But if noncognitivists reclaim *all* of the words that we might use in order to state the difference between cognitivism and noncognitivism, then we will no longer be able to tell the difference between the two views. Evaluate

the extent to which we should be worried about this problem. Is this worry premature?

10  D *New problem* (continuing from exercise 9): Although earlier noncognitivists were sometimes happy to say that moral sentences can't be true or false and that moral thoughts are not beliefs, Simon Blackburn made a big deal out of his proposal that expressivists attempt to mimic the kinds of things that realists can say (including that moral sentences can be true, and that moral thoughts are beliefs). He called this idea 'Quasi-Realism'. Quasi-Realism is sometimes described as if it is a special theory, but really it is just the articulation of a set of aims for a research program for noncognitivism. But distinguish between two possible such research programs. The aims of the first are to account for pre-theoretical data, including that some moral claims seem to be true and others seem to be false, and that we really do seem to have moral beliefs. The aims of the second research program, in contrast, are not just to account for the pre-theoretical data, but to account for whatever it is that realists are led to say in the course of offering their own theories. These two research programs overlap with respect to accounting for moral truth and for moral belief, but may diverge over other topics. For what topics might these two research programs diverge? Which program is it more important for noncognitivists to be successful at? Which program needs to be successful, in order for there to be a problem of 'creeping minimalism', as in exercise 9?

11  D *Branching out*: It is highly plausible that it is not the case that stealing and not stealing are both wrong. In this exercise, you'll provide a transcendental argument for this claim, within the following expressivist theory: first, assume that there is a state of mind called *being for*, which is *inconsistency-transmitting* (see Chapter 7, if you don't remember what this is). Second, assume that if 'X' denotes X, then 'X is wrong' expresses the state of being for avoiding X. Prove that it is rationally inconsistent to accept the sentence, 'stealing is wrong and not stealing is wrong', and explain why this is what you need for the requisite transcendental argument.

12  D *Extensions*: Prove Intersubstitutability, given the assumptions that |[it is true that P]| = |[P]| and that |[it is false that P]| = |[~P]|. The proof should be by *induction on formula complexity*. This means that you start by showing that Intersubstitutability holds for simple sentences of the form, 'it is true that P' or 'it is false that P'. Then you show that if Intersubstitutability holds

for one sentence, it also holds for that sentence's negation. And then you show that if Intersubstitutability holds for two sentences, it also holds for their disjunction. That way, you show that it holds for any sentence which is made up out of such simple sentences, by means of '~', '∨', and anything that is definable in terms of '~' and '∨'.

13    D  *New problem*: The purpose of this exercise is to generalize the disagreement-class approach to 'true' in order to use 'true' to apply to *sentences*. Importantly, someone who accepts 'S is true', where 'S' refers to a sentence, is only committed to accepting 'P', if she believes that S means that P – that is, accepts 'S means that P'. This observation leads to the idea that the meaning of 'S is true' can be approximated by an infinitely long sentence like '(if S means that A, then A)&(if S means that B, then B)&(if S means that C then C)& ... &(S means that A or S means that B or S means that C or ...)'. Use this idea, along with the other tools of the disagreement-class approach of Gibbardish semantics, from Chapter 7, to derive a formula for |[S is true]|.

14    D  *Extensions*: Use your formula for |[S is true]| from exercise 13 to argue that 'P' and 'S is true' are intersubstitutable for someone who accepts 'S means that P'.

15    D  *Branching out*: As the last two exercises illustrate, disagreement classes can be quite an unwieldy tool. A better way to think about things is in terms of *commitment tables*. Think of a commitment table as like a truth table, but instead of showing us how the truth-value of a complex sentence depends on the truth-values of other sentences, they tell us how the attitude that you are committed to having toward a complex sentence depends on the attitudes that you have toward other sentences. It is useful, in thinking about commitment tables, to leave open the possibility that in addition to the attitudes of *acceptance* and *denial*, there may also be a third possible attitude, of *rejecting* a sentence. Rejection is to be understood as a third attitude that is rationally inconsistent with both acceptance and with denial. Construct a commitment table for '~', which shows which attitude you are committed to having toward '~P', on the basis of which attitude you have toward 'P'.

16    A  *Extensions*: Let's say that a complex sentence is *commitment-functional* just in case the attitude you are committed to having toward it is a function

of the attitudes you have toward its parts (the last exercise involves showing that sentences formed by '~' are commitment-functional). Using the following portion of a commitment table for 'true' (where 'A' stands for 'accept', 'R' for 'reject', and 'D' for 'deny'), prove *Sentential Intersubstitutability*:

*Sentential Intersubstitutability*: If you accept 'S means that P', then if S* is any commitment-functional sentence of which P is a part, then you are rationally committed to having the same attitude toward S* as toward the sentence which is like S*, except that it replaces 'P' with 'S is true'.

| P | S means that P | S is true |
|---|----------------|-----------|
| A | A | A |
| R | A | R |
| D | A | D |
| A | R | |
| R | R | |
| D | R | |
| A | D | |
| R | D | |
| D | D | |

17   A *Branching out*: The following formula is known as the *sentential T-schema*:

If S means that P, then S is true just in case P.

First, substitute 'Liar' everywhere for 'S' and 'Liar is not true' everywhere for 'P', and explain why accepting the resulting sentence leads to paradoxical results, if Liar really is a name for the sentence, 'Liar is not true'. Then, use Sentential Intersubstitutability (from exercise 16) to show that it is rationally inconsistent to deny any instance of the sentential T-schema. If it's rationally inconsistent to accept it, and rationally inconsistent to deny it, what should you do? (This problem is less difficult, but draws on the previous exercise.)

## Partial answers

6   The obvious candidate for [it is true that P] in order to guarantee that |[it is true that P]| = |[P]| is simply [P]. The theory that [it is true that P] = [P] is an expressivist version of what is known as the *redundancy* theory of truth, according to which 'it is true that P' has the very same meaning as 'P', which is why they can be used to agree with one another. One problem with the redundancy theory is that it seems possible to think that P, without thinking that it is true that P. Another problem has to do with more interesting uses of the word 'true', such as those which allow you to agree with everything the Bible says, without needing to repeat it all. Can you explain what this problem is?

## References

Blackburn, Simon (1984). *Spreading the Word*. Oxford: Oxford University Press.

Dreier, James (1990). 'Internalism and Speaker Relativism.' *Ethics* 101(1): 6–25.

Gibbard, Allan (2003). *Thinking How to Live*. Cambridge, MA: Harvard University Press.

Hare, R.M. (1981). *Moral Thinking: Its Levels, Method, and Point*. Oxford: Oxford University Press.

Kant, Immanuel (1997). *Groundwork for the Metaphysics of Morals*. Mary Gregor, trans. Cambridge: Cambridge University Press.

Korsgaard, Christine (1996). *The Sources of Normativity*. Cambridge: Cambridge University Press.

Smith, Michael (1994b). 'Why Expressivists about Value Should Love Minimalism about Truth.' *Analysis* 54(1): 1–12.

# 9

# EPISTEMOLOGY: WISHFUL THINKING

## 9.1 Wishful thinking

So far we have been looking at a serious set of problems that confront noncognitivist theories, most of which have arisen in the philosophy of language, though some arose in the philosophy of mind. As we've seen, the Frege–Geach problem is a very central issue that has faced noncognitivist theories, and it has occupied most of our attention, as well as much of the attention of the literature. But noncognitivist theories also face significant challenges from other areas of philosophy, and in this chapter we'll turn our attention to explore one important problem that arises for noncognitivist theories in the area of *epistemology*, the study of when and how we know or are justified in believing things. In particular, we'll focus on a particular problem identified by Cian Dorr (2002) known as the *wishful thinking problem*. Fortunately, in contrast to the Frege–Geach problem, about which thousands of pages have been written over at least seventy years, the wishful thinking problem is a relatively new problem, and very little has been written about it, so it is possible to very quickly get up to speed.

The idea behind the wishful thinking problem is that intuitively, we ordinarily think that forming beliefs about what the world is like only on the basis of your desires about how you would like things to be is a kind of irrationality – it is 'wishful thinking'. But if expressivism is right, then it should sometimes be rational to form beliefs about what the world is like on the basis, essentially, of desires. You do this whenever you accept the conclusion of a *moral-descriptive modus ponens* argument on the basis of accepting its premises.

For example, consider the following moral-descriptive *modus ponens* argument, borrowed from Dorr's original article:

**P1**  If lying is wrong, the souls of liars will be punished in the afterlife.
**P2**  Lying is wrong.
**C**   The souls of liars will be punished in the afterlife.

It is intuitively possible for someone (let's follow Dorr in calling him 'Edgar') to rationally come to accept the conclusion of this argument, for the very first time, on the basis of reasoning from these premises. For example, Edgar might start by accepting P1 and at the time have no other evidence for C, and then later come to accept P2 – at which point he may rationally go on to infer C.

All of this is very intuitive. But it presents expressivists with a dilemma. Either all of this is right, and Edgar really *can* rationally come to accept C on the basis of P2, having started out only by accepting P1, or it is not right, and Edgar cannot rationally come to accept C on this basis. If it is *not* right, then that is its own problem, because on the face of it, this is a completely rational inference. So on the first fork of the dilemma, the expressivist fails to explain the rationality of what is intuitively a perfectly rational inference. But if it *is* right, then by expressivism's lights, it is rational for Edgar to form an ordinary descriptive belief about the world – for after all, to accept C is to have an ordinary descriptive belief about what will happen to the souls of liars in the afterlife – on the basis of a desire-like attitude – for after all, according to expressivists, to accept P2 is simply to have a desire-like attitude. But in that case, it looks like wishful thinking. So on the second fork of the dilemma, the expressivist is committed to allowing that wishful thinking is sometimes rational.[1]

The problem, as stated, is a problem specifically for expressivism, rather than for other forms of noncognitivism. It is expressivists who think that coming to accept P2 involves coming to want something – to have a certain desire-like attitude. And the charge, on the second fork of the dilemma, is that it is *wishful thinking* to come to accept a conclusion about the world on the basis of a change in what you want. So the charge is one that applies specifically to expressivists. But there is a related problem for other kinds of noncognitivist view. Suppose, for example, that coming to accept P2 is a matter of issuing a special sort of command, or of trying to create a special sort of influence, as other kinds of noncognitivist views hold. Now, someone who changes her mind about what the world is like only in order to fit better with the commands she is issuing, or only in order to fit better with the influence that she is trying to create, is not engaged in something that we would ordinarily call 'wishful thinking', precisely. But it does not appear to be any more rational of her to do so. Moreover, *any* view on which coming to accept P2 is different from coming to have any new belief or other cognitive state would appear to have this same general property – how could that make it rational to draw a conclusion about how things are? So it looks like the wishful thinking problem generalizes to a problem for any sort of noncognitivist view. Nevertheless, I will focus on the case of expressivism, just to fix the issues.

## 9.2 The shape of the problem

It is important to appreciate the difference between the wishful thinking problem, which invites expressivists to explain the rationality of inferring C on the basis of P1 and P2, and the problem of explaining the *inference-licensing property*, discussed in Chapters 6 and 7. An argument has the inference-licensing property just in case someone who accepts its premises is ration-ally committed to going on to accepting its conclusion. Famously, it doesn't follow from this that it is actually rational for him to go on and accept the conclusion; it could be that the only rational course would be for him to stop accepting one of the premises. For example, if Edgar has much better evidence against C than he has for P1 or P2, then the rational thing is not to accept C, but to give up on P1 or P2. Or alternatively, if the only reason Edgar accepts P1 is that he is confident that P2 is false (compare: 'if the moon is made of green cheese, then I'm a billy goat'), the rational response to coming to accept P2 is to stop accepting P1 – not to accept C, even in the absence of other evidence against C.

So the inference-licensing property applies to *every* case of a *modus ponens* argument – *whenever* you accept the premises, you are rationally committed to accepting the conclusion. But only in some cases is it rational for you to discharge this commitment by going on to accept the conclusion. In other cases, the only rational way of dealing with the commitment is to give up on one of the premises.

We saw in Chapter 6 that it has been a part of the traditional Frege–Geach problem to explain the inference-licensing property, which applies to each and every case, because one of the desiderata of the Frege–Geach problem is to explain the *validity* of moral arguments, and noncognitivists have proposed to turn the usual order of explanation on its head, and to explain validity in terms of the inference-licensing property, rather than following the usual strategy of expecting the inference-licensing property to be explained by validity. But the wishful thinking problem concerns only the rationality of actually going on to accept the conclusion, which applies only in some cases. So the wishful thinking problem is not a problem about logic or about validity; it is a problem in epistemology – about justification.[2]

As just noted, the inference-licensing property applies to *every* case of a *modus ponens* argument – *whenever* you accept the premises, you are rationally committed to accepting the conclusion. But only in some cases is it rational for you to discharge this commitment by going on to accept the conclusion. In other cases, the only rational way of dealing with the commitment is to escape it by giving up on one of the premises. The problem considered in Chapters 6 and 7 was to explain the inference-licensing property, which applies to each and every case. But the wishful thinking problem concerns only the rationality of actually going on to accept the conclusion, which applies only in some cases. So I'm going to introduce a distinction between the cases in which it *is* intuitively rational for Edgar to go on to accept C – which I'll unimaginatively call the *target-included* cases – and the cases in which it is *not* intuitively rational for Edgar to go on to accept C – which I'll call the *target-excluded* cases.

Using this terminology, the first fork of the dilemma, as Dorr puts it, is that not all cases are target-excluded cases. At least some cases are *target-included* cases. We can then think of the dilemma as arising separately for each of the target-included cases. Either – on the first fork – our expressivist theory denies that it is really rational for Edgar to accept the conclusion in that case, or – on the second – our expressivist theory claims that it *is* rational for Edgar to accept the conclusion in that case, in which case Dorr argues, first, that the conclusion is adopted only because of a change in desire-like attitudes, and second, that it consequently counts as a case of wishful thinking.

It is helpful to think of the dilemma as arising separately for each case, because one way of responding to the problem is to make further assumptions about Edgar's case, and to try to use those assumptions in order to explain why Edgar's rationality in coming to accept C is not just a case of wishful thinking, because *in that case* Edgar has independent, ordinary, descriptive evidence for C, so that it is supported on the basis of Edgar's other, ordinary, descriptive beliefs, and hence not only supported on the basis of P2, his desire-like attitude. In evaluating each of the proposals that this might be the case, the important thing for us to be keeping track of is not so much whether any such explanation *works*, as whether some such explanation works for *every* target included case. All that it takes for there to be a problem is that there are *some* target-included cases for which no such explanation is possible. On the other hand, a solution to the problem along these lines would not need to offer a one-size-fits-all solution which needs to apply to each and every case – it could be that different solutions work for different sorts of case, but each target-included case is adequately covered by *some* such solution. So what we should be looking for, in evaluating these solutions, is whether they *jointly cover* the target-included cases. The closer they come to jointly covering the target-included cases, the less unintuitive residue will remain. But if any target-included cases are left over, then the wishful thinking problem will not have been completely discharged.

Now, in principle several different responses to the wishful thinking problem are possible. The first is to embrace the first fork, biting the bullet and allowing that even though a given case is *intuitively* one in which it is rational for Edgar to accept C, in fact this is really not so. A second response is to embrace the second fork, biting the bullet and agreeing that wishful thinking really is sometimes rational. A third response – which I'll say more about later on – is to agree that it is rational to accept C on the basis of no further evidence than P2 (together with P1), but to deny that this is really *wishful thinking*. But the main sort of response to the problem, offered in both published responses to date, is to try to find a way between the forks of the dilemma by arguing that in every target-included case, Edgar is in possession of ordinary descriptive evidence for C, which can justify his concluding C without it being a case of wishful thinking.

This last strategy, of course, requires an account of where Edgar's descriptive evidence for C comes from. We can distinguish two possibilities for how this might happen. Since the only thing that changes when Edgar comes to accept P2 is that he comes to have a certain desire-like attitude, the first possibility is that the *fact that Edgar has this attitude* is itself ordinary descriptive evidence that Edgar comes by for C, by coming to accept P2. David Enoch (2003) has tried to exploit this possibility, by arguing that anyone who is *justified* in accepting P1 would also be justified in inferring C from the fact that he has the attitude expressed by P2.

A second possibility is that since Edgar is *rational* in coming to accept P2 (otherwise this wouldn't be a target-included case), he must have some evidence for it. So perhaps it is Edgar's evidence for P2 which is also evidence for C, and hence which guarantees that Edgar's acceptance of C is, because it is supported by ordinary descriptive evidence, not merely wishful thinking. This second possibility is exploited by James Lenman (2003) in his response to Dorr. In section 3 we'll look at how far the first of these two possibilities can take us; then in section 4 we'll turn to the second.

## 9.3  Enoch on accepting P2

Enoch's idea is that in every target-included case, when Edgar comes to accept P2, he comes to have available an independent, purely descriptive argument for C, which can justify him in accepting C without any wishful thinking. The new premise which becomes available to Edgar when he comes to accept P2 is P2*:

**P2\***   I disapprove of lying.

And so to get a descriptive argument for C, Edgar must also have available the additional premise P1*:

**P1\***   If I disapprove of lying, the souls of liars will be punished in the afterlife.

So for Enoch's strategy to work, every target-included case must be one in which Edgar is justified in accepting P1*.

His strategy for establishing this is piecemeal; noting that it can be rational for Edgar to conclude C on the basis of P1 and P2 only if he is justified in accepting P1, Enoch proposes to consider the different ways in which Edgar could be justified in accepting P1, and for each, to argue that if that is how Edgar is justified in accepting P1, then he would also be justified in accepting P1*.[3] In this way, he proposes to cover all of the target-included cases. Rather than going through every case that Enoch considers, we can fruitfully see the flavor of his strategy by looking at one illustrative case – that in which Edgar's justification for P1 comes from inductive evidence for its universal generalization, $\forall$P1:

$\forall$**P1**   For any action A, if it is wrong to do A, then the souls of those who do A will be punished in the afterlife.

So let's walk through this case and evaluate whether someone with inductive evidence for $\forall$P1 would also have to have inductive evidence for $\forall$P1*, as Enoch claims. (The exercises will invite you to work through Enoch's arguments for his other cases.)

∀**P1*** For any action A, if I disapprove of doing A, then the souls of those who do A will be punished in the afterlife.

The reason why Enoch thinks that anyone with inductive evidence for ∀P1 would also have inductive evidence for ∀P1* is straightforward. It is that getting inductive evidence for ∀P1 involves having come across a significant series of cases of actions A, for which he thinks, 'doing A is wrong and the souls of those who do A will be punished in the afterlife', without having come across any actions, B, for which he thinks, 'doing B is wrong and the souls of those who do B will *not* be punished in the afterlife'. But, Enoch reasons, every case in which Edgar thinks, 'doing A is wrong and the souls of those who do A will be punished in the afterlife' is one in which he is in a position to recognize that he disapproves of doing A, and hence in a position to think, 'I disapprove of doing A and the souls of those who do A will be punished in the afterlife', thereby collecting inductive evidence for ∀P1*.

This is clearly a very clever idea. But we should be suspicious of it. For one thing, the very same sort of reasoning would seem to predict that anyone is justified in accepting the following thesis:

**hubris**    For any action A, doing A is wrong just in case I disapprove of doing A.

But surely expressivists should not accept a 'friendly suggestion' which leads to this hubristic prediction – in fact, as we saw in Chapter 4, one of the primary initial motivations for expressivism is to *avoid* endorsing claims like hubris.

In fact it turns out not to be hard to see that Enoch's reasoning is problematic in at least a couple of places. First, whenever Edgar thinks that doing A is wrong without thinking that he disapproves of doing A, he will collect inductive evidence for ∀P1 without collecting inductive evidence for ∀P1*. Second, it is possible – even rationally possible – for Edgar to be wrong about what he disapproves of. Suppose, for example, that Edgar does not disapprove of viewing pornography, but that consultation with his trusted psychotherapist has led him to believe that he does. And suppose, moreover, that Edgar further thinks that the souls of pornography-viewers are not, as it turns out, punished in the afterlife. In that case, Edgar will accept 'I disapprove of viewing pornography and the souls of pornography-viewers will not be punished in the afterlife' and hence be in possession of conclusive counterevidence for $\forall P1^*$, without being in possession of any counterevidence for $\forall P1$. So he could be inductively justified in accepting $\forall P1$ without being inductively justified in accepting $\forall P1^*$.

Enoch's reasoning can also go wrong in a third way. Even if Edgar justifiably thinks that he disapproves of something in precisely all and only the cases in which he does justifiably disapprove of it, things can still go wrong. And that is because the appropriateness of inductive inferences depends on the suitability of the predicates that are being applied – on their *projectability*. Observation of a series of eagles to determine whether they fly will lead to a successful generalization to the effect that eagles fly. But observation of the same series of birds to see whether birds fly will not lead to a successful generalization. You might observe many birds which do fly, and generalize that all do, but the class of birds is heterogeneous with respect to locomotion in a way that the class of eagles is not. Enoch's reasoning requires the inductive evidence to work equally well when Edgar generalizes on what he thinks, as when he generalizes on what is wrong. But there does not seem to be any *a priori* reason to think that this is so. In fact, Edgar may explicitly think that it is not.

So in conclusion, it doesn't look like Enoch's account could apply to *all* cases in which Edgar is inductively justified in accepting P1. Of course, it might, for all that, apply to *some* such cases. But it doesn't look like it will succeed at covering the full range of target-included cases. Some of the exercises will guide you through generalizing this result to some of the other ways in which Edgar could be justified in accepting P1 and through following up on some of the details.

## 9.4  Lenman on evidence for P1 and P2

On the face of it, it shouldn't be too surprising that Enoch's strategy ran into trouble. For it doesn't even make use of the full set of resources that ought to be available for explaining how Edgar is justified in accepting C. As Enoch points out, it is rational for Edgar to accept C on the basis of P1 and P2 only if he is *justified* in accepting P1 and P2. But Enoch's explanations only appeal to the assumption that Enoch is justified in accepting P1 – no work is done by the assumption that Edgar is justified in accepting P2 – only by the assumption that Edgar *does* in fact accept P2. This means that Enoch's strategy both overgeneralizes and leaves explanatory resources on the table – it over-generalizes, because it explains why Edgar is rational to draw the conclusion even in target-excluded cases in which Edgar is unjustified in accepting P2, and it leaves explanatory resources on the table, because it makes no use of the assumption that Edgar is justified in accepting P2. So a different strategy hopes to explain why Edgar always has ordinary descriptive evidence for C in target-included cases, by trying to show that the evidence Edgar has for P1 and P2 must itself be descriptive evidence for C. I think this is the right way to understand the strategy taken by James Lenman (2003), in his reply to Dorr.

Lenman actually adopts a very strong version of this strategy; he holds that whenever Edgar is justified in accepting both P1 and P2, it is on the basis of beliefs which, *independently of P1 and P2*, can be used to directly argue for C. The clearest example that he gives for how this might work is the following argument:

R1    Derek never contravenes the Decalogue.
R2    All and only contraventions of the Decalogue are wrong.
R3    Therefore: Derek never does anything wrong.
R4    Therefore: if looking at a woman with lustful intent is wrong, then Derek never looks at a woman with lustful intent.
R5    Looking at a woman with lustful intent contravenes the Decalogue.
R6    Therefore: Looking at a woman with lustful intent is wrong.
R7    Therefore: Derek never looks at a woman with lustful intent.[4]

In the example, R4 and R6 constitute a moral–descriptive *modus ponens* argu-ment for R7 (just like Edgar's argument for C). But R4 is justified on the basis of R1 and R2, and R6 is justified on the basis of R2 and R5, and R1 and R5 (which are part of the justification of R4 and R6) constitute an inde-pendent, direct, descriptive argument for R7. So given the way that R4 and R6 are justified, coming to accept R7 on the basis of R4 and R6 can't lead Edgar any more astray than his beliefs have already led him – because it is independently supported by R1 and R5.

Lenman's case shows that there are at least *some* examples of target-included cases which needn't involve wishful thinking in any objectionable way. So it solves the problem for at least some cases. But recall that there is still a problem, unless Lenman's solution covers *all* target-included cases. This is exactly what Lenman claims his solution can do. He alleges that *all* target-included cases are like this case, except perhaps simply a little bit more complicated. What Lenman says is that if Edgar does *not* have background beliefs which guarantee that he is in possession of an independent descriptive argument for C, then

> in *that* case the noncognitivist may readily concede that Edgar, so characterized, is irrational. Such a concession is altogether harmless, as it is *independently* highly plausible – *whether we are noncognitivists or not*. If Dorr insists on considering a case where this disconnection is total, we get irrationality by *anybody's* standards.[5]

Lenman is saying here that every case which doesn't meet the condition laid down in his account should be classified as being a target-*excluded* case – one in which it is intuitively irrational for Edgar to come to accept the conclusion of the argument, anyway.

This is intuitively quite a surprising claim. There is no reason to suspect that in *non-moral* arguments, someone is rational in accepting their conclusion only if they are in possession of some further, different argument which would independently justify its conclusion. In fact, that *can't* be the case, because it would lead to a vicious regress. Some arguments have to support their conclusions without the help of further arguments, or no arguments would support their conclusions at all. So if Lenman's assumption is true of moral–descriptive *modus ponens* arguments, that would be quite a surprising and restrictive conclusion.

It is important to distinguish Lenman's thesis that the evidence for P1 and P2 must provide an *independent* justification for C from the weaker and more plausible thesis that the evidence for P1 and P2 must provide a justification for C. This latter thesis is compelling because since C follows from P1 and P2, any evidence sufficient to justify both of them would also be sufficient, *derivatively*, to justify C by way of justifying P1 and P2. What Lenman's solution requires is the stronger thesis that there must be a *direct* argument from the evidence for P1 and P2 to C, as in his Decalogue case. This is what we've seen no reason to think is satisfied in the full range of target-included cases.[6]

Still, a weaker way of pursuing a strategy similar to Lenman's would be to agree that even if C is only justified *through* P1 and P2, this isn't really wishful thinking, if these are ultimately based on further descriptive evidence. The problem with this line – and presumably the reason why Lenman doesn't take it – is that it means that forming beliefs about the world *by way of* desire-like attitudes is non-conservative, in the sense that it can take you to conclusions about the world which you could not otherwise reach. This does seem to have the full flavor of Dorr's worry about wishful thinking.

Even so, there is a deeper limitation to this approach, as well. It is one thing to point out that Edgar isn't rational in accepting C on the basis of P1 and P2 unless he is justified in accepting P1 and in accepting P2. And it is one thing to argue that Edgar is justified in accepting P2 only if he has evidence for P2. But it is another thing to claim that Edgar's evidence for P2 must all be ordinary descriptive evidence, based in beliefs about the world, rather than in further normative judgments. If Edgar's evidence for P2 itself comes from a further normative premise, then we have merely put off the problem – not solved it. So someone who wants to pursue this strategy must hold that it is not normative evidence all of the way down.

In contrast, an ordinary cognitivist theorist can happily accept that our evidence for moral theories can itself be normative – at least in part – all of the way down, without needing to be ultimately justified by ordinary descriptive evidence. Or she can remain neutral on whether this is possible. (In fact, one way of understanding David Hume's famous observation that no 'ought' can be derived from an 'is', sometimes called 'Hume's Law', is as the observation that part of the evidence for any normative claim *must* in fact be some further normative claim.) So this means that adopting this strategy is highly constraining for an expressivist. It forces her to accept conditions which – contra Lenman – it is not at all clear that cognitivists would want to accept, or even clear that they are at all plausible.

## 9.5 The second fork?

So it seems that neither Enoch's nor Lenman's suggestions do quite what they are presented as doing. But it does seem to me that it is worth thinking about the merits of the second fork of the dilemma. A first observation is that 'wishful thinking' is something of a persuasive definition. True cases of wishful thinking are cases of wanting it to be the case that p, and coming to believe that p. That is clearly a bad way of going, and deserves a special name. But it is not obvious that the connection between P2 and C looks like this, unless it turns out that 'lying is wrong' expresses the state of wanting the souls of liars to be punished in the afterlife. So it could be that some cases of getting to descriptive conclusions from, among other things, a desire-like attitude, are not as bad as the paradigm cases of wishful thinking, and hence the name of the problem is itself efficacious in dissuading us from the second fork. If so, it would seem, we should be cautious.

A second observation is that even though Dorr describes cases in which Edgar starts by accepting P1 and comes to accept P2, his acceptance of P1 is not, itself, irrelevant to the justification for C. But though it is clear that accepting P2 is just having a desire-like attitude, it is not clear what sort of state is involved with accepting P1, until an adequate expressivist solution to the embedding problem and account of logical inconsistency and logical entailment is on the table. Whatever such a state turns out to be like, it will have to have the property that it can be involved in joint inconsistency with both beliefs and desire-like attitudes at the same time. It must turn out, for example, that it is inconsistent to be in the state expressed by P1, the desire-like attitude expressed by P2, and the belief expressed by the negation of C. It is very puzzling how there could be any state that could make this so, and that is an important part of why an especially hard part of the embedding problem is to give an account that deals with mixed moral–descriptive conditionals.

It is possible, therefore, that expressivists should embrace the second fork of the dilemma and argue that this is nevertheless sufficiently different from the ordinary cases of wishful thinking that it is not at all obvious that whatever is so bad about such ordinary cases carries over. This strategy would need to be explored much further in order to see whether it could be viable.

## 9.6 Other problems in epistemology

In this chapter, we've considered one significant problem for noncognitivism in epistemology – the wishful thinking problem. I have focused on it because it is relatively new and interesting and because the responses to date on behalf of noncognitivism have been intriguing but less than convincing and it is not clear what satisfactory view could come out of it. But there are a variety of other significant problems for noncognitivists in epistemology. For example, throughout the discussion in this chapter, Enoch and Lenman assumed that within a noncognitivist framework, it will make sense to talk about 'evidence' for P1 and P2, and assumptions that 'justify' Edgar in accepting one or the other. But it is very obscure what account can be given of evidence for P2, on an expressivist view, or of what it is to be justified in one's moral views, as opposed to being justified in an ordinary descriptive belief.

Moreover, it would appear that a complete noncognitivist epistemology would need to provide a single account of evidence that would apply to both descriptive and moral conclusions. If we use a single word, 'evidence', to talk about both, this would require giving a semantics for 'evidence' from which both the proper account of descriptive evidence and the proper account of moral evidence fall out as special cases. And then this account would need to defend its account of moral evidence against objections of the form that it fails to validate standard platitudes about evidence, such as that evidence that p must be a true consideration that makes it more likely that p. And of course, in order to evaluate that, we would first need to know what it would be for a moral claim to be likely or unlikely.

Similarly, noncognitivists owe a special account of how to make sense of justification and knowledge within a noncognitivist framework. Allan Gibbard has begun to spell out an expressivist account of knowledge (2003, chapter 11), but his account leaves several puzzles and many questions unanswered. All in all, noncognitivists are only beginning to tackle the issues that arise in epistemology, given their view. And with good cause: if someone knows something only if they truly believe it, then providing an expressivist account of knowledge will be at least as hard as providing an expressivist account of belief and providing an expressivist account of truth, put together – but we spent two chapters, Chapters 5 and 8, just working on those topics. And that still leaves out whatever further condition is required to turn true belief into knowledge, which epistemologists have had enough trouble understanding, even on the assumption that noncognitivism is false. So all told, there are excellent reasons to expect the epistemological issues facing expressivism to be very difficult, as well as being particularly difficult to resolve without first resolving the issues about logic, truth, and belief considered in earlier chapters. Still, despite their difficulty, these are distinct and further problems for noncognitivists.

## Chapter summary

In this chapter we encountered Cian Dorr's wishful thinking problem for noncognitivism. We explored the responses given by David Enoch and James Lenman, as well another kind of response. And we saw how the problem is connected to more general problems in epistemology for noncognitivism, and some of the reasons why those problems are extremely difficult.

## Further reading

This chapter is designed to be read along with Dorr (2002), Enoch (2003), and Lenman (2003). For further reading on noncognitivist views in epistemology, a good place to start is Gibbard (2003, chapter 11).

Ridge (2006) discusses incidentally the ability of his hybrid noncognitivist view to avoid the wishful thinking problem, an issue that will come up in Chapter 10.

## Exercises

1    E *Comprehension*: What is the difference between the wishful thinking problem and the problem of explaining the inference-licensing property?

2    E *Comprehension*: Why shouldn't the expressivist just say that Edgar is *not* ever justified in inferring C under conditions like this?

3    E *Extensions*: One of the problems with Enoch's proposal in section 3 was that how appropriate an inductive argument is depends on the *projectability* of the predicate that is being observed. One predicate is more *projectable* than another just in case it makes inductive inferences more appropriate. Nelson Goodman illustrated this problem by considering a predicate like 'grue', which is defined to mean: 'either first observed before January 1, 2100 and green, or first observed only after January 1, 2100 and blue'. Every emerald that has ever been observed has been green – so that is evidence that all emeralds are green. But every emerald that has ever been observed has also been first observed before January 1, 2100, and so they are also all grue. So that would seem to be evidence that every emerald is grue. What color do you expect emeralds discovered in the twenty-second century to be – green or blue? Why is this evidence that some predicates must be more projectable than others?

4    M *Extensions*: Induction is not the only way of being justified in accepting P1; another way of being justified in accepting P1 is by understanding the underlying mechanism that makes it true. For example, as Enoch puts it, 'Perhaps we know enough about God's character to know that it guarantees that the souls of all and only wrong-doers will be punished in the afterlife.' If so, Enoch argues, 'If God's character guarantees that all wrong-doers will be punished in the afterlife, it likewise guarantees (assuming noncognitivism, as we are entitled to do in replying to Dorr's challenge) that all those towards whom I have a certain non-cognitive attitude – the one I express by calling them wrong-doers – will be punished in the afterlife.' First explain what is tempting about Enoch's reasoning, here, and then explain what is problematic about it.

5   M *Extensions*: In section 3 I claimed that the inset thesis, hubris, can be justified by the same sort of argument that Enoch uses to justify $\forall P_1*$. Explain how this argument would go. Can you think of any reasons why one of these arguments would be more vulnerable than the other?

6   M *Extensions*: Jeremy accepts the moral theory of utilitarianism, according to which an action is wrong just in case it does not maximize happiness. Jeremy does not accept this theory because it systematizes or makes sense of his other moral beliefs, but rather started by accepting utilitarianism, and only accepts other claims about what is wrong, or what follows, if something is wrong, on the basis of this theory. Consequently, nothing could lead him to revise this theory, because his only basis for evaluating any question that has to do with morality is by reference to this theory. Evaluate Lenman's proposed solution to the wishful thinking problem by discussing whether Lenman's solution could ever fail in Jeremy's case. Would Lenman's solution work, if we were all like Jeremy? Would we *have* to be all like Jeremy in order for Lenman's solution to work? Why or why not?

7   M *Extensions*: Enoch on testimonial evidence for $P_1$, part 1. Enoch suggests that in order to be justified in accepting $P_1$ on the basis of testimony from Jon, he must be justified in thinking that Jon is reliable – that is, in accepting $R_1$:

**R1**   If Jon thinks that if lying is wrong then the souls of liars are punished in the afterlife, then if lying is wrong then the souls of liars are punished in the afterlife.

Explain how Edgar could be justified in accepting $P_1\dagger$, if he were justified in accepting both $R_1$ and $R_2$:

**R2**   If Jon thinks that lying is wrong, then lying is wrong.
**P1†**   If Jon thinks that lying is wrong, then the souls of liars are punished in the afterlife.

Would you expect someone with a justification for $R_1$ to also have a justification for $R_2$? Why or why not? Under what conditions?

8   M *Extensions*: Enoch on testimonial evidence for $P_1$, part 2. The last exercise concerns how Edgar could be justified in accepting $P_1\dagger$, a descriptive–descriptive conditional. But in order to get from there to actually being

justified in accepting C, Edgar needs a justification for accepting the ante-cedent of P1† – that Jon thinks that lying is wrong. Argue, using the kind of reasoning that Enoch exploits elsewhere, that Edgar could get this if he had a justification for accepting R3 (below). Can you come up with any explana-tion of why we should expect Edgar to have a justification for R3?

**R3**  If I think that lying is wrong, then Jon thinks that lying is wrong.

9  M  *Extensions*: Enoch on testimonial evidence for P1, part 3. Show how Edgar could get a justification for accepting the antecedent of P1† from a justification for R4:

**R4**  If lying is wrong, then Jon thinks that lying is wrong.

Enoch suggests that this is how Edgar is justified in accepting the ante-cedent of P1†, and claims that Edgar should be justified in accepting R4 because he is in a position to get testimonial evidence from Edgar about P1. Is this plausible or not? Explain either why Edgar must be at least as justified in accepting R4 as R2, or why he need not be justified in accepting R4, even though he is justified in accepting R2.

10  M  *Extensions*: Enoch on testimonial evidence for P1, part 4. Observe that R4 is, like P1, a normative–descriptive conditional, from which it follows that Enoch's new justification for normative–descriptive *modus ponens* arguments contains a normative–descriptive *modus ponens* argument as a proper part. Does this lead to a vicious regress? Why or why not? If not, does it raise any other problems? If so, what, and how serious are they?

11  D  *Extensions*: In section 3 we observed that Enoch's argument requires that 'the souls of people who do X will be punished in the afterlife' projects just as well with respect to 'I disapprove of X' as with respect to 'X is wrong'. Look for evidence against this thesis by translating 'I disapprove of X' as 'I believe that X is wrong', since the expressivist view is that believing that X is wrong is just disapproving of X.

## Partial answers

4  Hint: Try replacing 'all those towards whom I have a certain attitude – the one I express by calling them wrong-doers' with 'all those whom I believe to be wrong-doers'.

7    Hint: Could Jon be a reliable source of information about P1 without being a reliable source of information about P2?

9    Hint: Some people are rarely wrong in their views, but only because they don't have views about very many things. Explain why this is relevant.

## Morals

8    In the case in which P1 is inductively justified, from the main text, Enoch claims that Edgar's evidence for C derives from the fact that he accepts P2. But this exercise suggests that the analogous thesis is implausible in the case of knowledge by testimony. That is why Enoch resorts to a different view in the case of knowledge by testimony, explored in exercises 9 and 10.

## References

Dorr, Cian (2002). 'Non-Cognitivism and Wishful Thinking.' *Noûs* 36(1): 97–103.

Enoch, David (2003). 'How Noncognitivists Can Avoid Wishful Thinking.' *Southern Journal of Philosophy* 41: 527–45.

Gibbard, Allan (2003). *Thinking How to Live*. Cambridge, MA: Harvard University Press.

Lenman, James (2003). 'Noncognitivism and Wishfulness.' *Ethical Theory and Moral Practice* 6: 265–74.

Ridge, Michael (2006). 'Ecumenical Expressivism: Finessing Frege.' *Ethics* 116(2): 302–36.

# 10

# THE HYBRID GAMBIT

## 10.1 Pejoratives and license for optimism

In Chapters 2 through 9 we have encountered both the earlier generation of noncognitivist theories, including the emotivist theories of Ayer and Stevenson and the prescriptivism of Hare, and their more contemporary counterpart, expressivism. We also encountered major problems facing noncognitivist theories in metaphysics, epistemology, the philosophy of mind, and especially the philosophy of language. We saw the shape of these problems and where they come from, the kinds of tools available to noncognitivists of various kinds in dealing with them, and some of the reasons why noncognitivists remain optimistic that they will be able to solve these problems, even if they haven't yet done so.

The arguments that noncognitivists give that there must be some solution to their problems, even if they haven't been able to develop one, yet, are what I have called arguments for *license for optimism*. Rather than showing directly how to solve the problems for noncognitivism, arguments for license for optimism try to show that there is some other uncontroversial phenomenon which behaves much like the noncognitivists believe that moral thought or moral language behaves, but must be able to overcome the problems, somehow. So, for example, when Hare argued that there must be some way for noncognitivists to account for the meanings of complex sentences and the logical relationships between them, because there are complex imperative sentences and there are logical relationships between them, he was offering an argument for license for optimism.

In the last decade or so, some philosophers with sympathies for noncognitivism have begun to look in a different place for license for optimism. Rather than looking to expressive terms or punctuation, like Ayer, or to imperatives, like Hare, they have begun looking to pejoratives or slur terms as a model for what the meaning of moral words might be like – a development with which Stevenson, along with other early noncognitivists, would have been perfectly at home. The unfortunate thing about this development, at least for discussions in polite company, is that the slur terms which provide the best illustration of the phenomena which provide the grounds for license for optimism are quite offensive. So I won't name them, here. But you know the ones that I mean – slur words used for people of a certain race or sexual orientation are among the most powerful. Imagine, therefore, that '***' is one such offensive slur, which is applied to people who belong to a certain racial or ethnic group, which I'll just call 'R'.

Slurs like '***' provide a provocative argument for license for optimism about noncognitivism, first of all because their meaning does not seem to be exhausted by their ordinary truth-conditional content. To call someone '***', after all, is to say that they are R, but it is also to do more than that; you don't really understand the meaning of '***' unless you know that it is used only if you have a contemptuous attitude toward people who are R. This aspect of the meaning of '***' plausibly seems like it may go over and above what would be captured by a truth-conditional theory of meaning. So '***' is a good candidate for a word with at least some of the important features that noncognitivists have wanted to claim that moral words have.

Moreover, it is straightforward to observe that there are no problems about '***' corresponding to many of the problems that we have encountered for noncognitivism over the course of this book. For example, there is no puzzle about what it is to believe that Al is a ***, or why someone who believes that Al is a *** disagrees with someone who believes that Al is not a ***. Nor is there a puzzle about why believing that Al is a *** intrapersonally disagrees with believing that Al is not a ***, or about how it is possible to be more or less confident in whether Al is a ***, or to hope that or wonder whether Al is a ***, or about why believing that Al is a *** and wanting to avoid ***s is the kind of state to motivate one to avoid Al. So the problems that we encountered for noncognitivism in the philosophy of mind in

Chapter 4 all seem like they don't arise for '***', or at least like if they do, they must have solutions.

It is also easy to see that complex sentences involving '***' are straight-forwardly meaningful, no matter how they are constructed – using 'not', 'and', 'or', or 'if ... then', for example. Moreover, valid arguments involving '***' straightforwardly have both the inconsistency property and the infer-ence-licensing property. Compare:

1    Al's mother is a ***.
2    If Al's mother is a ***, then Al is a ***.
3    Al is a ***.

Someone who accepts both premises of this argument and denies its conclu-sion is intrapersonally inconsistent, and someone who accepts both of its premises is committed to its conclusion. So valid arguments involving '***' seem to have both the inconsistency property and the inference-licensing property.

Together, all of these observations license optimism that if 'wrong' were like '***', then similarly, there should be no problem about complex sentences involving 'wrong' being meaningful, or about valid arguments involving 'wrong' having the inconsistency or inference-licensing proper-ties, or about what is involved in believing that something is wrong, or why that state of mind is so much like ordinary descriptive belief.

Noncognitivist theories which attempt to make good on this source for license for optimism are known as hybrid theories, because they share some important features both with expressivist theories and with ordinary cogni-tivist theories. In particular, hybrid theories generally hold that there are two parts to the meanings of moral sentences, one of which is basically an ordi-nary descriptive content – the same sort of content as ordinary non-moral sentences have – and one of which is something extra that is special to moral sentences. Hybrid theories are not an entirely new development – we saw in Chapter 2, for example, that Stevenson's view had a 'hybrid' character, as did some other earlier noncognitivist views. But it is recently that proponents have offered the hybrid gambit more explicitly as an alternative to 'pure' noncognitivist views, able to respond to some of their problems.

Quite a few different hybrid theories have been advanced in the last decade or so, all of which in some fashion try to take advantage of the idea that the meanings of moral sentences are hybrid in this way, and many of which explicitly model themselves on pejoratives or slurs. Surveying all of these views and the particular issues that they face would be too much for this chapter, so in this chapter I will simplify things somewhat by focusing on hybrid theories which are versions of *expressivism*. Such theories hold, as do the pure expressivist theories that we encountered in earlier chapters, that the meaning of sentences is given by the mental states that they express. But rather than holding that sentences express only one state of mind, the hybrid theory holds that sentences can express more than one state of mind, and that one of these states of mind is always an ordinary descriptive belief.

So, 'Al is a ***' differs in meaning from 'Al is R', because while both express the ordinary descriptive belief that Al is R, 'Al is a ***' also expresses a certain further attitude. Consequently, someone who accepts 'Al is a ***' has more than the ordinary descriptive belief that Al is R – she also has this certain further attitude. Similarly, hybrid expressivists will say, 'murder is wrong' may have some ordinary non-moral counterpart sentence, 'murder is K', such that both express the ordinary descriptive belief that murder is K. But they differ in meaning, because 'murder is wrong' also expresses a certain further desire-like attitude. Consequently, someone who accepts 'murder is wrong' has more than an ordinary descriptive belief that murder is K – she also has a certain further desire-like attitude.

## 10.2 Cheap advantages of hybrid theories

It turns out that hybrid expressivist theories – that is, theories according to which moral sentences express both ordinary descriptive beliefs and also desire-like attitudes – can solve all of the problems for noncognitivism about which the example of pejorative terms like '***' gives us license for optimism. But it is important to understand *how* hybrid theories evade these problems, and why. Understanding this will help us to understand why pejoratives do not give rise to those problems, and also to understand which of the advantages of traditional noncognitivist theories can be retained by hybrid theories.

It is useful to divide the problems for ordinary noncognitivist theories which the hybrid theories evade into two categories. In the first category are problems which hybrid theories evade simply because they are hybrid: that is, simply because they hold that moral sentences express beliefs. The solutions to these problems are indifferent to the fact that moral sentences also express desire-like attitudes; they are neither helped nor hindered by any desire-like attitude expressed by moral sentences, and it does not matter whether moral sentences express desire-like attitudes, or which desire-like attitudes they express, if they do, in order for us to understand why hybrid theories escape these problems. In the second category are problems which hybrid theories can evade if they make the right assumptions about which desire-like attitude is expressed by moral sentences. The assumption which enables hybrid theorists to evade the problems in the second category is one which models them closely on pejoratives. In the remainder of section 2, we'll see how hybrid theories escape the problems in the first category; then in section 3 we'll see why the problems in the second category are still left over, and what further assumption is needed to avoid them.

We may start by noting how the descriptive component in slur terms is enough, by itself, to explain the inconsistency and disagreement relations between sentences involving them. To see why, compare the following two sentences involving '***', each of which is paired with its descriptive component, along with 'something extra':

| sentence | meaning involves: | descriptive content | 'something extra' |
|---|---|---|---|
| **3** Al is a ***. | $\Rightarrow$ | Al is R. | +?+?+ |
| **4** Al is not a ***. | $\Rightarrow$ | Al is not R. | +?+?+ |

If accepting a sentence containing a slur like '***' involves having an ordinary descriptive belief in its descriptive content, then if Bert accepts 'Al is a ***' and Ernie accepts 'Al is not a ***', Bert and Ernie's disagreement can be explained in terms of the fact that they have ordinary descriptive beliefs with inconsistent contents, and hence in terms of the disagreement properties of ordinary descriptive belief. To get this explanation to work, we don't need to make any assumptions about any other kind of attitude involving disagreement, and we don't even need to know what the 'something extra' involved in pejorative sentences is. Similarly, the fact that it would be intrapersonally inconsistent for Bert to accept both 'Al is a ***' and 'Al is not a ***' at one and the same time can be explained in terms of the fact that to do so would involve having ordinary descriptive beliefs with inconsistent contents – and hence in terms of the properties of ordinary descriptive belief. To get this explanation to work, we don't need to make any assumptions about any other kind of attitude being subject to intrapersonal inconsistency, and we don't even need to know what the 'something extra' is.

The same sort of reasoning allows us to see why valid arguments involving slur terms like '***' have the inconsistency property, as we can observe by diagramming two more sentences:

| sentence | meaning involves: | descriptive content | 'something extra' |
|---|---|---|---|
| **1** Al's mother is a ***. | ⇒ | Al's mother is R. | +?+?+ |
| **2** If Al's mother is a ***, then Al is a ***. | ⇒ | If Al's mother is R, then Al is R. | +?+?+ |

Sentences 1 and 2 together make a valid argument for 3, so it should be rationally inconsistent to accept 1, accept 2, and deny 3 – that is, accept 4. But it is easy to see why that would be: accepting 1 involves having the ordinary descriptive belief that Al's mother is R, accepting 2 involves having the ordinary descriptive belief that if Al's mother is R, then Al is R, and accepting 4 involves having the ordinary descriptive belief that Al is not R. But those three ordinary descriptive beliefs are rationally inconsistent to have at the same time. So valid arguments involving slurs like '***' have the inconsistency property for the very same reason that valid arguments involving ordinary descriptive terms do. Whatever extra is involved with the distinctive meaning of the slur doesn't hinder this, and it doesn't help, either – it is just an extra wheel.

Let's look at one more advantage of the slur model that does not turn on what the 'something extra' amounts to – on what desire-like attitude is expressed by moral sentences. In Chapter 9 we learned about Cian Dorr's challenge to noncognitivists to address the charge that they license wishful thinking. The problem arose as a result of moral–descriptive *modus ponens* arguments like the following:

P1    If lying is wrong, the souls of liars will be punished in the afterlife.
P2    Lying is wrong.
C     The souls of liars will be punished in the afterlife.

The problem was that it is sometimes rational to come to accept the conclusion of arguments like this one on the basis of accepting their premises. But according to ordinary, pure expressivism, someone who starts by accepting only P1, and then comes to accept P2, only changes in their desire-like attitudes. So coming to accept C on that basis seems to be like a case of wishful thinking – forming a belief about what the world is like only on the basis of what one wants it to be like.

Fortunately, it is easy to see how hybrid theories solve this problem. And like the last couple of problems, all that we need to know, in order to see how, is that moral words have some descriptive content. If moral words have a descriptive content, coming to accept P2 is *not* just a matter of coming to have a desire-like attitude. It is a matter of coming to have an *ordinary descriptive belief* plus something else. As with the problems just discussed, we don't even need to know what the 'something else' is, in order to see why this helps. Since coming to accept P2 involves coming to have a belief, accepting C on the basis of accepting P1 and P2 is ipso facto not a case of wishful thinking – for it is based in part on an ordinary descriptive belief.

In this section we've been seeing why slurs do not lead to problems about inconsistency or disagreement, why there is no problem about how arguments involving slurs could have the inconsistency property, and why arguments involving slurs do not license wishful thinking. All of these things can be easily explained simply on the basis of the assumption that sentences involving slurs have ordinary descriptive contents. If there is more to the meaning of slur terms than these ordinary descriptive contents, it neither helps nor hinders these explanations. So if moral terms are like slur terms in both having ordinary descriptive contents and also having 'something extra' to their meanings, then that would explain the facts about inconsistency, disagreement, and wishful thinking for *moral* arguments. But in section 3 we'll turn our attention to our second category of potential advantages of hybrid theories, where it turns out that the fact that there is 'something extra' to the meaning of slur terms definitely has the potential to get in the way.

## 10.3  What is the 'something extra'?

Any ordinary cognitivist theory holds that when you accept 'stealing is wrong', you have an ordinary descriptive belief. In section 2 we saw why, by endorsing this view as well, hybrid theorists can solve many of the problems facing ordinary noncognitivists – in particular, the problems relating to inconsistency and disagreement and the wishful thinking problem. But what distinguishes hybrid theories from ordinary cognitivist theories is that they hold that there is something *more* going on with moral sentences – in particular, that you need to do more in order to accept a moral sentence than to have an ordinary descriptive belief – you also need to have a certain desire-like attitude. In this section we'll see why some of the potential advantages of hybrid theories depend on *what* this desire-like attitude turns out to be.

If an argument has the inconsistency property, then it is inconsistent for someone who accepts the premises to *deny* the conclusion. So if there is some kind of rational pressure to *either* accept or deny the conclusion, or at least to do one if the other is not an option, then someone who accepts the premises will be under rational pressure to accept the conclusion. So for any argument with a conclusion which people are committed to either accepting or denying, having the inconsistency property is sufficient for having the inference-licensing property. But unfortunately, if accepting a moral sentence requires *more* than just having a belief, then we should not expect moral sentences to be ones which people are committed to either accepting or denying.

To see why, consider the sentence, 'Al is a *** or Al is not a ***'. If you don't have the contemptuous attitude toward people who are R that is expressed by 'Al is a ***', then you won't accept either 'Al is a ***' or 'Al is not a ***' – '***' simply won't be one of your words. So you won't accept 'Al is a *** or Al is not a ***', either. Consequently, the fact that it would be rationally inconsistent of you to accept 'Al is not a ***' wouldn't do anything to show that you are rationally committed to accepting 'Al is a ***'. So the inconsistency property is not enough, by itself, to establish the inference-licensing property, when sentences express more than one attitude.

Let's remind ourselves of what it would take for a hybrid theory to establish the inference-licensing property. Recall that according to the hybrid theory, sentences involving 'wrong' express both an ordinary descriptive belief and a desire-like attitude, and that accepting the sentence requires having both the ordinary descriptive belief and the desire-like attitude. For example, if the descriptive content of 'wrong' is K, then the sentences involved in a moral *modus ponens* argument might look like this:

| sentence | expresses: | belief | attitude |
|---|---|---|---|
| **5** Stealing is wrong. | $\Rightarrow$ | Stealing is K. | $D_1$ |
| **6** If stealing is wrong, then murder is wrong. | $\Rightarrow$ | If stealing is K, murder is K. | $D_2$ |
| **7** Murder is wrong. | $\Rightarrow$ | Murder is K. | $D_3$ |

This argument has the inference-licensing property just in case accepting its premises commits someone to accepting its conclusion – that is, just in case the ordinary descriptive beliefs that stealing is K and that if stealing is K, then murder is K, together with desire-like attitudes D1 and D2, commit someone to the ordinary descriptive belief that murder is K and desire-like attitude D3.

It is easy to see how accepting the premises commits someone to the belief expressed by the conclusion, because the relationship between the three beliefs is the same as that in an ordinary, non-moral *modus ponens* argument. So as long as ordinary, non-moral arguments have the inference-licensing property, accepting the premises of this argument will commit someone to having the *belief* expressed by its conclusion. So the argument will have the inference-licensing property *full stop* just in case it is possible to explain why they would also be committed to having desire-like attitude D3. Notice that this *depends on what D3 is*. None of the advantages of hybrid theories canvassed in section 2 depended on what desire-like attitudes are expressed by moral sentences, but the inference-licensing property depends closely on what D1, D2, and D3 turn out to be.

The easiest way to see how to solve this problem is to look to the example of pejoratives, which we saw *did* satisfy the inference-licensing property. The reason why arguments involving pejoratives like '\*\*\*' have the inference-licensing property is that in arguments involving pejoratives, the desire-like attitude expressed by the conclusion is always expressed by one of the premises. And that is because every sentence involving a slur like '\*\*\*' expresses the very same contemptuous attitude toward people who are R. If you say 'Al is a \*\*\*' you express this contemptuous attitude toward people who are R, and if you say 'Al is not a \*\*\*' you express the same attitude. Similarly, you express this attitude if you say 'if I'm not mistaken, then Al is a \*\*\*', or 'if Al's mother is a \*\*\*, then Al is a \*\*\*', or 'if Al is a \*\*\*, then I'm not going to talk to him'. It doesn't matter where '\*\*\*' appears in a sentence – sentences involving '\*\*\*' always express one and the same contemptuous attitude.

That is why someone who accepts the premises of the following argument is rationally committed to its conclusion:

1    Al's mother is a \*\*\*.
2    If Al's mother is a \*\*\*, then Al is a \*\*\*.
3    Al is a \*\*\*.

Even though it takes both a belief and a desire-like attitude to accept 3, someone who accepts 1 and 2 already has the contemptuous attitude needed in order to accept 3. So the only thing it takes for *her* to accept 3 is to form the belief that Al is R. But that belief is one that she is committed to, in virtue of the beliefs that she has by accepting 1 and 2 – namely, the beliefs that Al's mother is R, and that if Al's mother is R, then Al is R. So someone who accepts the premises of this argument is committed to its conclusion.

So hybrid theories according to which every sentence containing 'wrong' – no matter where it appears in the sentence – expresses the very same attitude can also account for the inference-licensing property of *modus ponens*, and more generally, of other valid arguments (although see the exercises for one important qualification). This is an advantage of hybrid theories over ordinary noncognitivist views, because as we saw in earlier chapters, ordinary noncognitivist views actually have significant trouble explaining why moral arguments have the inference-licensing property.

This is a very different view about the desire-like attitudes expressed by moral sentences than that of ordinary, non-hybrid expressivism – which is a very important thing to understand, in order to appreciate the differences between these two kinds of views. According to ordinary, non-hybrid, expressivist theories, such as those of Blackburn and Gibbard, 'stealing is wrong' and 'lying is wrong' express different attitudes – one toward stealing, and one toward lying. They have to say this, because on their view, what makes the two sentences have different meanings is that they express different states of mind, and the only state of mind they express is a desire-like attitude. Hence, the desire-like attitudes that they express must be different. Hybrid theories which take their cue from pejoratives, in contrast, hold that 'stealing is wrong' and 'lying is wrong' have different meanings because their *descriptive* component is different. But both express the very same desire-like attitude, an attitude which is neither toward stealing nor toward lying.

Moreover, this same idea – that all sentences containing 'wrong' express the very same desire-like attitude – also makes the Frege–Geach problem far, far, easier. If complex sentences containing moral words express the very same attitudes as their parts do, then the compositional rules for the meanings of complex sentences will be very simple, and will consist of two parts. The first part will compose the descriptive part of the meaning of the complex sentence as a function of the descriptive contents of its parts – and for these recipes, the hybrid theorist can simply use the very same recipes that are used by the ordinary truth-conditional semanticist. And the second part will simply say that if any of the parts express a desire-like attitude, then the complex sentence expresses that desire-like attitude, too. This is about as simple as a noncognitivist recipe for the meaning of complex sentences could be, and it is at least highly plausible that something like this is going on with the meanings of pejorative words like '***'.

## 10.4  The advantages of noncognitivism

So far in this chapter, we've seen that a hybrid theory which models moral words like 'wrong' on the meaning of pejoratives like the racial slur '***' can avoid some of the potential pitfalls facing other noncognitivist theories. The tradeoff facing hybrid theories, however, is that it is not clear whether they can retain the advantages which interested us in noncognitivism in the first place. Recall that we were interested in noncognitivism for two different kinds of potential theoretical advantages. First, there were the domain-neutral *core questions* from metaphysics, epistemology, the philosophy of language, and the philosophy of mind which noncognitivism held promise of helping us to evade. And second, there were the domain-specific problems of metaethics, specifically including the motivation problem. On both counts, a hybrid theory which models moral terms closely on pejoratives loses some of the distinctive features of noncognitivism which made it look like an answer to, or a way of evading, these problems.

Take first the problem from moral metaphysics, of being able to say what it is for something to be wrong. Ordinary 'pure' noncognitivist theories could evade this question by saying that there is nothing that it is for something to be wrong — calling it 'wrong' or thinking that it is wrong is just having or expressing or advocating a certain attitude toward it. Let's try this out in terms of '***':

> There is nothing that it is for someone to be a *** — calling her 'a ***' or thinking that she is a *** is just having or expressing or advocating a certain attitude toward her.

Unfortunately, that's not exactly right. Someone can't be a *** unless she is R — so there is something that it is to be a ***. Of course, in a sense that's not *all* it is to be a *** — to call someone a *** is to do more than simply say that she is R — it is also to express a certain contemptuous attitude toward people who are R. But it is also, at least in part, to say that she is R. So if moral terms work like '***', then there will be something that it is for something to be wrong, too. And whatever that is, we can still ask our question about moral metaphysics about it: what is it for something to be this way – the way that we are saying it is, when we say that it is wrong?

In addition to the question about metaphysics, this leaves us with our original question about moral epistemology, as well. If there is some way that we are (at least in part) saying that things are, when we say that they are wrong, then how do we find out that something is this way? And similarly, we still get our old questions from the philosophy of mind and the philosophy of language: how do we manage to talk about this way that things are, and how do we manage to think about it, in the first place?

We are also still left with a problem about moral motivation. This is somewhat surprising, because you might think that if thinking that something is wrong involves having a desire-like attitude as well as an ordinary descriptive belief, then that should lead to an explanation of why someone who thinks that something is wrong would be motivated not to do it – the desire-like attitude, along with the belief, motivates her not to do it. That sounds, on the face of it, like the right kind of thing to explain why someone who thinks that stealing is wrong would be motivated not to do it.

Unfortunately, however, if moral terms are like pejoratives like '***', then that doesn't work. According to the pejorative model which enabled our explanation of the inference-licensing property in section 3, recall, every sentence containing 'wrong' expresses the very same desire-like attitude. And you accept a moral sentence only if you have that desire-like attitude. So there must be some desire-like attitude that is shared by everyone who has ever had a view about whether something is wrong or not – or even a view about under what conditions something would be wrong, or about what would follow, if something were wrong. Anyone who has ever accepted any sentence involving 'wrong' at all, that is, must have some desire-like attitude in common.

The problem is that to assume that there is some desire-like attitude that has been shared by everyone who has ever accepted any sentence involving 'wrong' is an extraordinary empirical assumption. And once we make that assumption, the further assumption that this desire-like attitude is expressed by 'wrong' doesn't appear to do any extra work in explaining why people are motivated by their moral judgments. The reason why not is that for every hybrid theory, there is a corresponding non-hybrid, ordinary cognitivist theory, according to which moral sentences have exactly the same ordinary descriptive content as the hybrid theory claims, but do not express any desire-like attitude. But like the hybrid theory, the ordinary cognitivist theory assumes that there is some desire-like attitude that is so widespread that it has been shared by everyone who has ever accepted any sentence involving the word 'wrong'. Given this assumption, the ordinary cognitivist theory can explain why people are motivated by their moral judgments just as well as the hybrid theory can – they are motivated by their beliefs, along with the background desire-like attitude that nearly everyone has.

Since every hybrid theory has an ordinary cognitivist counterpart which can offer exactly the same explanation of why moral judgments motivate as it does, the hybrid part of the theory doesn't actually do any work in solving the motivation problem. What does all of the work, is the strong empirical assumption that there is some desire-like attitude that has been shared by nearly everyone in human history – including everyone who has ever had any views about what is wrong or not. So the very assumption which enables hybrid theories to explain inference-licensing and to avoid the problems in providing a compositional semantics, as we saw in section 3, means that hybrid theories do not help explain moral motivation, after all. This is a hard dilemma for hybrid theories; the more closely they model themselves on pejoratives, the clearer it is that they escape some of the traditional problems for noncognitivism, but the less clear it is that they attain any of noncognitivism's traditional advantages.

## 10.5 The Big Hypothesis and judgment internalism

In the last section we saw that there are obstacles to a hybrid theory's being able to attain the same advantages as other noncognitivist theories, with respect to the core questions and with respect to the motivation problem. This made it look like even though hybrid theories give us excellent license for optimism about some of the problems facing other noncognitivist theories, the move to a hybrid theory also involves sacrificing some of the theoretical payoffs of noncognitivism. There are, however, some subtle advantages that hybrid theories can offer over ordinary cognitivist theories.

One of the chief of these is related to the motivation problem. According to some philosophers, it is not just an important fact that we generally expect people to be motivated to avoid doing what they think is wrong – it is somehow a conceptual truth that people will be motivated not to do what they think is wrong. In the last section we saw that each hybrid theory has an ordinary cognitivist competitor, which assigns moral sentences the very same descriptive meaning, but holds that that is all there is to their meaning, rather than requiring, as the hybrid theory does, that there is 'something more' to the meaning of moral sentences – for example, that they express a desire-like attitude. Both the hybrid theory and the ordinary cognitivist theory assume that there is some desire-like attitude that is shared by almost everyone who has ever lived, and appeal to that desire, along with the ordinary descriptive belief that someone has when she accepts a moral sentence, to explain what she is motivated to do, because she accepts that moral sentence. Both theories are committed to the empirical assumption that there is such a desire-like attitude, and so neither theory is more successful than the other at explaining why individual people are motivated by their moral judgments. But the hybrid theory can explain why it is a *conceptual truth* that people are motivated by their moral judgments.

The reasoning behind the hybrid explanation of why this is a conceptual truth goes like this: if 'stealing is wrong' expresses two mental states – both a belief and a desire-like attitude – it follows that to accept 'stealing is wrong' requires being in both mental states – having the belief and having the desire-like attitude. So (the reasoning goes) 'Elly thinks that stealing is wrong' must mean that Elly has both the belief and the desire-like attitude. In contrast, if 'stealing is wrong' expresses only one mental state – a belief – it follows that to accept 'stealing is wrong' requires being in only one mental state – having the belief. So 'Elly thinks that stealing is wrong' must mean only that Elly has the belief. So on a hybrid view, it would be *built into the meaning* of 'Elly thinks that stealing is wrong' that she has a desire-like attitude, whereas on its cognitivist counterpart, it would merely be an empirical background fact that Elly has this desire-like attitude. Consequently, a hybrid theory could claim that it follows from the *meaning* of 'wrong' that someone who thinks that stealing is wrong will be motivated not to steal, whereas according to a cognitivist theory, this is merely an empirical fact.

Notice that even the hybrid theory can say that it is at least in part due to the meaning of 'wrong' that we expect people to be motivated not to do what they think is wrong. If 'wrong' had meant something else – for example, if it had meant *unusual*, or if it had meant *required* – then beliefs about what is wrong would not have engaged a background desire-like attitude that nearly everyone has, in order to motivate people not to do what they judged 'wrong'. So what is distinctive about this hybrid explanation is not that it lets us say that it is *partly* due to the meaning of 'wrong' that we expect people to be motivated not to do what they think is wrong. The distinctive thing which this hybrid explanation lets us capture is the idea that it is wholly due to the meaning of 'wrong' that it is true that people will be motivated not to do what they think is wrong.

So if you are attracted to the idea that not only do we generally expect people to be motivated not to do what they think is wrong, but that this can be entirely predicted from the meaning of 'wrong', then this is an advantage for the hybrid theory over its ordinary cognitivist counterpart. It is important to stress that this is a subtle advantage, and it is worth being careful about whether it is one that it is really worth having. But some hybrid theorists, particularly including Daniel Boisvert, believe that this advantage, along with some other similarly subtle advantages, is worth preferring a hybrid theory to an ordinary cognitivist theory.

The chief assumption needed in order to explain why it is a conceptual truth that moral judgments motivate was the assumption that 'Elly thinks that stealing is wrong' means that Elly has both the belief expressed by 'stealing is wrong' and the desire-like attitude expressed. I call this assumption the Big Hypothesis, because it is not at all clear that pejoratives obey the analogous assumption. The analogue of the Big Hypothesis for a racial slur like '***' is the assumption that 'Annette thinks that Al is a ***' means that Annette both believes that Al is R and has the relevant contemptuous attitude toward people who are R.

To see why this is not obviously true, imagine that Bigot is a stereotypical bigot, and has a contemptuous attitude toward people who are R, whereas Nice Guy is a stereotypical nice guy, and has no contemptuous attitude whatsoever toward people who are R. Both believe that Al is R, and both recognize about each other that they have this belief, as well as that Bigot is a bigot and that Nice Guy is a nice guy. Now imagine that you ask Nice Guy what race Bigot thinks Al is. If the Big Hypothesis holds for '***', we would expect that the appropriate answer would be 'Bigot thinks that Al is a ***' – for after all, this is what most accurately describes Bigot's view – he both believes that Al is R and has a contemptuous attitude toward people who are R, and that is what 'Bigot thinks that Al is a ***' means, according to the Big Hypothesis. But intuitively, Nice Guy would never say such a thing. He would retreat to saying, 'Bigot thinks that Al is R', and wouldn't use '***', even in describing Bigot's views. Similarly, imagine that you ask Bigot what race Nice Guy thinks Al is. If the Big Hypothesis holds for '***', we would expect that it would be inappropriate – because false – for Bigot to answer, 'Nice Guy thinks that Al is a ***', because that means not only that Nice Guy believes that Al is R, but that Nice Guy has a contemptuous attitude toward people who are

R – which Bigot knows that he does not. But intuitively, Bigot would be completely comfortable describing Nice Guy's attitude in this way. Indeed, it would be quite strange for a bigot like Bigot to make a point of saying, 'Nice Guy thinks that Al is R'.

These observations about Bigot and Nice Guy don't lend support to the idea that '***' obeys the Big Hypothesis. On the contrary, they lend support to the alternative theory that 'Annette thinks that Al is a ***' expresses two states of mind – the belief that Annette believes that Al is R and a contemptuous attitude toward people who are R. According to this alternative theory, if you don't have a contemptuous attitude toward people who are R, then '***' shouldn't be one of your words – *even to describe what other people think*. In order to glean the subtle advantage of explaining how motivational internalism could be a conceptual truth, hybrid theorists therefore need to depart from the analogy of pejoratives. Rather than being *completely* like pejoratives, hybrid theorists who want this subtle advantage should say that the desire-like attitudes expressed by moral sentences obey the Big Hypothesis.

One good example of a term which behaves in roughly the way that this kind of hybrid theorist wants is 'but'. Compare the following three sentences:

**8**   Shaq is huge but agile.
**9**   It is not the case that Shaq is huge but agile.
**10**   If Shaq is huge, then Shaq is huge but agile.
**11**   Marv thinks that Shaq is huge but agile.

As philosophers and linguists have observed for some time, the word 'but' serves in some way to indicate a contrast, but is otherwise alike in meaning to 'and'. So someone who asserts 8 indicates that Shaq is huge and agile, and also that she sees some contrast between being huge and being agile. Sentences 9 and 10 illustrate that this contrast 'projects' through environments like negation and conditionals, so that even in complex sentences in which the speaker is not committed to the truth of 'Shaq is huge and agile', she is still committed to there being a contrast between being huge and being agile. This is just like the negative attitude that is associated with slurs like '***'. But sentence 11 illustrates that when 'but' appears inside a verb like 'thinks that', the speaker is not committed to the contrast, but rather to saying that Marv thinks there is a contrast. This is like the Big Hypothesis and unlike the behavior of '***', which as we've observed in this section appears to 'project' even though attitude-ascriptions like 'thinks that'.

The most promising kind of hybrid theory, then, will not take the analogy with pejoratives too far. It will say that moral terms are in *some* ways like pejoratives, but in some ways like 'but'. They will be like pejoratives in being associated with a desire-like attitude, rather than with an assumed contrast, as 'but' is. But they will be like 'but', in that this associated desire-like attitude is expressed by *some* kinds of complex sentences involving the terms, but not by others. In particular, attitude-ascriptions like 'believes that' will report that their subject has the attitude, rather than expressing the attitude themselves. This kind of theory has yet to be fully developed, but several theorists have made progress in outlining what it would be like, and many other hybrid theories have recently been defended.

## Chapter summary

In this chapter we learned about hybrid noncognitivist theories, whose license for optimism about the problems facing noncognitivism comes largely from consideration of pejoratives like racial slurs. We saw that despite intuitively not having only purely descriptive meanings, racial slurs do not lead to many of the problems that we have seen are faced by other noncognitivist theories in the rest of this book. For each of those problems facing other noncognitivist views, we diagnosed *why* slurs do not give rise to those problems, and hence why the right sort of hybrid view can avoid them. And then we looked back at the theoretical advantages that noncognitivist theories were supposed to provide, and started to look at which of these a hybrid theory can still provide, and given what further assumptions.

## Further reading

This chapter may profitably be read along with Boisvert (2008), whose hybrid theory closely resembles the one discussed here, and Copp (2001), which played a large role in igniting the current interest in hybrid meta-ethical theories. For a significantly different sort of hybrid theory, which owes much less to the analogy with pejoratives, see Ridge (2007a,b). And for a more detailed discussion of some of the general issues facing hybrid theories, see Schroeder (2009).

# Exercises

1    E *Comprehension*: According to Michael Ridge, 'stealing is wrong' expresses approval of an ideal observer, and the belief that that ideal observer disapproves of stealing. Explain how Ridge would explain why it is rationally inconsistent to both think that stealing is wrong and think that stealing is not wrong.

2    E *Comprehension*: According to Daniel Boisvert, 'torturing the cat is wrong' is used to assert that torturing the cat is F and to express an attitude toward things that are F. Apply the explanation of why hybrid theories don't license wishful thinking to Boisvert's view.

3    E *Extensions*: 'Jerk' is another word which one might think is partly descriptive and partly expressive. Does 'jerk' obey the Big Hypothesis? Why or why not?'

4    M *Extensions*: In section 4 we observed one subtle advantage of hybrid theories. In this exercise, show how hybrid theories which accept the Big Hypothesis can attain another subtle advantage, by considering the following sentences:

   1    Max thinks that stealing fails to maximize happiness, but does Max think that stealing is wrong?
   2    Max thinks that stealing is wrong, but does Max think that stealing is wrong?
   3    Max thinks that stealing is wrong, but does Max think that stealing fails to maximize happiness?

   Assuming that the descriptive content of 'wrong' is 'fails to maximize happiness', use the Big Hypothesis to translate what each of these sentences means. Use the result to explain why sentence 1 feels 'open' in a way that neither sentence 2 nor 3 does.

5    M *New problem*: Consider the following argument:

   1    Everything Jack said is true.
   2    Jack said that stealing is wrong.
   3    Stealing is wrong.

This argument is valid. So if the hybrid theory is to explain why it has the inference-licensing property in the way that was explained in section 3, then either sentence 1 or sentence 2 needs to express the same desire-like attitude as sentence 3. What are the advantages and costs of saying that it is sentence 1? What are the advantages and costs of saying that it is sentence 2?

6   M *New problem* (continuing from exercise 5): Distinguish the inference-licensing property that an argument has just in case accepting its premises *commits* you to accepting its conclusion, from the property an argument has when accepting its premises actually makes it rational to go on and accept its conclusion (as in the wishful thinking problem). An argument can have the inference-licensing property without having this further property, if it is never rational to accept its premises because that would commit one to accepting its conclusion, and it is never rational to accept its conclusion. Explain why the argument in exercise 5 might be a good example of an argument which has the inference-licensing property but never makes it rational to go on and accept its conclusion. Does this make a difference in what is needed in order to explain why it has the inference-licensing property? Why or why not?

7   M *New problem* (continuing from exercises 5 and 6): The answer to 5 sheds light on the question of whether 'wrong' sentences obey the Big Hypothesis. Is it evidence for the Big Hypothesis, or against it? Why?

8   M *Extensions*: In earlier sections we saw reasons to think that belief ascriptions like 'Annette thinks that Al is a \*\*\*' express the contemptuous attitude toward people who are R, rather than reporting that Annette has that contemptuous attitude. Does 'Annette said that Al is a \*\*\*' work in the same way, or differently? What is your evidence?

9   M *New problem*: In Chapter 8 we encountered the transcendental noncognitivist strategy for arguing for *bivalence* for moral sentences – that is, that they are either true or false. If moral sentences express more than one state of mind, however, as hybrid theorists claim, that raises a question about whether we really should expect them to be bivalent. First illustrate this problem by discussing the case of slurs like '\*\*\*', and then consider whether it makes a difference, if, unlike slurs, moral terms obey the Big Hypothesis.

10   M *Branching out*: Recall that an argument has the inference-licensing property just in case accepting its premises rationally commits you to accepting its conclusion. In classical logic, the argument with no premises but whose conclusion is any sentence of the form 'P or ~P' is valid. If we have pejorative terms like '***' in our language, should it turn out that all classically valid arguments have the inference-licensing property? Explain why or why not.

11   M *New problem* (continuing from exercise 10): Try to use the trick from section 3 in order to explain why the argument with no premises but whose conclusion is 'stealing is wrong or stealing is not wrong' has the inference-licensing property. Do you run into trouble? Why or why not? Should this argument turn out to have the inference-licensing property, intuitively speaking? Why or why not?

12   M *Qualifications*: In section 3 of Chapter 2, we discussed whether Stevenson's theory, which had some hybrid features, still retained the advantages of noncognitivism. In this chapter, we discussed whether hybrid theories retain the advantages of noncognitivism. In Chapter 2, we concluded that since for Stevenson answering ordinary descriptive questions doesn't suffice to answer moral questions, he still retains these advantages. Does a hybrid theory which models itself closely on pejoratives, like the one discussed in this chapter, agree that answering ordinary descriptive questions doesn't suffice to answer moral questions? Why or why not?

13   D *Extensions*: In section 3 we saw that the assumption that every sentence containing 'wrong' expresses the same attitude allows us to explain the inference-licensing property, by predicting that someone who accepts the premises of a valid argument must already accept its conclusion. In this and the following exercises, you'll show why it seems like this is the only way for a hybrid theorist to be able to explain the inference-licensing property. First, in this exercise, show that if one of the premises of a *modus ponens* argument always expresses the same attitude as its conclusion, it must be the conditional premise. Show this in two different ways: first, by considering a *modus ponens* argument with a descriptive–moral conditional, and second, show that for any *modus ponens* argument in which 'P→Q' is the conditional premise, there is another *modus ponens*

argument in which it is the non-conditional premise. Explain why this proves the point.

14  D *Extensions*: Think back to the motivation problem from Chapter 1 and explain why assuming that the attitude expressed by the conclusion is identical to some combination of beliefs undermines one of the important arguments for noncognitivism.

15  D *Extensions* (continuing from exercise 14): Explain why assuming that the beliefs themselves rationally commit to the desire-like attitude expressed by the conclusion undermines one of the important arguments for noncognitivism.

16  D *Extensions* (continuing from exercises 14 and 15): Explain why assuming that the desire-like attitudes expressed by the premises *commit* to the attitude expressed by the conclusion turns the problem of explaining the inference-licensing property into the same problem that was faced by ordinary, pure expressivists.

17  D *Extensions* (continuing from exercise 16): What about the idea that the beliefs and desires *jointly* commit to the attitude expressed by the conclusion? Is that a more promising idea? Why or why not? How would it go?

18  D *Extensions* (continuing from exercises 14–17): Even if one of the preceding is a viable strategy, explain why the hypothesis that every sentence containing 'wrong' expresses the very same desire-like attitude drastically simplifies what a compositional semantics needs to do.

## Partial answers

10  Since every argument with no premises but whose conclusion has the form, 'P or ~P' is classically valid, it follows that if every classically valid argument has the inference-licensing property, then everyone whatsoever is committed to accepting every sentence of the form, 'P or ~P'. Why is that problematic, if 'P' involves a slur like '***'?

# References

Boisvert, Daniel (2008). 'Expressive-Assertivism.' *Pacific Philosophical Quarterly* 89: 169–203.

Copp, David (2001). 'Realist-Expressivism: A Neglected Option for Moral Realism.' *Social Philosophy and Policy* 18: 1–43.

Ridge, Michael (2007a). 'Ecumenical Expressivism: The Best of Both Worlds.' In Russ Shafer-Landau, ed., *Oxford Studies in Metaethics*, vol. II.

—— (2007b). 'Epistemology for Ecumenical Expressivists.' *Proceedings of the Aristotelian Society*, supplementary volume 81: 83–108.

Schroeder, Mark (2009). 'Hybrid Expressivism: Virtues and Vices.' *Ethics* 119(2): 257–309.

# 11

## PROSPECTS AND APPLICATIONS

### 11.1 What we've learned so far

In the last nine chapters we've seen that noncognitivist theories both promise a significant philosophical payoff and also face daunting problems. Both the payoff and the problems derive from noncognitivism's differences from truth-conditional theories of meaning. Truth-conditional theories of meaning explain what words mean by saying what they are *about*, and explain what sentences mean by saying what it takes for them to be *true*. Noncognitivist theories hold, on the contrary, that knowing what a moral term is about is either unnecessary or insufficient to understand what it means, and that knowing what would make a moral sentence true is either unnecessary or insufficient to understand what it means. On the plus side, this allows noncognitivist theories to finesse or evade the 'core questions' of metaethics, and to explain why moral thoughts have a special, more intimate, connection to motivation than ordinary non-moral thoughts. But on the minus side, the departure from truth-conditional semantics also means a departure from all of the great successes of truth-conditional semantics at accommodating the compositional constraint and at explaining the semantic properties of complex sentences.

Along the way, we've explored at least three different kinds of noncognitivist theory – the speech act theories of Ayer, Stevenson, and Hare, the expressivist theories of Blackburn and Gibbard, and contemporary hybrid theories. These views differ greatly from one another, but they share the basic core idea of noncognitivism: that moral words have a different kind of meaning from ordinary non-moral words. At their best, we saw that these views model themselves closely on grounds for *licensed optimism* that some words *have* to be able to have the kind of meaning that they attribute to moral words, by modeling themselves on examples taken from non-moral language. These arguments from license for optimism frame fruitful research programs, because they focus our energies by telling us where we need to look, in order to evaluate whether these views really can work, and they direct us toward what we need to improve about our theories of meaning in order to accommodate the meanings of moral words.

Just as the potential payoffs of noncognitivism come from all of the core areas of philosophy, we also saw that the problems noncognitivism faces arise in all of the core areas of philosophy, and we spent chapters focusing on problems in each of the philosophy of mind, philosophy of language, metaphysics, and epistemology. But what were plausibly the largest of those problems came from the philosophy of mind and the philosophy of language.

The problem in the philosophy of mind was to explain the nature of moral thought. This task ran into three main difficulties. The first was the *Many Attitudes* problem. The Many Attitudes problem wasn't so much its own problem, as it was an estimate of the enormous *size* of the noncognitivist task of explaining the nature of moral thought. This is a *huge* problem, because noncognitivists must not only explain the nature of moral beliefs, but also of moral hopes, moral fears, moral desires, and so on, for each and every one of the many, many attitudes that there are. The second main difficulty facing this task was the *Multiple Kinds* problem. The Multiple Kinds problem was that according to noncognitivism, for each of these attitudes, there are really at least two different *kinds* of attitude – both moral belief and ordinary descriptive belief, to take one example, and both moral hope and ordinary descriptive hope, to take another.

Noncognitivists think that these are in some way very different kinds of attitude, but in other respects they are strikingly similar. For example, moral and descriptive beliefs share the interpersonal and intrapersonal disagreement properties, as well as many features of their phenomenology, and very similar functional roles. Noncognitivists must explain why such different underlying kinds of mental state turn out to have such strikingly similar properties, and this task does not look to be made easier by the fact that from the point of view of noncognitivism, this looks like a coincidence. And the idea of inferential commitment theories that there is really an infinite hierarchy of attitudes called 'belief', rather than simply two, makes this look like a *massive* coincidence. Finally, the third main difficulty facing noncognitivist accounts of the nature of moral thought was the One Word problem. The One Word problem was really a task in the philosophy of language – it was to explain how we manage to talk about such different kinds of mental state using a single word – 'believes that'. Given the Many Attitudes problem, the sheer size of these other tasks is clearly daunting.

Meanwhile, the central problem in the philosophy of language – the Frege–Geach problem – also remains without a satisfactory solution. We saw that there were serious flaws with the kinds of *constructive* approach to this problem that are exhibited by Higher-Order Attitude accounts. We saw that there is no *formal* obstacle to inferential-commitment accounts, which pass the buck to the philosophy of mind, but we also saw that these accounts are crucially unexplanatory, and involve writing many (infinitely many, in fact) checks that they are structurally unable to cash. Finally, we saw *why* expressivists seem pushed to inferential-commitment accounts and the hierarchy of attitudes; it was the problem diagnosed by Unwin, that expressivist accounts lack sufficient *structure* to enable them to give constructive recipes for the meanings of complex sentences.

Both of these sets of problems – from the philosophy of mind, and from the philosophy of language – are quite discouraging about the prospects both of expressivism and of noncognitivism more generally. If expressivists can't solve these problems, then expressivism *can't* be true. And if it can't be true, then it doesn't matter how nice its philosophical payoff would be if it *was* true. So to the extent that expressivists have so far failed to adequately address these problems, we should be at best cautiously skeptical about the truth of expressivism.

Still, I think that we can do somewhat better for expressivism. In fact, I think that there is essentially one move that we can make in order to develop a version of expressivism that both essentially solves the negation problem and substantially diminishes the size and difficulty of the Multiple Kinds and One Word problems. In section 2 I'll sketch just the outlines of how this move works, and a little bit of why things look so much better for expressivism after we make this move. Then in sections 3 and 4 we'll take a look at potential applications of expressivism outside of metaethics, and close in section 5 by looking at the prospects for noncognitivism in general.

## 11.2  New directions

Thinking that grass is green involves bearing a certain sort of attitude toward grass. It involves believing it to be green, or for short, *believing-green* grass. It is an important fact about the attitude, *believing-green*, that it has a certain kind of structure. It is not just a primitive attitude; rather, it consists in a more general attitude, *ordinary descriptive belief*, and a contribution to the content of that belief – *green*. It turns out that many of the central problems for expressivism that we discussed in earlier chapters are due to, or at least exacerbated by, the fact that expressivists typically assume that thinking that stealing is wrong does not have this kind of structure. On ordinary expressivist views, thinking that stealing is wrong consists in a single, simple, attitude toward stealing – one which does not factor into a more general attitude and a contribution to its content.

The problem with this lack of structure is illustrated by Nicholas Unwin's characterization of the 'negation problem', discussed earlier in Chapter 7. There we distinguished the following four sentences, where each of n1–n3 is formed by inserting a 'not' into one of the places in w:

**w**   Max thinks that stealing is wrong.
**n1**  Max does not think that stealing is wrong.
**n2**  Max thinks that stealing is not wrong.
**n3**  Max thinks that not stealing is wrong.

The problem is that there are not, similarly, three places to insert a 'not' in w\*, the expressivist's translation of w:

**w\***   Max disapproves of stealing.
**n1\***  Max does not disapprove of stealing.
**n2\***  ???
**n3\***  Max disapproves of not stealing.

This means that the expressivist treatment of 'Max thinks that stealing is wrong' as attributing to Max a simple attitude toward stealing is precisely what makes it difficult to understand what it is to think that stealing is not wrong – and hence difficult to understand what 'stealing is not wrong' *means*, in an expressivist framework.

All of this, however, is due to the lack of structure in the attitude of disapproval. If we assume that to disapprove of stealing is really to have a complex attitude toward stealing, which consists in a more general attitude together with a contribution to its content, then we get the following sort of picture:

**w†**   Max is for blaming for stealing.
**n1†**   Max is not for blaming for stealing.
**n2†**   Max is for not blaming for stealing.
**n3†**   Max is for blaming for not stealing.

It is easy to see that this picture makes it possible to make all of the same distinctions as in n1–n3, and to do so in a way that intuitively tracks the differences between n1–n3.

Moreover, this picture leads to a very straightforward recipe for the mental states expressed by complex sentences on the basis of the states expressed by their parts. On this picture, if 'P' expresses being for $\pi$, then '~P' expresses being for $\sim\pi$. We've just seen that illustrated with the example of 'P' = 'stealing is wrong', but it very easily generalizes to other sentences. For example, consider 'stealing is not not wrong'. Since thinking that stealing is not wrong is being for not blaming for stealing, our rule tells us that thinking that stealing is not not wrong is being for not not blaming for stealing. Since not not blaming for stealing is equivalent to stealing, it is easy to see, on this picture, why someone who thinks that stealing is not not wrong is committed to accepting that stealing is wrong, and conversely. And finally, this idea lets us predict and explain why moral belief has the intrapersonal inconsistency property, by appealing to the assumption that the attitude of being for is inconsistency-transmitting. Rather than simply hoping that there is a mental state with the right properties, like the inferential commitment views discussed in Chapter 7, it therefore both tells us what the mental states are and explains why they have the right properties.

This observation is the core idea of biforcated attitude semantics, an expressivist semantic framework that I develop in my book, *Being For: Evaluating the Semantic Program of Expressivism*. Without getting too far into the details, biforcated attitude semantics offers a picture of the kind of structure that is possessed by the mental states expressed by sentences, which is suitable for allowing for a compositional semantics. The core idea of biforcated attitude semantics is that the problems for expressivism are centrally related to the lack of structure ordinarily assumed to belong to the attitudes that are associated with normative predicates. So the way to get around this is to have the right sort of view of the structure of the mental states that are expressed by sentences. Though explaining why would take us somewhat too far afield for our purposes here, it turns out that this approach leads very naturally to answers to the Multiple Kinds and One Word problems, at least for belief. So biforcated attitude semantics at least points in a profitable direction, which at least has some prospects to be able to make progress on some of the hardest problems we've encountered in this book.

## 11.3 Applications – epistemic modals

One reason why it is worth trying to better understand noncognitivism and its prospects, especially including the problems and prospects of expressivism, is that expressivism has important and promising applications in areas of philosophy other than metaethics. Indeed, my own view is that the potential applications of expressivism outside of metaethics are actually much more interesting than its application to solve the core questions of metaethics. This has partly to do with the fact that I am inclined to think that the core questions of metaethics have other solutions and partly to do with the difficulty of these problems from other areas of philosophy.

First take the case of the terms known as 'epistemic modals'. These include terms like 'might' and 'must' as in 'Max might be in Carpinteria right now.' Epistemic modals need to be understood as relative to some informational background. Given all of the facts, there is only one place where Max might be – the place where he actually is. But given incomplete information, which doesn't tell us for certain Max's current location, he might be in Carpinteria, or he might be in Ventura – we simply can't say for sure. So according to the conventional view, epistemic modals are context-dependent terms like 'I', 'you', and 'now', which need to be interpreted relative to a *context of utterance*. As we noted in Chapter 4, when different people use the word 'I', they say different things. When Max says 'I am tall' he says that Max is tall, whereas when Mary says 'I am tall' she says not that Max is tall, but that Mary is tall. Similarly, according to the conventional view of epistemic modals, someone who says 'Max might be in Carpinteria' always says that it is compatible with some particular informational background that Max is in Carpinteria – but in different conversations, different particular informational backgrounds might be the ones that are being spoken about. This conventional view is called *contextualism* about epistemic modals.

Contextualism about epistemic modals has much in common with speaker subjectivism, the theory about moral language that we briefly considered in Chapter 4 in the process of motivating expressivism. And consequently, it has some of the very same problems. In particular, contextualism about epistemic modals predicts that Maude, who is having a conversation with Clara in California, might say, 'Max might be in Carpinteria', and Hilda, who is having a conversation with George in New York, might say, 'it is not the case that Max might be in Carpinteria', and both might speak perfectly truly – for it might be compatible with all of Maude and Clara's information that Max is in Carpinteria, but it might be incompatible with Hilda and George's information – for example, they might have just run into him in Union Square. But this is a strange prediction. If for some reason Hilda and George later find out what Maude said, it would make sense for Hilda to say, 'that's false – it's not the case that Max might be in Carpinteria'. It also makes sense for a third-party observer to describe Maude and Hilda's assertions by saying, 'Maude and Hilda disagree about whether Max might be in Carpinteria.' But if contextualism about epistemic modals is right, then there is nothing that Maude and Hilda are disagreeing about. This is just the disagreement problem all over again – essentially the same problem as was faced by speaker subjectivism in ethics.

This sort of observation has led some philosophers to believe that contextualism is the wrong theory about how epistemic modals are relative to informational backgrounds. According to one prominent recent reaction to this observation, instead of talking about different things in their different conversations, Maude and Hilda are talking about one and the same thing – namely, whether Max might be in Carpinteria – but this is a thing which is only *relatively*, rather than absolutely, true. It is true relative to some informational backgrounds, and not relative to others. On this view, what Maude says is true relative to some informational backgrounds and not relative to others, and similarly what Hilda says is true relative to some informational backgrounds and not relative to others – but relative to any given informational background, what Maude says and what Hilda says can't both be true. This is why they are in disagreement. This theory is known as *relativism* about epistemic modals.[1]

Relativism about epistemic modals faces another problem, however. It says that there is a single proposition which Maude endorses and Hilda denies – namely, that Max might be in Carpinteria. But if 'Max might be in Carpinteria' expresses a single proposition that is independent of context, then 'Max might be in Carpinteria and he might not be in Carpinteria' must, too – unless the words 'and' or 'not' can make a sentence that does not otherwise depend on context into one that does depend on context. But this leads to a violation of a well-known and very plausible principle known as the *principle of reflection*.[2]

The idea behind the principle of reflection is that if you know that in the future you will have some belief, and you know that the only thing that will happen between now and that time in the future is that you will come by some more information and respond to it rationally, then the rational thing for you to do is to already have that belief. After all, knowing that you will have evidence to which the rational response is to have that belief is as good as already having (indirect) evidence to which the rational response is to have that belief. At any rate, so says the basic idea behind the highly plausible principle of reflection.

But now suppose that presently you don't know Max's whereabouts, and so are unsure whether he is in Carpinteria. Intuitively, you think that he might be in Carpinteria and he might not be in Carpinteria. But in the next few minutes, you expect Max to call and tell you where he is. Once he calls, you will come to possess more information – namely, about Max's whereabouts – and you expect yourself to rationally respond to that information. Either Max will tell you that he is in Carpinteria, in which case you will come to believe that he is in Carpinteria and hence to deny that he might not be in Carpinteria, or else Max will tell you that he is not in Carpinteria, in which case you will come to believe that he is not in Carpinteria, and hence to deny that he might be in Carpinteria. But either way, you will deny that he might be in Carpinteria and he might not be in Carpinteria. So if there is a single proposition expressed by 'Max might be in Carpinteria and Max might not be in Carpinteria' which you believe now and expect yourself not to believe in the future after Max tells you where he is, then you are violating the highly plausible principle of reflection.

Expressivism about epistemic modals promises to avoid the disagreement problem for contextualism about epistemic modals, without leading to a violation of reflection. According to expressivism about epistemic modals, to believe that Max might be in Carpinteria is not to have an ordinary descriptive belief whose content is that Max is in Carpinteria; rather, it is simply to have a positive level of confidence in the proposition that Max is in Carpinteria – and the meaning of 'Max might be in Carpinteria' is that it expresses this positive level of confidence, rather than an ordinary, all-out belief. If expressivism were a viable semantic theory, then this could therefore be an attractive alternative to both contextualism and relativism.

## 11.4  Applications – truth and conditionals

Another promising application of expressivism outside of metaethics is to
the theory of truth. To see why a truth-conditional theory of the meaning
of 'true' looks problematic, we need only to consider once more the famous
example of the liar:

> Liar   'Liar is not true.'

Liar says of itself that it is not true. But this makes it look impossible to
assign it any stable set of truth-conditions. For it to be true, it must not
be true. And for it not to be true, it has to be true. So there seem to be no
conditions either under which it could be true, or under which it could not
be true. Yet it is clearly meaningful; someone might easily believe that Liar
is not true – particularly if she does not realize what Liar says.

Because expressivism is a nondescriptivist theory of meaning, and hence
seeks to explain the meanings of sentences by different means than by
saying what it would take for them to be true, it has reasonable prospects
of being the right kind of theory of meaning for 'true' to avoid this kind
of problem. The basic idea behind an expressivist theory of truth would be
to notice that someone who thinks that a sentence, S, means that P should
be committed to having the same view about 'S is true' and about 'P' –
either accepting both, denying both, or rejecting both. That is, given that
you accept 'S means that P', accepting 'S is true' disagrees with any attitude toward 'P' but acceptance, and accepting 'P' disagrees with any attitude
toward 'S is true' but acceptance. The expressivist project would then be to
say what mental state is expressed by 'S is true' in such a way as to predict
that it has these properties. An inferential-commitment theory would do
so simply by stipulation: saying that 'S is true' expresses that mental state,
whatever it is, which has these disagreement properties.

Yet another potentially interesting application for expressivism is to
conditional sentences. Throughout this book we have been making the
simplifying assumption that 'if A, then B' means the same as 'not both A and
not B'. But it turns out that this simplifying assumption, though useful for
many purposes, is problematic as a theory about what 'if ... then' actually
means in natural languages like English.

Philosophers have offered a variety of interesting arguments against the
thesis that this is what 'if ... then' means, and even against the thesis that
there can be any truth-conditional theory of the meaning of 'if ... then' at

all. But one of the most interesting is based on the observation that your confidence in 'if A, then B' is the same as your conditional confidence in B, conditional on A. Your conditional confidence in B, conditional on A is just the confidence that you are prepared to have in B, should you become completely convinced of A. But in a famous and influential argument, in the 1970s David Lewis proved that there is *no* proposition such that it makes sense to have the same confidence in that proposition as your conditional confidence in B, conditional on A. So one natural conclusion to draw from this – a conclusion that a number of philosophers who work on understanding conditionals have drawn – is that truth-conditional theories of meaning are the wrong way to try to account for the meanings of conditional sentences.

Expressivism offers a very direct alternative. It tells us to explain the meaning of 'if A, then B' by explaining what it is to think that if A, then B. But the observation that we have already been discussing tells us what it intuitively is to think that if A, then B. Rather than being a matter of having a high confidence in any single proposition, it is a matter of having a high *conditional* confidence in B, conditional on A. An expressivist theory of meaning is therefore very well cut-out in order to explain why having a high confidence in the conditional 'if A, then B' lines up with having a high conditional confidence in B, conditional on A – it is because they are *identical*.

In this and the last section I have barely touched the surface of many complicated issues surrounding truth, conditionals, and epistemic modals. Nothing I have said here suffices – by any means – to show that we need an expressivist semantic theory in order to account for any of these domains. But they do offer at least initial promise as potential applications for expressivism outside of metaethics. And the more promising we take these applications to be, the closer we are to a 'license for optimism' argument that it is worth trying harder to solve the problems facing expressivism, even if we are currently having trouble doing so.

## 11.5 Directions for progress

If this book has read more like a litany of open problems facing noncognitivist theories than like an introduction to what moral language is like if noncognitivism is true, that is at least true to the state of the art. Ultimately, the fundamental question which animated both the original noncognitivists and contemporary expressivists was not the project of understanding *what* moral words mean, but the project of understanding *what is the best way to say* what words mean, in general. The fundamental idea animating noncognitivists of every persuasion is that truth-conditional semantics is very successful and promising *within its domain*, but that we need a more flexible and general framework for understanding linguistic meaning, if we are to have any realistic shot at coming to an adequate understanding of the full range of words in natural languages like English.

This is why the arguments for license for optimism about the various noncognitivist theories that we have considered along the way have so often taken us to looking at words and linguistic constructions which test the boundaries of truth-conditional approaches to the theory of meaning, regardless of whether they have anything directly to do with moral language. For example, Ayer's original discussion drew our attention to expressives like 'damn', Hare's arguments for license for optimism focused on mood, including the imperative mood, and the hybrid theorists' arguments focused on pejoratives and racial slurs. Stevenson and Gibbard, meanwhile, got us started in thinking about intentions or plans as a model for moral thought. And as we've seen in the last two sections, part of the grounds for assessing expressivism will come from assessing its other potential applications, including to epistemic modals, conditionals, and truth. None of these topics looks like it has anything directly to do with morality, and none of them are well understood, in their own right – which leaves both plenty of room for controversy and plenty of room for progress. Nevertheless, what noncognitivism shows us is that understanding all of these other things better will lead to being in a better position to understand moral language – whether noncognitivism turns out to be right or not. Investigating all of these other topics is simply part of the task of coming to a better understanding of the prospects for noncognitivism of any kind.

This is essentially the prescience of the early noncognitivists: the project of trying to understand all of these other kinds of linguistic construction is as live and open today as it was in the 1930s or 1950s. If anything, independent progress in the philosophy of language and linguistic semantics is now making it possible to make more fruitful progress in addressing these topics. Noncognitivism benefits from the fruits of this progress, and it is possible that the efforts of noncognitivists will yet help us toward a better understanding of these other aspects of linguistic meaning, as well. Certainly each gives us a fruitful place to look for progress on the other.

## Chapter summary

In this chapter we rehearsed some of the main issues that have come up for noncognitivist theories in this book. We briefly saw how an expressivist theory can solve the *negation problem* from Chapter 7, which was the key reason why existing expressivist theories have faced a tradeoff between *constructiveness* and *formal adequacy*. And we encountered new potential applications for expressivism, in the theories of truth, of conditionals, and of epistemic modals.

## Further reading

This chapter can fruitfully be read alongside David Kaplan's challenging but provocative unpublished manuscript, 'Meaning as Use'. For further discussion of the connection between epistemic modals and the principle of reflection, see Ross and Schroeder (unpublished), for discussion of the motivations for non-truth-conditional approaches to conditionals, see Edgington (1986), and for a challenging introductory discussion of the technical issues surrounding truth and paradox, see Field (2008).

## Exercises

1   E *Comprehension*: Why is it helpful for evaluating the prospects for noncognitivism to investigate things like mood, pejoratives, and swear words?

2   E *Comprehension*: How do noncognitivist theories promise to help us gain a better understanding of things like mood, pejoratives, and swear words?

3   M *Comprehension*: Suppose that you now know that you are not in Carpinteria, so you don't accept 'I might be in Carpinteria.' But suppose that you also know that you are about to take a 'forgetting pill', which will make you forget where you are. After you take the pill, you expect to no longer know that you are not in Carpinteria, and hence to accept 'I might be in Carpinteria.' Do you violate the principle of reflection? Why or why not? What makes this similar to or different from the cases which motivate the basic idea behind the principle of reflection?

4   M *Extensions*: Consider the sentence schema, 'if S means that P, then S is true just in case P'. Can you think of any counterexamples? What would a

counterexample have to be like? What about 'if Liar means that Liar is not true, then Liar is true just in case Liar is not true'. Is *this* sentence true? Even if you say 'no', do you still feel the 'pull' behind the intuition that it has to be true?

5   M *Extensions*: The following diagram is a map of Max's *confidence space*. Each proposition corresponds to some region of the diagram, and Max's confidence in that proposition corresponds to the area of that region. His confidence in ~P corresponds to the area of the rectangle outside of that region. And his confidence in P&Q corresponds to the area of overlap between the regions associated with P and with Q. For example, the left-hand circle represents the proposition that P, and Max's confidence in P corresponds to its area. Since the area of the circle is much smaller than the area of the whole rectangle, Max is much less confident in P than in ~P. Similarly, he is less confident in Q than in ~Q, less confident in P than in Q, and much less confident that P and Q are both true (corresponding to their overlap) than he is in either P or Q by itself.

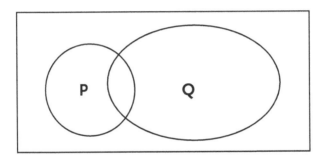

Assign plausible numbers, given their areas, to each region, in such a way that the area of the whole rectangle adds to 1. Then use these numbers to calculate two things. First, find the total area associated with the region for ~(P&~Q). This is the 'material conditional' definition for 'P→Q' that we have been assuming for most of this book. Second, divide the area associated with P&Q by the area associated with P. This number is what it known as the *conditional confidence* or *conditional probability* of Q, given P. It represents how confident Max would be in Q, if he found out for certain that P. Are these two numbers the same, or is one larger than the other? Can you change the sizes of the respective areas in such a way as to make the other number larger? Why or why not?[3]

## Morals

3    Most philosophers agree that the principle of reflection needs to be qualified, because it doesn't apply if you expect to forget something or expect
to be irrational in the future. But the case in the argument from section 3
wasn't like that, so the argument appears to survive counterexamples like
this one.

5    If 'if P, then Q' just means '~(P&~Q)', then we should expect Max's confidence in 'if P, then Q' to be the same as his confidence in '~(P&~Q)'. But if
that is right, then his confidence in 'if P, then Q' can be much higher than
the confidence that he expects to have in Q, should he find out for certain
that P. This is strange – and is a part of the evidence that 'if P, then Q'
doesn't mean '~(P&~Q)', after all.

## References

Edgington, Dorothy (1986). 'Do Conditionals Have Truth-Conditions?' *Critica*
18: 3–39.

Egan, Andy, John Hawthorne, and Brian Weatherson (2003). 'Epistemic
Modals in Context.' In Gerhard Preyer and Georg Peter, eds., *Contextualism
in Philosophy: Knowledge, Meaning, and Truth.* Oxford: Oxford University
Press.

Field, Hartry (2008). *Saving Truth from Paradox.* Oxford: Oxford University
Press.

Kaplan, David (unpublished). 'Meaning as Use.' Unpublished manuscript.

MacFarlane, John (forthcoming). 'Epistemic Modals are Assessment-Sensitive.'
Forthcoming in a volume on epistemic modals edited by Andy Egan and
Brian Weatherson.

Ross, Jacob, and Mark Schroeder (unpublished). 'Reflections on Epistemic
Modals.' Unpublished draft manuscript, available online at www-rcf.usc.
edu/~maschroe/research/Reflections_on_Epistemic_Modals.pdf

van Fraassen, Bas (1984). 'Belief and the Will'. *Journal of Philosophy* 81:
235–56.

# GLOSSARY

**antecedent** *see* **conditional**

**atomic**  A sentence is *atomic* when it is a simple subject–predicate sentence. Contrast *molecular*.

**basic expressivist maneuver**  To try to see how to solve a problem for expressivism by seeing how to raise an analogous problem for a non-expressivist theory. See Chapter 4.

**Big Hypothesis**  The hypothesis that belief-ascriptions (sentences like 'Jones believes that ...') report that their subject (Jones) has any attitude expressed by their complement ('...'), rather than themselves expressing that attitude.

**cognitivism about instrumental reason**  The thesis that the rational and disagreement relationships between intentions can be explained by appeal to the assumption that intention involves belief.

**communicative constraint**  The idea that a theory of what a sentence means needs to give us the resources in order to be able to explain how it is used to communicate.

**compositional constraint**  The idea that a theory of meaning must explain how we are able to understand the meanings of complex sentences on the basis of understanding the meanings of their parts and how they are put together.

**conditional**  An 'if ... then' sentence. The 'if' part is called the *antecedent* and the 'then' part is called the *consequent*.

**conjunction**   An 'and' sentence.

**consequent** *see* **conditional**

**contextualism**   A theory according to which what some sentence says can vary from one context of use to another. For example, speaker subjectivism.

**core questions**   The central questions from *metaphysics*, *epistemology*, the *philosophy of language*, and the *philosophy of mind* which motivate *noncognitivism*.

**descriptivism**   A theory according to which the meanings of sentences can be explained in terms of what they are about.

**direction of fit**   A state of mind has *mind-to-world* direction of fit if its job is to match the world. Its direction of fit is *world-to-mind* if its job is to make the world match it.

**disagreement**   *Interpersonal* disagreement is disagreement between people; *intrapersonal* disagreement is the kind of rational inconsistency that is involved in thinking that P and also thinking that ~P.

**disagreement class**   The *disagreement class* of a mental state M, denoted |M|, is the set of states of mind that you land yourself in disagreement with by being in M.

**disagreement problem**   This was a problem for speaker subjectivism. It is the problem that speaker subjectivism cannot explain how people who have conflicting moral views really disagree.

**disjunction**   An 'or' sentence.

**domain-specific/domain-neutral**   A problem is *domain-specific* if it arises as a result of special features of a particular topic. For example, the paradox of the Liar is a domain-specific problem for theories of truth, and the motivational problem is a domain-specific problem in ethics. A problem is *domain-neutral* if it arises for any topic. The core questions give rise to domain-neutral problems.

**ecumenical expressivism**   Michael Ridge's *hybrid* noncognitivist theory; see Chapter 10.

**emotivism**   The earliest noncognitivist theories, including those of Ayer and Stevenson, were known as emotivism.

**epistemic modals**   Words like 'might' and 'must'.

**epistemology**   The study of knowledge and rational belief.

**expressive-assertivism**   Daniel Boisvert's *hybrid* noncognitivist theory; see Chapter 10.

**expressivism**   The contemporary noncognitivist theory according to which the right way to explain the meaning of a sentence, 'P', is to say what it is to think that P.

**formally adequate**   A noncognitivist account of the meanings of complex sentences is *formally adequate* if it generates the right predictions about which arguments are valid and which pairs of sentences are inconsistent.

**Frege–Geach problem**   The problem of accounting for the meanings of complex sentences as a function of the meanings of their parts.

**Gibbardish semantics**   The variant on Allan Gibbard's expressivist theory developed in section 2 of Chapter 7.

**Higher-Order Attitude theories**   Expressivist answers to the Frege–Geach problem, like Blackburn's (1984) theory, according to which the mental states expressed by complex sentences are attitudes toward the attitudes expressed by their parts.

**hybrid theories**   Theories which incorporate both noncognitivist elements and ordinary truth-conditional elements.

**illocutionary act**   An act that you perform in saying something; see exercise 4 of Chapter 2.

**imperative** *see* **mood**

**inconsistency property**   An argument has the *inconsistency property* just in case someone who accepts the premises but denies the conclusion suffers from *intrapersonal disagreement*.

**inconsistency-transmitting**   An attitude is *inconsistency-transmitting* just in case two states involving this attitude intrapersonally disagree just in case they are cases of having this attitude toward inconsistent contents.

**indicative** *see* **mood**

**induction**   To perform an inference by induction is to accept a generalization like 'all swans are white' on the basis of having observed many white swans without having observed any swans of any other color.

**inference-licensing property**   An argument has the *inference-licensing property* just in case someone who accepts the premises of the argument is committed to accepting its conclusion.

**inferential-commitment theories**   These expressivist theories tell us what mental state is expressed by complex sentences by picking them out by means of their inferential commitments or disagreement properties; see Chapter 7.

**internalism, motivational**   According to *motivational internalism*, someone who makes a moral judgment will tend to be motivated to act accordingly.

**interpersonal disagreement** *see* **disagreement**

**interrogative** *see* **mood**

**intrapersonal disagreement** *see* **disagreement**

**judgment internalism** *see* **internalism, motivational**

**language, philosophy of**   The philosophy of language asks questions about the nature and structure of language, including but not limited to questions about what kind of meaning words have, and how words come to have the meanings that they do.

**license for optimism**   A common noncognitivist strategy is to offer arguments for *license for optimism* that one of their problems should be solvable. Such arguments don't show what the solution to the problem is, but they try to establish that we should expect there to be some solution, and they often give us some ideas of where to look for one.

**locutionary act**   The act of uttering a sentence with a given meaning.

**Many Attitudes problem**   The problem arising from the fact that a noncognitivist account of moral thought must not only account for moral belief, but must also account for moral desire, moral hope, moral wondering, and so on, for each other kind of attitude.

**metaethics**   The study of *metaphysics, epistemology, philosophy of language,* and *philosophy of mind,* insofar as they intersect with questions about ethics.

**metaphysics**   The philosophical study of the nature of reality–of what exists and what it is like.

**mind, philosophy of**   The philosophical study of the mind.

**modal problem**   A problem for *speaker subjectivism*. The problem is that speaker subjectivism yields the wrong predictions about sentences involving modal terms and/or tense.

*modus ponens*   Any argument of the form, P, if P then Q; therefore Q.

**molecular**   A sentence is *molecular* when it is constructed by combining one or more *atomic* sentences by use of connectives like 'not', 'and', 'or', or 'if … then'.

**mood**   A feature of natural-language sentences, dividing them into *indicative* (ordinarily used for ordinary assertions), *interrogative* (ordinarily used to ask questions), or *imperative* (ordinarily used to issue commands or suggestions).

**Moorean inconsistency**   You are Moorean inconsistent if you believe something but believe you don't believe it.

**motivation problem**   The problem of explaining why people would be motivated in accordance with their moral judgments, as *motivational internalism* claims.

**motivational internalism** *see* **internalism, motivational**

**Multiple Kinds problem**   This is the problem arising for *noncognitivism* in the *philosophy of mind* as a result of the fact that noncognitivists think that there are *multiple kinds* of belief–two at the least, and for some views infinitely many–which coincidentally share many of the same properties.

**negation**    A 'not' sentence.

**negation problem**    The problem for *expressivism* of explaining what mental state is expressed by 'not' sentences in a way that allows for an explanation of why accepting 'P' and accepting '~P' intrapersonally disagree–illustrated by Unwin's n1–n3. An exactly analogous problem arises for other noncognitivist theories.

**noncognitivism**    A class of nondescriptivist theories about moral language which have prospects for helping to solve the *motivational problem* and evade the *core questions*.

**non-constructive**    An expressivist theory is *non-constructive* if it picks out the mental states expressed by complex sentences only by means of definite descriptions, rather than telling us what those states are and explaining why they satisfy those definite descriptions.

**nondescriptivism**    Nondescriptivist theories seek to explain the meaning of words by other means than by saying what they are about.

**One Word problem**    The problem arising for *noncognitivism* in the *philosophy of mind* as a result of the fact that we use a single word for both moral and *ordinary descriptive belief*, a single word for both moral and ordinary descriptive hope, and so on for each of the other attitudes.

**ordinary descriptive belief**    The kind of belief you have when you believe that grass is green – with mind-to-world *direction of fit*. According to noncognitivists, this contrasts with moral belief, which is a different kind of mental state, typically assumed to have world-to-mind *direction of fit*.

**pejoratives**    Words which, in addition to describing something as being a certain way, cast it in a negative light. Pejoratives include racial slurs like 'kraut', 'wop', and others that are more offensive.

**performativism, Geachian**    The theory that what makes a sentence mean what it does is the speech act that it is used to perform on that particular occasion.

**perlocutionary act**    An act that you achieve *by* saying something, but which depends on the results of saying it.

**pragmatics**    The study of what we manage to communicate by means of general principles of communication, rather than the specific rules associated with the meanings of particular words.

**predicate**    An adjective or verb phrase. Each *atomic* sentence is formed by the combination of a subject (or noun) with a predicate.

**prescriptivism**    Hare's noncognitivist theory.

**propositions**    Propositions are the objects of belief, desire, assertion, and the other attitudes, and the bearers of truth and falsity.

**relativism**   According to relativism about some subject matter, the sentences of that subject matter are associated with the same *proposition* in different contexts of utterance, but that *proposition* may vary in its truth when evaluated from different points of view.

**semantic property**   A semantic property of a sentence is a feature that it has in virtue of the meaning of its terms. For example, 'stealing is not wrong' has the property of being inconsistent with 'stealing is wrong' in virtue of the meaning of 'not'.

**semantic theory**   A theory which says what kind of meaning each sentence has.

**semantics**   The study of meaning.

**speaker subjectivism**   The theory that 'stealing is wrong' has the same sort of meaning as 'I disapprove of stealing'.

**target-excluded cases**   In the *wishful thinking problem*, a case in which intuitively it is not rational for Edgar to come to accept the conclusion on the basis of the premises.

**target-included cases**   In the *wishful thinking problem*, a case in which intuitively it is rational for Edgar to come to accept the conclusion on the basis of the premises.

**testimony**   When you learn something on the basis of someone else telling you.

**token**   An individual instance. For example, there are two tokens of 't' in 'attack'.

**truth-conditional semantics**   According to this kind of *semantic theory*, the way to explain the meaning of a sentence is to say under what conditions it would be true.

**truth conditions**   The truth conditions of a sentence are just the conditions under which it is true.

**truth tables**   A truth table tells us the conditions under which a complex sentence is true, as a function of the conditions under which its parts are true.

**type** *see* **token.**   Even though there are two tokens of 't' in 'attack', they belong to the same type.

**van Roojen problem**   A problem for *Higher-Order Attitude* expressivist theories. The problem is that they classify too many arguments as valid.

**wishful thinking**   Believing something because you want it to be true.

**wishful thinking problem**   Cian Dorr's objection that noncognitivists are committed to thinking that wishful thinking is sometimes rational.

# NOTES

## 1 The problems of metaethics

1 I obtain this number by comparing the WHO's estimate that each year 3 million girls in Africa are at risk for genital cutting (see http://www.who.int/reproductive-health/publications/fgm/fgm_statement_2008.pdf) to their estimate that 10 percent of genital cutting procedures are type III.

2 See http://www.who.int/reproductive-health/publications/articles/lancetfgm.pdf, figures 1 and 2, p. 3.

3 Ibid., figure 2, p. 3.

4 See http://www.who.int/reproductive-health/publications/fgm/fgm_statement_2008.pdf, p. 29.

5 According to the US State Department: http://www.state.gov/g/wi/rls/rep/crfgm/10047.htm

6 See, for example, de Waal (1996); Haidt (2001); Greene *et al.* (2001); Greene and Haidt (2002); Nichols (2004); and Joyce (2006).

7 http://www.care.org/

8 http://www.oxfamamerica.org/

9 Though this view is often called the Humean Theory of Motivation, not everyone agrees that Hume really believed it.

10 The shopping-cart analogy is from Anscombe (1957, 56–7). Smith (1994, chapter 4) is another important and classic discussion of the Humean Theory of Motivation, and I take its name from him.

## 2 The noncognitivist turn

1 Etymologically, the name appears to be derivative from Ogden and Richards' (1923) characterization of some uses of language as 'emotive'.

2 The description that I have given of Ayer's view in the main text is controversial; see

exercises 8 and 9 for further discussion.

3   See Stevenson (1944, 82).

4   Ibid., 206.

5   It is a little bit anachronistic to see Ayer and Stevenson as reacting directly to this Very Big Idea; nevertheless, I think that it is particularly instructive to understand their views in opposition to it.

6   See also Hare (1952, 11–12).

## 3 The Frege–Geach problem, 1939–70

1   It is worth noting that noncognitivist treatments of 'boo!' *do* trivially satisfy the compositional constraint, because 'boo!' doesn't really figure in complex sentences. What is difficult about the Frege–Geach problem is that moral words like 'wrong' and 'should' *do* figure in complex sentences – all of the very same kinds of complex sentences as non-moral words like 'quick' and 'large'. This is what noncognitivists need to be able to explain.

2   See, for example, Strawson (1949).

3   See Wittgenstein (2005).

4   There are two ways to think about the symbols that I will be introducing, such as '∼'. One is to treat them as an artificial language in which their meaning is stipulated to be captured by the truth tables. If we think about them that way, then it is uncontroversial (because true by stipulation) that '∼' obeys the truth tables, but controversial whether 'not' just means '∼'. This is the way of thinking usually employed in logic textbooks. On another way of proceeding, however – the way I use in this book – '∼' is stipulated to be a kind of shorthand for 'it is not the case that', and what is controversial is whether its meaning can be captured by the truth table.

5   The idea that imperatives can be characterized as performatives in this way comes from Karttunen (1977).

6   Faith-based conditionals are discussed in Dreier (2009).

## 4 Expressivism

1   A mental state *type*.

## 6 The Frege–Geach problem, 1973–88

1   It is worth noting that nearly everything is controversial in philosophy, and the validity of *modus ponens* has been questioned by some philosophers – for example, see McGee (1985); Lycan (2001); and Kolodny and MacFarlane (unpublished). I'll continue to assume for our purposes in this book, however, that *modus ponens* is valid; if it turns out that *modus ponens* is valid only under restricted circumstances, then that is what noncognitivists would need to explain instead.

2   Careful readers will note that '&' and '∼' are here being used as a different kind of connective, so that '[P]&∼[Q]' picks out the state of being in the state of mind expressed by 'P' and not being in the state of mind expressed by 'Q'. Elsewhere in the text, '&' and '∼' are sentential connectives. If we were going to discuss Blackburn's

HOA account at any greater length, it would be important to distinguish between them.

3    I am grateful to Johannes Schmitt for the idea behind exercises 5–8.


## 7  The Frege–Geach problem, 1988–2006

1    Just to be clear about the notation: putting square brackets around a sentence yields a name for a mental state, and putting vertical lines around a name for a mental state yields a name for a disagreement class.


## 8  Truth and objectivity

1    Observe that this kind of transcendental argument does not assume any kind of transcendental *idealism* – that is, it does not assume that if it is rationally inconsistent to think something, then it is true. The 'transcendental turn' in the argument is not justified by any further assumption that makes the transcendental argument valid; it merely makes rational sense in that given what the argument has established so far, it is rationally inconsistent to deny the argument's conclusion. So the transcendental step of the argument is more like the step from realizing that it is irrational to throw money down the toilet to the decision not to throw money down the toilet, than like the step from realizing that P and that if P, then Q, to drawing the conclusion that Q.

2    Compare Kant (1997); Hare (1981); and Korsgaard (1996).


## 9  Epistemology

1    Note that neither Dorr nor either of his commentators, Enoch (2003) or Lenman (2003), characterizes the problem as a dilemma; all assume that the second fork is obviously to be avoided.

2    Another way of seeing that the wishful thinking problem is distinct from the Frege–Geach problem – a point which Dorr himself highlights – is that the Frege–Geach problem arises in full force for expressivist theories in any domain – including theories about probability judgments, epistemic modals, or indicative conditionals. For example, an expressivist about probability judgments might hold that to think that the probability of P is 60 percent is to have a credence of 60 percent in P, an expressivist about epistemic modals might hold that to think that Jack might be in Seattle is to have a positive credence that Jack is in Seattle, and an expressivist about indicative conditionals might hold that to have a confidence of $n$ that if you ask, she'll say 'yes', is to have a conditional credence of $n$ in the proposition that she'll say 'yes', conditional on the proposition that you ask. (For more on expressivist theories in other domains, see Chapter 11.)

    All of these theories face the traditional Frege–Geach problem, and need to explain how the sentences of which they seek to provide a special account can combine in complex sentences with the right semantic properties – including validating the right arguments. The Frege–Geach problem is a *general* problem for expressivist theories. But none of these theories face the wishful thinking problem or any analogue of it, for there is nothing problematic about the idea that a subject could come to be justified in forming an ordinary descriptive belief about a matter of fact, on the basis of having a credence of 60 percent in P, on the basis of having a positive credence that Jack is in Seattle, or on the basis of having full credence in the proposition that she'll say 'yes', conditional on the proposition that you ask. Forming beliefs on the basis of other cognitive attitudes – such as levels of credence or conditional credence – is not intuitively problematic in the way that wishful thinking is, so there is no second fork to the dilemma. So this further supports the view that the wishful thinking problem is a distinct problem facing expressivist views in *metaethics*, and arising in *epistemology*, rather than from considerations from the philosophy of language.

3   Things are slightly more complicated in the case in which Edgar is justified in accepting P1 only on the basis of testimony. See exercises 6–9.

4   Lenman (2003, 272).

5   Ibid., 269 (italics in original).

6   A further limitation of Lenman's strategy derives from an important distinction between what epistemologists call *propositional* and *doxastic* justification. You have a propositional justification for believing that *p* if you have evidence that would make it rational for you to believe that *p* – even if you do not actually believe *p*, or if you believe that *p*, but only on the basis of evidence that does not really support it. But you are *doxastically* justified *in* believing that *p* only if you are rational in believing *p*, because you believe it on the basis of your evidence that supports it. On a natural way of understanding Lenman's strategy, it explains why Edgar has a *propositional* justification for drawing the conclusion, but it can explain why Edgar is doxastically justified in accepting the conclusion only if Edgar actually *relies* on the more complicated reasoning that Lenman appeals to. But even if the rest of Lenman's claims are right, this further claim is even more implausible.

## 10  The hybrid gambit

1   I am grateful to Ryan Hay for this exercise.

## 11  Prospects and applications

1   See, in particular, Egan *et al.* (2003) and MacFarlane (forthcoming).

2   For the principle of reflection, see van Fraassen (1984).

3   This exercise is borrowed from Edgington (1986).

# BIBLIOGRAPHY

Items are organized topically rather than alphabetically for ease of use as a resource. Some entries are duplicated, as a result. Within each group, entries are in chronological order of publication.

## General works in metaethics

Moore, G.E. (1903). *Principia Ethica*. Cambridge: Cambridge University Press.

Harman, Gilbert (1977). *The Nature of Morality*. Oxford: Oxford University Press.

Mackie, J.L. (1977). *Ethics: Inventing Right and Wrong*. New York: Penguin, especially chapters 1 and 2.

Smith, Michael (1994a). *The Moral Problem*. Oxford: Basil Blackwell.

Darwall, Stephen, Allan Gibbard, and Peter Railton, eds. (1997). *Moral Discourse and Practice: Some Philosophical Approaches*. Oxford: Oxford University Press.

Miller, Alexander (2003). *An Introduction to Contemporary Metaethics*. Cambridge: Polity.

Copp, David, ed. (2006). *The Oxford Handbook of Ethical Theory*. Oxford: Oxford University Press.

Fisher, Andrew, and Simon Kirchin, eds. (2006). *Arguing about Metaethics*. New York: Routledge.

Shafer-Landau, Russ, and Terence Cuneo, eds. (2007). *Foundations of Ethics: An Anthology*. Oxford: Basil Blackwell.

## Empirical work on moral judgment and philosophical discussions of its connection to metaethics

de Waal, Frans (1996). *Good Natured: The Origins of Right and Wrong in Primates and Other Animals*. Cambridge, MA: Harvard University Press.

Greene, J.D., R.B. Sommerville, L.E. Nystrom, J.M. Darley, and J.D. Cohen (2001). 'An fMRI Investigation of Emotional Engagement in Moral Judgment.' *Science* 293: 2105–8.

Haidt, Jonathan (2001). 'The Emotional Dog and Its Rational Tail: A Social Intuitionist Approach to Moral Judgment.' *Psychological Review* 108: 814–34.

Greene, J.D., and J. Haidt (2002). 'How (and Where) Does Moral Judgment Work?' *Trends in Cognitive Sciences* 6: 517–23.

Nichols, Shaun (2004). *Sentimental Rules*. Oxford: Oxford University Press.

Joyce, Richard (2006). *The Evolution of Morality*. Cambridge, MA: MIT Press.

## Historical noncognitivism

Ogden, C.K., and I.A. Richards (1923). *The Meaning of Meaning*. New York: Harcourt Brace.

Barnes, W.H.F. (1933). 'A Suggestion about Value.' *Analysis* 1: 45–6.

Broad, C.D. (1933). 'Is "Goodness" the Name of a Simple Non-Natural Quality?' *Proceedings of the Aristotelian Society* 34: 249–68.

Carnap, Rudolf (1935). *Philosophy and Logical Syntax*. Bristol: Thoemmes Press.

Ayer, A.J. (1936). *Language, Truth, and Logic*. New York: Dover.

Stevenson, C.L. (1937). 'The Emotive Meaning of Ethical Terms.' Reprinted in Stevenson (1963), *Facts and Values*. Westport, CT: Greenwood Press.

Moore, G.E. (1942). 'A Reply to My Critics.' In Paul Schilpp, ed., *The Philosophy of G.E. Moore*. Evanston: Northwestern University Press.

Stevenson, C.L. (1942). 'Moore's Arguments against Certain Forms of Ethical Naturalism.' In Paul Schilpp, ed., *The Philosophy of G.E. Moore*. Evanston: Northwestern University Press.

Stevenson, C.L. (1944). *Ethics and Language*. Oxford: Oxford University Press.

Hare, R.M. (1952). *The Language of Morals*. Oxford: Oxford University Press.

Hägerström, Axel (1953). *Inquiries into the Nature of Law and Morals*. Edited by Karl Olivecrona and translated by C.D. Broad. Stockholm: Almqvist and Wiksell.

Edwards, Paul (1955). *The Logic of Moral Discourse*. Glencoe, IL: The Free Press.

Hare, R.M. (1963). *Freedom and Reason*. Oxford: Oxford University Press.

Stevenson, C.L. (1963). *Facts and Values*. Westport, CT: Greenwood Press.

Urmson, J.O. (1968). *The Emotive Theory of Ethics*. New York: Oxford University Press.

Hare, R.M. (1972). *Practical Inferences*. Los Angeles: University of California Press.

Hare, R.M. (1981). *Moral Thinking: Its Levels, Method, and Point*. Oxford: Oxford University Press.

Smart, J.J.C. (1984). *Ethics, Persuasion, and Truth*. Oxford: Oxford University Press.

Satris, Stephen (1987). *Ethical Emotivism*. Dordrecht: Martinus Nijhoff Publishers.

## Truth-conditional semantics

Larson, Richard, and Gabriel Segal (1995). *Knowledge of Meaning: An Introduction to Semantic Theory*. Cambridge, MA: MIT Press.

Heim, Irene, and Angelica Kratzer (1998). *Semantics in Generative Grammar*. Oxford: Basil Blackwell.

## Speaker subjectivism and related theories

Moore, G.E. (1903). *Principia Ethica*. Cambridge: Cambridge University Press.

Perry, R.B. (1926). *General Theory of Value: Its Meaning and Basic Principles Construed in Terms of Interest*. Cambridge, MA: Harvard University Press.

Stevenson, C.L. (1937). 'The Emotive Meaning of Ethical Terms.' Reprinted in Stevenson (1963), *Facts and Values*. Westport, CT: Greenwood Press.

Dreier, James (1990). 'Internalism and Speaker Relativism.' *Ethics* 101(1): 6–25.

Timmons, Mark (1999). *Morality without Foundations*. Oxford: Oxford University Press.

Finlay, Stephen (2004). 'The Conversational Practicality of Value Judgment.' *Journal of Ethics* 8: 205–23.

## Expressivism

Blackburn, Simon (1984). *Spreading the Word*. Oxford: Oxford University Press.

Gibbard, Allan (1990). *Wise Choices, Apt Feelings*. Cambridge, MA: Harvard University Press.

Blackburn, Simon (1993). *Essays in Quasi-Realism*. Oxford: Oxford University Press.

Blackburn, Simon (1998). *Ruling Passions*. Oxford: Oxford University Press.

Horgan, Terry, and Mark Timmons (2000). 'Nondescriptivist Cognitivism: Framework for a New Metaethic.' *Philosophical Papers* 29: 121–53.

Gibbard, Allan (2003). *Thinking How to Live*. Cambridge, MA: Harvard University Press.

Horgan, Terry, and Mark Timmons (2006). 'Cognitivist Expressivism.' In Horgan and Timmons, eds., *Metaethics after Moore*. Oxford: Oxford University Press.

## The nature of the expression relation

Jackson, Frank, and Philip Pettit (1998). 'A Problem for Expressivism.' *Analysis* 58(4): 239–51.

Barker, Stephen (2000). 'Is Value Content a Component of Conventional Implicature?' *Analysis* 60(3): 268–79.

Copp, David (2001). 'Realist-Expressivism: A Neglected Option for Moral Realism.' *Social Philosophy and Policy* 18: 1–43.

Joyce, Richard (2002). 'Expressivism and Motivation Internalism.' *Analysis* 62(4): 336–44.

Jackson, Frank, and Philip Pettit (2003). 'Locke, Expressivism, and Conditionals.' *Analysis* 63(1): 86–92.

Smith, Michael, and Daniel Stoljar (2003). 'Is There a Lockean Argument against Expressivism?' *Analysis* 63(1): 76–86.

Dreier, James (2004). 'Lockean and Logical Truth Conditions.' *Analysis* 64(1): 84–91.

Finlay, Stephen (2005). 'Value and Implicature.' *Philosophers' Imprint* 5(4), available online at www.philosophersimprint.org/005004/.

Boisvert, Daniel (2008). 'Expressive-Assertivism.' *Pacific Philosophical Quarterly* 89: 169–203.

Schroeder, Mark (2008a). 'Expression for Expressivists.' *Philosophy and Phenomenological Research* 76(1): 86–116.

## Cognitivism about instrumental reason

Harman, Gilbert (1976). 'Practical Reasoning.' Reprinted in Harman (1999), *Reasoning, Meaning, and Mind*. Oxford: Oxford University Press.

Davis, Wayne (1984). 'A Causal Theory of Intending.' *American Philosophical Quarterly* 21: 43–54.

Bratman, Michael (1987). *Intention, Plans, and Practical Reason*. Cambridge, MA: Harvard University Press.

Setiya, Kieran (2007). 'Cognitivism about Instrumental Reason.' *Ethics* 117(4): 649–73.

Bratman, Michael (2009). 'Intention, Belief, Theoretical, Practical.' Forthcoming in Simon Robertson, ed., *Spheres of Reason: New Essays in the Philosophy of Normativity*. Oxford: Oxford University Press.

Ross, Jacob (2008). 'How to Be a Cognitivist about Practical Reason.' Forthcoming in *Oxford Studies in Metaethics*.

## The Frege–Geach problem

### *Before Geach and Searle*

Acton, H.B. (1936). 'The Expletive Theory of Morals.' *Analysis* 4: 42–5.

Ross, W.D. (1939). *Foundations of Ethics*. Oxford: Clarendon Press, chapter 2.

Hare, R.M. (1952). *The Language of Morals*. Oxford: Oxford University Press, especially chapter 2.

### *The classical problem*

Geach, Peter (1958). 'Imperative and Deontic Logic.' *Analysis* 18: 49–56.

Geach, Peter (1960). 'Ascriptivism.' *Philosophical Review* 69: 221–5.

Searle, John (1962). 'Meaning and Speech Acts.' *Philosophical Review* 71: 423–32.

Geach, Peter (1965). 'Assertion.' *Philosophical Review* 74: 449–65.

Searle, John (1969). *Speech Acts: An Essay in the Philosophy of Language*. Cambridge: Cambridge University Press.

Hare, R.M. (1970). 'Meaning and Speech Acts.' *Philosophical Review* 79(1): 3–24.

### *Early approaches and responses*

Blackburn, Simon (1973). 'Moral Realism.' Reprinted in Blackburn (1993), *Essays in Quasi-Realism*. Oxford: Oxford University Press.

Zimmerman, David (1980). 'Force and Sense.' *Mind* 89: 214–33.

Blackburn, Simon (1984). *Spreading the Word*. Oxford: Oxford University Press.

Schueler, G.F. (1988). 'Modus Ponens and Moral Realism.' *Ethics* 98(3): 492–500.

Zangwill, Nick (1992). 'Moral Modus Ponens.' *Ratio* (NS) 5(2): 177–93.

Hale, Bob (1993). 'Can There Be a Logic of Attitudes?' In John Haldane and Crispin Wright, eds., *Reality, Representation, and Projection*. New York: Oxford University Press.

van Roojen, Mark (1996). 'Expressivism and Irrationality.' *Philosophical Review* 105(3): 311–35.

Sinnott-Armstrong, Walter (2000). 'Expressivism and Embedding.' *Philosophy and Phenomenological Research* 61(3): 677–93.

Kölbel, Max (2002). *Truth without Objectivity*. New York: Routledge.

## Deflationist responses

Horwich, Paul (1993). 'Gibbard's Theory of Norms.' *Philosophy and Public Affairs* 22: 67–78.

Stoljar, Daniel (1993). 'Emotivism and Truth Conditions.' *Philosophical Studies* 70: 81–101.

Price, Huw (1994). 'Semantic Deflationism and the Frege Point.' In S. L. Tsohatzidis, ed., *Foundations of Speech Act Theory: Philosophical and Linguistic Perspectives*. London: Routledge.

Dreier, James (1996). 'Expressivist Embeddings and Minimalist Truth.' *Philosophical Studies* 83(1): 29–51.

## Inferential-commitment strategies

Blackburn, Simon (1988). 'Attitudes and Contents.' *Ethics* 98(3): 501–17.

Gibbard, Allan (1990). *Wise Choices, Apt Feelings*. Cambridge, MA: Harvard University Press.

Dreier, James (1999). 'Transforming Expressivism.' *Noûs* 33(4): 558–72.

Horgan, Terry, and Mark Timmons (2000). 'Nondescriptivist Cognitivism: Framework for a New Metaethic.' *Philosophical Papers* 29: 121–53.

Björnsson, Gunnar (2001). 'Why Emotivists Love Inconsistency.' *Philosophical Studies* 104(1): 81–108.

Gibbard, Allan (2003). *Thinking How to Live*. Cambridge, MA: Harvard University Press.

Horgan, Terry, and Mark Timmons (2006). 'Cognitivist Expressivism.' In Horgan and Timmons, eds., *Metaethics after Moore*. Oxford: Oxford University Press.

Schroeder, Mark (2008c). *Being For: Evaluating the Semantic Program of Expressivism*. Oxford: Oxford University Press.

### The negation problem

Unwin, Nicholas (1999). '*Quasi*-Realism, Negation and the Frege–Geach Problem.' *Philosophical Quarterly* 49(196): 337–52.

Unwin, Nicholas (2001). 'Norms and Negation: A Problem for Gibbard's Logic.' *Philosophical Quarterly* 51(202): 60–75.

Gibbard, Allan (2003). *Thinking How to Live*. Cambridge, MA: Harvard University Press, chapter 4.

Dreier, James (2006). 'Negation for Expressivists: A Collection of Problems with a Suggestion for Their Solution.' In Russ Shafer-Landau, ed., *Oxford Studies in Metaethics*, vol. I. Oxford: Oxford University Press.

Schroeder, Mark (2008c). *Being For: Evaluating the Semantic Program of Expressivism*. Oxford: Oxford University Press.

Schroeder, Mark (2008d). 'How Expressivists Can and Should Solve Their Problem with Negation.' *Noûs* 42(4): 573–99


### Noncognitivism and truth

Blackburn (1984). *Spreading the Word*. Oxford: Oxford University Press.

Horwich, Paul (1990). *Truth*. Oxford: Oxford University Press.

Wright, Crispin (1992). *Truth and Objectivity*. Cambridge, MA: Harvard University Press.

Divers, John, and Alexander Miller (1994). 'Why Expressivists about Value Should *not* Love Minimalism about Truth.' *Analysis* 54(1): 12–19.

Horwich, Paul (1994). 'The Essence of Expressivism.' *Analysis* 54(1): 19–20.

Jackson, Frank, Graham Oppy, and Michael Smith (1994). 'Minimalism and Truth-Aptness.' *Mind* 103: 287–302.

Smith, Michael (1994b). 'Why Expressivists about Value Should Love Minimalism about Truth.' *Analysis* 54(1): 1–12.

Smith, Michael (1994c). 'Minimalism, Truth-Aptitude, and Belief.' *Analysis* 54(1): 21–6.

Schroeder, Mark (forthcoming a). 'How to Be an Expressivist about Truth.' Forthcoming in Nikolaj Jang Pedersen and Cory Wright, eds., *New Waves in Truth*.


### The wishful thinking problem

Dorr, Cian (2002). 'Non-Cognitivism and Wishful Thinking.' *Noûs* 36(1): 97–103.

Enoch, David (2003). 'How Noncognitivists Can Avoid Wishful Thinking.' *Southern Journal of Philosophy* 41: 527–45.

Lenman, James (2003). 'Noncognitivism and Wishfulness.' *Ethical Theory and Moral Practice* 6: 265–74.

Ridge, Michael (2007a). 'Ecumenical Expressivism: The Best of Both Worlds.' In Russ Shafer-Landau, ed., *Oxford Studies in Metaethics*, vol. II. Oxford: Oxford University Press.

Budolfson, Mark (unpublished). 'Non-Cognitivism and Rational Inference.' Unpublished paper.

## Other epistemological issues for noncognitivism

Gibbard, Allan (2003). *Thinking How to Live.* Cambridge, MA: Harvard University Press, especially chapter 11.

Chrisman, Matthew (2007). 'From Epistemic Contextualism to Epistemic Expressivism.' *Philosophical Studies* 135(2): 225–54.

Lenman, James (2007). 'What s Moral Inquiry?' *Proceedings of the Aristotelian Society*, supplementary volume 81: 63–81.

Ridge, Michael (2007b). 'Epistemology for Ecumenical Expressivists.' *Proceedings of the Aristotelian Society*, supplementary volume 81: 83–108.

## Hybrid theories

Stevenson, C.L. (1944). *Ethics and Language.* Oxford: Oxford University Press.

Hare, R.M. (1952). *The Language of Morals.* Oxford: Oxford University Press.

Stevenson, C.L. (1963). *Facts and Values.* Westport, CT: Greenwood Press.

Alm, David (2000). 'Moral Conditionals, Noncognitivism, and Meaning.' *Southern Journal of Philosophy* 38(3): 355–77.

Barker, Stephen (2000). 'Is Value Content a Component of Conventional Implicature?' *Analysis* 60(3): 268–79.

Copp, David (2001). 'Realist-Expressivism: A Neglected Option for Moral Realism.' *Social Philosophy and Policy* 18: 1–43.

Finlay, Stephen (2004). 'The Conversational Practicality of Value Judgment.' *Journal of Ethics* 8: 205–23.

Finlay, Stephen (2005). 'Value and Implicature.' *Philosophers' Imprint* 5(4), available online at www.philosophersimprint.org/005004/.

van Roojen, Mark (2005). 'Expressivism, Supervenience, and Logic.' *Ratio* 18(2): 190–205.

Ridge, Michael (2006). 'Ecumenical Expressivism: Finessing Frege.' *Ethics* 116(2): 302–36.

Alm, David (2007). 'Noncognitivism and Validity.' *Theoria* 73(2): 121–47.

Ridge, Michael (2007a). 'Ecumenical Expressivism: The Best of Both Worlds.' In Russ Shafer-Landau, ed., *Oxford Studies in Metaethics*, vol. II.

Ridge, Michael (2007b). 'Epistemology for Ecumenical Expressivists.' *Proceedings of the Aristotelian Society*, supplementary volume 81: 83–108.

Boisvert, Daniel (2008). 'Expressive-Assertivism.' *Pacific Philosophical Quarterly* 89: 169–203.

Bar-On, Dorit, and Matthew Chrisman (2009). 'Ethical Neo-Expressivism.' In Russ Shafer-Landau, ed., *Oxford Studies in Metaethics*, vol. IV. Oxford: Oxford University Press.

Ridge, Michael (2009). 'Truth for Ecumenical Expressivists.' In David Sobel and Stephen Wall, eds., *Reasons for Action*. Cambridge: Cambridge University Press.

Schroeder, Mark (2009). 'Hybrid Expressivism: Virtues and Vices.' *Ethics* 119(2): 257–309.

Finlay, Stephen (2009). 'Oughts and Ends.' In *Philosophical Studies* 143: 315–40.

Copp, David (unpublished). 'In Defense of Realist Expressivism and Conventional Simplicature.' Unpublished draft of December 2007.

## Pejoratives and related linguistic issues

Dummett, Michael (1973). *Frege: Philosophy of Language*. London: Duckworth.

Hornsby, Jennifer (2001). 'Meaning and Uselessness: How to Think about Derogatory Words.' In Peter A. French and Howard K. Wettstein, eds., *Figurative Language* (Midwest Studies in Philosophy, vol. XXV). Oxford: Basil Blackwell.

Boghossian, Paul (2003). 'Blind Reasoning.' *Proceedings of the Aristotelian Society*, supplementary volume 77: 225–48.

Williamson, Timothy (2003). 'Blind Reasoning.' *Proceedings of the Aristotelian Society*, supplementary volume 77, 249–93.

Barker, Stephen (2004). *Renewing Meaning*. Oxford: Oxford University Press.

Potts, Christopher (2005). *The Logic of Conventional Implicature*. Oxford: Oxford University Press.

Potts, Christopher (2007). 'The Expressive Dimension.' *Theoretical Linguistics* 33(2): 165–97.

Richard, Mark (2008). *When Truth Gives Out*. Oxford: Oxford University Press, chapter 1.

Hom, Christopher (2008). 'The Semantics of Racial Epithets.' In *Journal of Philosophy* 105: 416–40.

Kaplan, David (unpublished). 'Meaning as Use.' Unpublished manuscript.

## Mood, imperatives, and imperative logic

Ross, Alf (1941). 'Imperatives and Logic.' *Theoria* 7: 53–71.

Hare, R.M. (1952). *The Language of Morals*. Oxford: Oxford University Press, chapter 2.

Rescher, Nicholas (1966). *The Logic of Commands*. New York: Dover.

Stenius, Erik (1967). 'Mood and Language-Game.' *Synthese* 17(1): 254–74.

Hare, R.M. (1971). 'Wanting: Some Pitfalls.' Reprinted in Hare (1972), *Practical Inferences*. Los Angeles: University of California Press.

Hare, R.M. (1972). *Practical Inferences*. Los Angeles: University of California Press.

Karttunen, Lauri (1977). 'Syntax and Semantics of Questions.' *Linguistics and Philosophy* 1: 3–44.

Huntley, Martin (1984). 'The Semantics of English Imperatives.' *Linguistics and Philosophy* 7(2): 103–33.

Smart, J.J.C. (1984). *Ethics, Persuasion, and Truth*. Oxford: Oxford University Press.

Sadock, Jerrold and Arnold Zwicky (1985). 'Speech Act Distinctions in Syntax.' In Timothy Shopen, ed., *Language Typology and Syntactic Description*, vol. I, *Clause Structure*. Cambridge: Cambridge University Press.

Searle, John, and Daniel Vanderveken (1985). *Foundations of Illocutionary Logic*. Cambridge: Cambridge University Press.

Harnish, Robert (1994). 'Mood, Meaning, and Speech Acts.' In S. L. Tsohatzidis, ed., *Foundations of Speech Act Theory: Philosophical and Linguistic Perspectives*. London: Routledge.

Hare, R.M. (1999). 'Imperatives, Prescriptions, and Their Logic.' In Hare, *Objective Prescriptions and Other Essays*. Oxford: Oxford University Press.

Boisvert, Daniel, and Kirk Ludwig (2006). 'Semantics for Nondeclaratives.' In B. Smith and E. Lepore, eds., *The Oxford Handbook of the Philosophy of Language*. Oxford: Oxford University Press.


## Epistemic modals, conditionals, and truth


### *Epistemic modals*

Egan, Andy, John Hawthorne, and Brian Weatherson (2003). 'Epistemic Modals in Context.' In Gerhard Preyer and Georg Peter, eds., *Contextualism in Philosophy: Knowledge, Meaning, and Truth*. Oxford: Oxford University Press, 131–68.

MacFarlane, John (forthcoming). 'Epistemic Modals are Assessment-Sensitive.' Forthcoming in a volume on epistemic modals edited by Andy Egan and Brian Weatherson.

Ross, Jacob, and Mark Schroeder (unpublished). 'Reflection, Disagreement, and Invariance.' Unpublished draft manuscript, available online at www-rcf. usc.edu/~maschroe/research/Reflections_on_Epistemic_Modals.pdf


### Conditionals

Adams, Ernest (1975). *The Logic of Conditionals: An Application of Probability to Deductive Logic*. Dordrecht: Reidel.

Gibbard Allan (1981). 'Two Recent Theories of Conditionals.' In William Harper, Robert Stalnaker, and Glenn Pearce, eds., *Ifs*. Dordrecht: Reidel.

McGee, Vann (1985). 'A Counterexample to Modus Ponens.' *Journal of Philosophy* 82(9): 462–71.

Edgington, Dorothy (1986). 'Do Conditionals Have Truth-Conditions?' *Critica* 18: 3–39.

Edgington, Dorothy (1995). 'On Conditionals.' *Mind* 104: 235–329.

DeRose, Keith, and Richard Grandy (1999). 'Conditional Assertions and Biscuit Conditionals.' *Noûs* 33(3): 405–20.

Lycan, William (2001). *Real Conditionals*. Oxford: Oxford University Press.

Bennett, Jonathan (2003). *A Philosophical Guide to Conditionals*. Oxford: Oxford University Press.

Dreier, James (2009). 'Practical Conditionals.' In David Sobel and Stephen Wall, eds., *Reasons for Action*. Cambridge: Cambridge University Press.

Kolodny, Niko, and John MacFarlane (unpublished). 'Ifs and Oughts.' Unpublished manuscript.


### Truth

Strawson, P.F. (1949). 'Truth.' *Analysis* 9: 83–97.

Horwich, Paul (1990). *Truth*. Oxford: Oxford University Press.

Soames, Scott (1999). *Understanding Truth*. Oxford: Oxford University Press.

Field, Hartry (2008). *Saving Truth from Paradox*. Oxford: Oxford University Press.


## Other work on noncognitivism by the author

Schroeder, Mark (2008a). 'Expression for Expressivists.' *Philosophy and Phenomenological Research* 76(1): 86–116.

Schroeder, Mark (2008b). 'What Is the Frege–Geach Problem?' *Philosophy Compass* 3/4: 703–20.

Schroeder, Mark (2008c). *Being For: Evaluating the Semantic Program of*

*Expressivism*. Oxford: Oxford University Press.

Schroeder, Mark (2008d). 'How Expressivists Can and Should Solve Their Problem with Negation.' *Noûs* 42(4): 573–99.

Schroeder, Mark (2009). 'Hybrid Expressivism: Virtues and Vices.' *Ethics* 119(2): 257–309.

Schroeder, Mark (forthcoming a). 'How to be an Expressivist about Truth.' Forthcoming in Nikolaj Jang Pedersen and Cory Wright, eds., *New Waves in Truth*.

Schroeder, Mark (forthcoming b). 'How Not to Avoid Wishful Thinking.' Forthcoming in Michael Brady, ed., *New Waves in Metaethics*.

Schroeder, Mark (forthcoming c). 'The Moral Truth.' Forthcoming in Michael Glanzburg, ed., *The Oxford Handbook to Truth*.

Ross, Jacob, and Mark Schroeder (unpublished). 'Reflections on Epistemic Modals.' Unpublished draft manuscript, available online at www-rcf.usc.edu/~maschroe/research/Reflections_on_Epistemic_Modals.pdf

# INDEX

# MORAL EPISTEMOLOGY – 'NEW PROBLEMS OF PHILOSOPHY'

## *Aaron Zimmerman*

How do we know right from wrong? Do we even have moral knowledge? Moral epistemology studies these and related questions about our under-standing of virtue and vice. It is one of philosophy's perennial problems, and has recently been the subject of intense debate as a result of findings in developmental and social psychology.

In this outstanding introduction to the subject Aaron Zimmerman covers the following key topics:

- What is moral epistemology? What are its methods?
- Skepticism about moral knowledge based on the anthropolog-ical record of deep and persistent moral disagreement, including contextualism
- Moral nihilism, including debates concerning God and morality and the relation between moral knowledge and our motives and reasons to act morally
- Epistemic moral scepticism, intuitionism and the possibility of inferring 'ought' from 'is,' discussing Locke, Hume, Kant, Audi, and many others
- How children acquire moral concepts and become more reliable judges
- Criticisms of those who would reduce moral knowledge to value-neutral knowledge or attempt to replace moral belief with emotion.

Throughout the book Zimmerman argues that our belief in moral knowl-edge can survive sceptical challenges. He also draws on a rich range of exam-ples from Plato's Meno and Dickens's David Copperfield to Bernard Madoff and Saddam Hussein.

Including chapter summaries and annotated further reading at the end of each chapter, Moral Epistemology is essential reading for all students of ethics, epistemology and moral psychology.

ISBN 13: 978-0-415-48553-1 (hbk)
ISBN 13: 978-0-415-48554-8 (pbk)
ISBN 13: 978-0-203-85086-2 (ebk)

Available at all good bookshops
For ordering and further information please visit:
www.routledge.com

Related titles from Routledge

# THE ROUTLEDGE COMPANION TO ETHICS

## *Edited by John Skorupski*

'Written by leaders in the field, and with depth as well as breadth, this is the ideal companion for anyone with an interest in philosophical ethics'

Roger Crisp, St.Anne's College, Oxford

The Routledge Companion to Ethics is an outstanding survey of the whole field of ethics by a distinguished international team of contributors. Over sixty entries are divided into six clear sections:

- The history of ethics
- meta-ethics
- perspectives from outside ethics
- perspectives in ethics
- morality
- debates in ethics.

The Routledge Companion to Ethics is a superb resource for anyone interested in the subject, whether in philosophy or related subjects such as politics, education, or law. Fully indexed and cross-referenced, with helpful further reading sections at the end of each entry, it is ideal for those coming to the field of ethics for the first time as well as readers already familiar with the subject.

ISBN 13: 978-0-415-41362-6 (hbk)
ISBN 13: 978-0-203-85070-1 (ebk)

Available at all good bookshops
For ordering and further information please visit:
www.routledge.com

# PHYSICALISM – 'NEW PROBLEMS OF PHILOSOPHY'

## *Daniel Stoljar*

'An elegant and insightful introduction to one of the most puzzling dogmas of contemporary metaphysics - much needed and highly recommended.'

Huw Price, *University of Sydney*, Australia

Physicalism, the thesis that everything is physical, is one of the most important yet divisive problems in philosophy. In this superb introduction to the problem Daniel Stoljar focuses on three fundamental questions: the interpretation, truth and philosophical significance of physicalism. In answering these questions, he covers the following key topics:

- A brief history of physicalism
- What a physical property is and how physicalism meets challenges from empirical sciences
- 'Hempel's dilemma' and the relationship between physicalism and physics
- Physicalism and key debates in metaphysics and philosophy of mind, such as supervenience, identity and conceivability
- Physicalism and causality.

Additional features include chapter summaries, annotated further reading and a glossary of technical terms, making Physicalism ideal for those coming to the problem for the first time.

ISBN 13: 978-0-415-45262-5 (hbk)

ISBN 13: 978-0-415-45263-2 (pbk)

ISBN 13: 978-0-203-85630-7 (ebk)

Lightning Source UK Ltd.
Milton Keynes UK
UKOW07f0914070115

244127UK00004B/79/P